ALTERED STATES OF AWARENESS

Readings from

**SCIENTIFIC
AMERICAN**

ALTERED STATES OF AWARENESS

with introductions by
Timothy J. Teyler
The University of California, Irvine

W. H. Freeman and Company
San Francisco

All of the SCIENTIFIC AMERICAN articles in
Altered States of Awareness are available as
separate Offprints. For a complete list of
approximately 700 articles now available as
Offprints, write to W. H. Freeman and Company,
660 Market Street, San Francisco, California
94104.

Printed in the United States of America

Library of Congress Catalog Card Number: 76–190436

Standard Book Number: 0–7167–0856–6 (cloth)
0–7167–0855–8 (paper)

9 8 7 6 5 4 3

PREFACE

It is becoming increasingly apparent that for man merely to exist on this planet he must react appropriately to the world and persons surrounding him. We are still threatened with the classical horrors of war, famine, and disease. How we perceive and react to these threats will determine the position of twentieth-century man in the history of the world and will influence the future of the earth as we know it.

Persons interested in the biology of behavior are acutely alert to the fact that our awareness of the world about us is not constant— rather, we constantly fluctuate from one state of awareness to another. Indeed, some states of awareness are hardly what the layman would refer to as "being aware" at all: while we are sleeping, for instance, we are certainly not cognizant of what is happening around us. Dreams are also perceived as being special or different from the perceptions and experiences of wakefulness. It can be argued, however, that sleeping and dreaming are merely different kinds or states of awareness. That is, they are *altered* states of awareness.

The purpose of this short reader is to provide the student of behavior with some insight into several states of awareness that are distinct from the "normal" state of alert wakefulness. It must be realized that we are referring to a continuum of phenomena. Anything that infringes upon an organism is either meaningful or not meaningful. A meaningful stimulus will, in some manner, change the organism, if only briefly. The state of awareness of the organism is thus continually modulating, and being modulated by, meaningful events. Some modulating influences are considerably more powerful than others. The most dramatic are those influences that act directly upon the brain. Drugs are powerful external modulators of awareness, capable of severely distorting the perceived world. There are equally potent internal modulators of awareness: for instance, those that give rise to the states of light sleep and dreaming represent two strong modulators of awareness that are independent of external agents.

There is great current interest in a topic called "biofeedback." The basic tenet of biofeedback is appealingly simple: if one is allowed to observe in himself some biological event of which he is normally unaware, such as the presence of the alpha rhythm in his own brain waves, then he can be trained to modify some aspect of that event. In the case of the alpha rhythm, the subject might be trained to produce more of the rhythm and its attendant state of awareness at will. Thus, one aspect of biofeedback is the training of individuals to control their own states of awareness. That we are capable of so modifying our own biological processes is in itself interesting (see Leo V. DiCara's article "Learning in the Autonomic Nervous System," p. 74), and it takes on added significance when we consider its practical applications. A person with high blood pressure, for example, might be trained to alleviate his condition through this kind of procedure. The allied area of biocybernetics is concerned with coordinating man and machine to utilize the best features of both in a synergistic system. This approach may effectively increase man's capabilities and level of awareness far beyond anything presently achieved. Many of the articles in this reader anticipated the current interest in biofeedback and biocybernetics, particularly those by S. Grey Walter, Mary A. B. Brazier, J. D. French, Leo V. DiCara, and Ivo Kohler.

December 1971   TIMOTHY J. TEYLER

CONTENTS

Note on cross-references: References to articles included in this book are noted by the title of the article and the page on which it begins; references to articles that are available as Offprints, but are not included here, are noted by the article's title and Offprint number; references to articles published by SCIENTIFIC AMERICAN, but which are not available as Offprints, are noted by the title of the article and the month and year of its publication.

I

BRAIN AND AWARENESS

I

BRAIN AND AWARENESS

INTRODUCTION

The brain is an immensely complicated tissue that is responsible for our every thought and action. The articles in this section were chosen to provide an understanding of how scientists study the brain's response to internal and external modulators of awareness.

A classical paper by W. Grey Walter, "The Electrical Activity of the Brain," is an introduction to the electroencephalogram (EEG), a basic tool for studying the brain. Walter discusses the "brain prints" attendant to various states of awareness and discusses some strategies for extracting more information from the EEG. The toposcope—an early instrument designed to ferret as much information as possible from the elusive brain waves—and the information gained from it are discussed in the final section of Walter's article.

In a continuation of the theme developed by W. Grey Walter, the article by Mary A. B. Brazier, "The Analysis of Brain Waves," plunges into the complex world of computer analysis of EEG. Several of the modern techniques that have been made possible by the advent of the high speed digital computer are discussed in this article—specifically, the use of averaging computers to extract a weak and variable signal from biological noise, the ability to construct poststimulus histograms, and the use of frequency analysis on the EEG. Brazier and Walter both liken the scalp-recorded human EEG to cryptography, in that the basic problem is to determine a pattern and decode or decipher it into a meaningful representation of a known process.

The reticular formation is a portion of the brain stem that has been implicated in a number of vital bodily functions, including the maintenance of the arousal level of an organism. J. D. French, in "The Reticular Formation," discusses the role of a functional system of this part of the brain, the reticular activating system (RAS), which has a critical role in determining the states of awareness and arousal level. The research to which French refers has had a profound effect on our understanding of the brain's functioning in arousal and attention, and helps to explain how an organism can effect directed or selective awareness, wherein it attends only to a particular stimulus or group of stimuli, rather than to all available stimuli.

The final paper in Section I is a somewhat speculative article by John Eccles, "The Physiology of Imagination." Eccles, who was awarded the Nobel Prize in 1963 for his work on synaptic neurophysiology, presents in this paper some of his thoughts about the activities of the brain that underlie higher mental processes. Eccles presents evidence that electrical waves, which travel over dynamic multilane pathways on the cortex of the brain, are the physical correlates of our higher mental functions, such as imagination and creativity. In this article, we are permitted to share the speculation of an eminent brain scientist concerning the operation of the brain in its most complex modes of action.

1

THE ELECTRICAL ACTIVITY OF THE BRAIN

W. GREY WALTER
June 1954

Twenty-five years ago Hans Berger, a German psychiatrist working in Jena, began to publish some strange little pictures consisting of nothing but wavy lines. They should have caused great excitement among his colleagues, because he claimed that they showed the electrical activity of a human brain. But in fact no one took them seriously. For several years no one even bothered to repeat his experiments.

Berger was naturally hurt and disappointed that his epoch-making discovery was ignored or ridiculed. But there were three understandable reasons why any well-trained scientist should have dismissed Berger's claims. First, it was not considered really respectable to study the activity of the brain with measuring tools. Classical scientific methods depend on measuring one thing at a time as exactly as possible, and it was plainly impossible to isolate the individual functions of the complex human brain. Second, the "brain waves" Berger published were altogether dull—merely a tiny electrical oscillation at about 10 waves per second. It was inconceivable that these simple, regular lines could disclose anything significant about so mysterious an organ as the human brain. Third, Berger had rather unwisely admitted that he was looking for what he claimed to have found; psychiatrists, rightly or wrongly, have a reputation for being able to find proof of their wildest ideas when it suits their beliefs.

This little episode in the history of brain research should be a lesson to everyone with a brain to study, for it shows that curiosity and imagination are too easily stifled by the usual scientific training, emphasizing self-criticism and technical skill. Berger was in fact a modest and careful observer; his misfortune was that his technique did not equal his enthusiasm. In the quarter-century since then the study of his little wavy lines has grown into a new department of science called electroencephalography. Today several hundred laboratories in the U. S. and a similar number in Europe are recording and interpreting charts of the electrical discharges of human brains. Their total annual output of charts would girdle the earth. Hospitals all over the world have accumulated thousands upon thousands of brainprints of their patients, for these recordings have proved to be a great help in the diagnosis and treatment of brain diseases.

Brain diseases leave prints as distinctive as a criminal's fingerprints, and the brainprints have been useful in medical practice for precisely the same purpose—to identify the culprit. Just as a fingerprint serves this purpose although its details reveal nothing about the criminal's character, so a brainprint may be put to use for identifying a brain disorder even though we do not understand what it may have to tell about what is going on in the brain. The detective work involved in tracking down the clues to brain diseases is so exciting that at first scientists were content to exploit this aspect of electroencephalography and to postpone more fundamental investigations. During the last few years, however, interest has been swinging round to use of the tool to study the working of the living brain itself.

By a fortunate coincidence—or perhaps it is not a coincidence—the designers of the new electronic computers have, at the same time, become more and more impressed with the similarities between their machines and the mechanisms of the brain. Physiologists have had the satisfaction of seeing engineers develop, with great labor and expense, systems which evolved naturally in living creatures millions of years ago. This convergence of interest—the cross-fertilization between communication engineering and biology—has been given the name cybernetics, originally used by the French physicist André Marie Ampère over a hundred years ago. Norbert Wiener, professor of mathematics at the Massachusetts Institute of Technology, focused interest on the subject with his book in 1949, and it has since been pursued at several conferences convened by the Josiah Macy Jr. Foundation. Through these discussions runs a thread of longing and conjecture—if only we could unravel by our physical methods the mystery of how the brain functions!

The Instrument

The machines that record the electrical rhythms in the brain have become elaborate and expensive. They contain dozens or even hundreds of radio tubes. A really elaborate research apparatus may have several hundred controls, set and adjusted by a team of highly skilled operators before and during each experiment. The cost of the equipment is usually defrayed by the fees earned in medical applications; the gigantic scale of this work could never have been achieved with the funds available for academic research. The astonishing thing is that with all this time and material we still do not understand even one part in a thousand of the frantic scribblings of our fine machines.

The standard electroencephalographic chart shows a set of eight or more wavy lines, each line being a graph of the electric signals from one region of the head. We may suppose—and it is only a supposition—that these signals are coded messages from the brain, and our task may be defined as a search for clues that will help us to break the cipher and read the messages. The usefulness of the brainprints in diagnosing disease lies in the fact that we have established that serious emergencies in the brain usually yield certain simple code messages in our machines.

The signals are usually classified by the frequency of the electrical pulsations in them. Berger's original oscillations, which he named *alpha* rhythms,

are in the frequency band between 8 and 13 cycles per second—that is, about as fast as you can move a finger. Their size, or amplitude, is around 30 millionths of a volt. Neither the frequency nor the amplitude is constant. Each individual has his own characteristic pattern of shifts in frequency and size; thus his brainprint is as distinctive as his signature. The alpha rhythms also can be identified by the part of the brain they come from; they are nearly always largest at the back of the head, where the nerve signals from the eyes reach the brain. They are usually larger and more regular when a person has his eyes shut and is not thinking. From this the inference has been drawn that activity of the visual imagination may suppress the alpha rhythms. One person in five shows no alpha rhythm at all—only small, complex, irregular pulsations from all parts of the brain, with no fixed frequency. In one in five also the alpha rhythms go on even when the eyes are open. Upon the basis of such personal differences we

have established a tentative classification of brain types in human beings. This system indicates differences in ways of thinking, rather than the relative success of people's thinking, as "intelligence tests" do.

Let it be said at once that nobody has yet been able to determine precisely the meaning of the alpha and other electrical rhythms of the brain. Nonetheless they are much too prominent, too individual, too persistent—and already too clearly related to mental activities—to be dismissed as "disappointingly constant," as they were when the brain physiologist E. D. Adrian demonstrated them at Cambridge University in 1934.

Some time ago I was struck by a peculiar coincidence. I had reflected a thousand times that the brain rhythms are a unique phenomenon: Nowhere else in nature are such intricate patterns to be found, such variety, such interweaving of differential frequencies in their ever-changing combinations and permutations. On the thousand and first

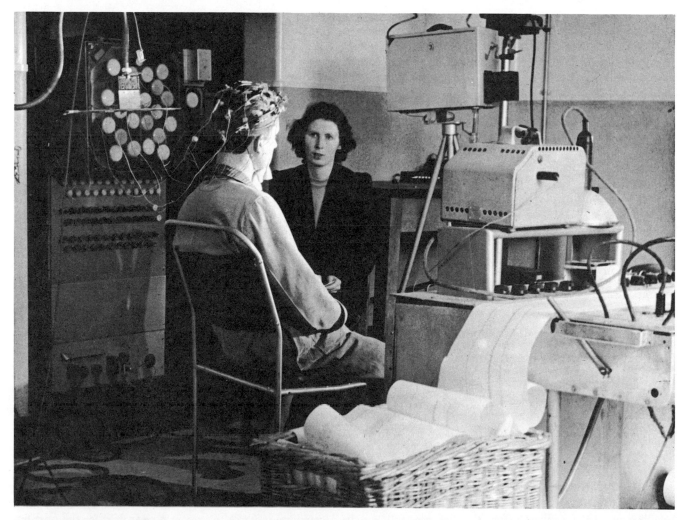

ELECTROENCEPHALOGRAM is made at the Burden Neurological Institute in Bristol, England. The electrodes are attached to the scalp of the subject, who is seated with an investigator. Where an electroencephalogram is normally recorded on a paper tape such as that in the foreground, here it is also displayed on a device called the Toposcope, the face of which is visible at the upper left.

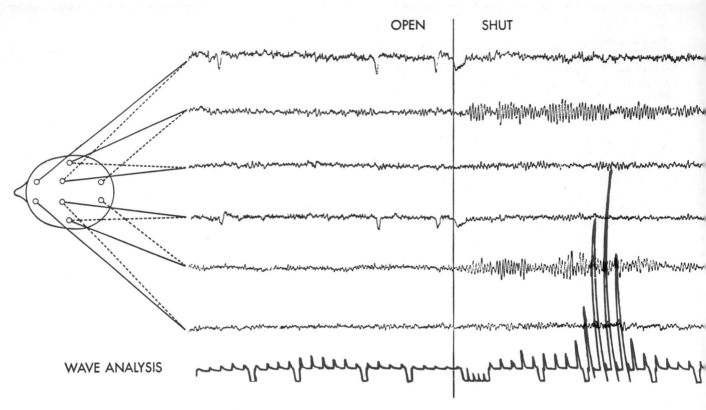

OPEN   SHUT

WAVE ANALYSIS

ALPHA RHYTHMS are recorded. Each curve in black represents the fluctuations of current from electrodes attached to the head as indicated by the drawing at left. The colored curve is drawn by a wave analyzer which periodically dissects the frequencies of which the fifth curve from the top is composed. Tallest colored spike on this page, for example, records the average amplitude of a frequency

reflection I followed up this thought with the question: What is the unique function of the brain? The brain's unique function is to learn. The conclusion from this seemed inescapable: probably there is some kind of coupling between learning and the brain's unique physical activity—its electrical rhythms.

Since then we have gone some way toward verifying the learning theory, as will be told later in this article. But the immediate problem that presents itself to the thoughtful reader will be: What is the physiological function of the electrical rhythms? Apart from such end results as learning, what are the rhythms for, what do they do, what is their special role in brain mechanisms?

The Brain's Communications

Let us concentrate on the alpha rhythms, definitely known to be associated with vision. One of the great physiological puzzles about vision is this: When an image is received by the brain, how is it passed on to the cognition areas? We know that a scene registered on the retina in the eye is projected on a section of the brain cortex by the optic nerve—a compact bundle of a million or so nerve fibers. From the visual projective cortex, information about the things seen is somehow trans-

ferred to billions of other cells in the brain. Can we imagine that the million points of projection are connected with all those billions of cells? It is quite inconceivable that anything like the necessary number of physical links could be housed in the head. We are therefore led to the suggestion, derived from the examples of radar and television, that communication between the projection and the cognition areas must be by a scanning mechanism.

This suggestion gains force when we consider what may have been the evolutionary origin of brain rhythms. Such a rhythm means that a group of millions of brain cells are firing together at regular intervals. The most primitive living example of cellular collaboration of this kind is the jellyfish. We may suppose that an early form of jellyfish depended for its existence upon the food signals received by its nerve net, which produced a convulsion (comparable to an epileptic seizure) that propelled the animal toward the exciting food. Such an action implies a combined discharge of many motor cells. The nerve net presumably consisted of specialized food-and-motor cells and steering cells. A cell receiving the food stimulus would pass it to the steering cells and these would transmit it to the other motor cells almost—but not quite—simultaneously. In other words,

besides the time lag always required for recharging the cells, there would be a time lag in the communication of the signal to all the cells. There is already here something suggestive of scanning; the whole of the forward nerve net would be open to suggestion and the impulse would be propagated by whichever cell first received the incentive.

Further evolutionary specialization might produce a system in which the signal or incentive was passed from the perceptive cells to the steering cells and from there to the motor cells, the steering cells thus assuming a primitive brain function. This is where one would have to look for a rhythmic discharge like that of the alpha rhythms. It has been suggested that the alpha rhythms may be a necessary periodical wiping out of the impressions received on the visual projection cortex. Such a process may seem plausible in a primitive perceptive-steering-motor system, but it would not account for the phenomena of the human brain. Moreover, for a primitive system such as the one described it would not be necessary. The discharge of the steering cells as they communicated their impulse to the motor cells would itself wipe out the previous impression and allow them to present a clear field for the next impulse. But again to carry the matter a step further in brain evolution, the time

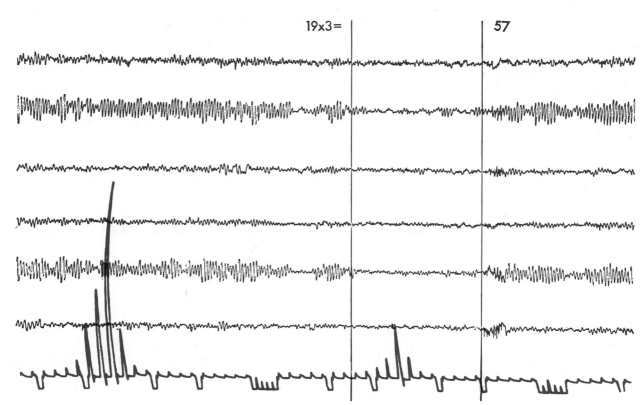

19x3=   57

of 10 cycles per second; the spikes to the left of it represent the amplitude of nine cycles, eight cycles, seven cycles and so on. To the left of the vertical black line on the opposite page the subject's eyes were open and the alpha waves are small; to the right, his eyes were closed and the waves are larger. When he was given a problem in arithmetic (*above*), waves were damped until he gave answer.

lag in transmission of the signals would establish an inherent rhythmic sympathy among all the steering cells, geared to the period of the passing of signals from the perception cells. Putting it very crudely, this is in effect what seems to be taking place in the human brain: the alpha waves sweep to and fro scanning the visual cortex in harmony with the period during which a scene is retained by the transmitting retina.

As already mentioned, the diversity of alpha rhythms is their most intriguing property. What, however, are we to say about the many people who display little or no alpha rhythm? According to the scanning hypothesis, their scanner must be working at very low amplitude, yet these are the people in whom visual imagery is most vivid and persistent. At first this seemed a crude paradox, but we were blinded by the vision of familiar machines. In a TV set, scanning of the field goes on continually whatever the picture may be; in certain radar sets designed to control artillery and in many target-seeking projectiles, a scanner is set to search for targets, but once an echo has been received the scanner stops and swings the gun or missile into a position of best attack. This simple system was incorporated into the toy robot, *Machina speculatrix*, which we made years ago to see how "scanning" would affect be-

havior [see "An Imitation of Life," by W. Grey Walter; SCIENTIFIC AMERICAN, May, 1950]. In systems such as these, the more active and excited the system is, the less regular and rhythmic the scanning cycle becomes. So perhaps within our heads we carry a bundle of target-seeking tissue—in origin primeval, but in function as penetrating and as precise as any imagined, even in the realms of science fiction. Here we can discern at work the organ of selection and imagination, first stages on the road to learning, understanding and foreseeing the shifting patterns of the outside world—and all contained in a cupful of tepid, pinkish-gray, electric jelly.

The Brainprint

To complete the panorama of the strange dark world within our heads, let us look at the brainprint itself. Learning to understand brainprints is rather like learning a foreign language from a number of acquaintances with different accents and dialects. Now there are two things which often astonish a visitor to a foreign land: (1) the ease with which young children speak the tongue, and (2) the similarity of baby talk in all countries. We are called mammals because "ma" is one of the first syllables human babies everywhere fix upon, and

they seem to apply it to the maternal organ which first regularly attracts their attention. There are similar characters in brainprints. At birth the brainprints of infants are generalized, but at an early age, around three or four, the child's brainprint acquires the individualistic features of an adult's. In a newborn babe there are slow, rhythmic swings of electric change in all areas of the brain, the different parts acting in the same way electrically but without much coordination. During sleep the brainprints of babies are very like those of sleeping adults: mainly large, slow, regular oscillations, called *delta* rhythms. Some time during the first few months of life an important mechanism appears—a transient outburst of fast and slow rhythms when the sleeping baby is half awakened by a noise or movement. Most parents are only too familiar with the transition from an infant who will sleep through almost any racket to one which stirs at the creak of a floor board. The same electrical response to stimuli when asleep is seen in adults. In most cases it seems to be connected with the brain mechanism that prevents a sleeper from being awakened too easily by trivial noises; it has been called the "K" complex. In later life these safety mechanisms are usually very sharply tuned, as it were, so that a mother may sleep through a thunder-

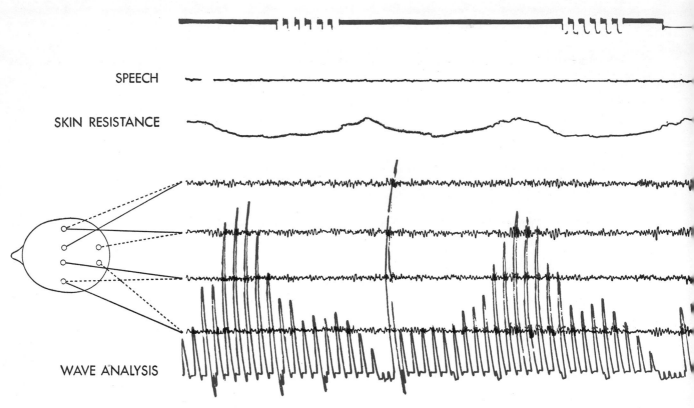

SPEECH

SKIN RESISTANCE

WAVE ANALYSIS

VERSATILITY of an individual brain is suggested by the variability of its rhythms over a relatively extended period. Constant
rhythms are associated with low versatility; variable rhythms, with
high versatility. In addition to the four electroencephalographic
curves on this record are curves for speech and the electrical resistance of the skin. Here tallest spikes on the colored curve of
the wave analyzer merely mark intervals of 40 seconds. Groups of
shorter colored spikes dissect the frequencies of the black curve

storm but wake when her baby
whimpers.

During the first few years of life the
slow rhythms get steadily smaller as the
nerve fibers in the brain complete their
growth. At about the end of the first year
another sort of rhythm appears. It has a
frequency of five or six per second and is
largest at the sides of the head. It seems
to be connected in some way with what
we call emotion, particularly with feelings of annoyance and frustration. In
children of about three years old it can
be evoked very easily by teasing—by
offering a piece of candy and then
snatching it away again. Another similar
rhythm can easily be evoked by simple
physical pleasure. These rhythms have
been called *theta* rhythms, because they
seem to be connected in some way with
the functioning of the thalamus, the midbrain where signals from the body are
relayed to the brain roof. The theta
rhythms usually appear at that phase of
development when children start to acquire self-control. The age at which this
happens varies, and so do the size and
character of the theta rhythms.

The first sign of alpha rhythms is seen
clearly during the second or third year,
but the faster components rarely appear
until the age of seven or eight. The theta
rhythms and alpha rhythms are present

together in varying proportions until the
age of 13 or 14. Consequently the interpretation of children's brainprints is particularly difficult, demanding appreciation of psychological and social factors
influencing the individual child. For instance, adults usually submit to electroencephalography calmly, but for children the mere fact of being in a hospital,
of not being allowed to sit on mother's
knee, of having to keep still and so forth,
has a startling effect on the brain activity. It is often possible to tell a good deal
about a child's fears and interests from
the way in which the brain rhythms
change during a recording or from one
examination to another. His brainprint
may even vary according to whether the
operator is wearing a white or a green
coat.

An adult whose brain becomes dis-
eased or injured, or who has a childish
personality, may revert to the slow delta
and theta rhythms of infancy and child-
hood. In certain conditions of strain unusually fast rhythms appear. In certain
types of epilepsy there is a characteristic
combination of enormous slow waves
and fast spikes. Naturally the exact location of these abnormal features is a very
important part of electroencephalography, for it can pinpoint a disturbance
for an operation by a brain surgeon.

This catalogue of the signals received
from the living brain may give a mislead-
ing impression of simplicity. Only in very
severe or advanced stages of a brain
disease are the brainprints so clear that
their features can be designated with
complete confidence. Far more often all
these slow and fast components appear
together intermittently or continuously
in various parts of the brain, all of them
varying with the state of the person
being studied. The record is usually more
like the score of a symphony or the tran-
script of conversations at a cocktail party
than a simple code message. Whenever
it takes on the character of a solo or a
monologue, one knows that something
has gone seriously wrong, either with the
brain or with the recording machine.

Disentangling the Signals

Using again the analogy with cipher
breaking, the difficulty with electroencephalography is not to pick up a message but that inevitably a great many
different messages are received at the
same time. This situation has demanded
several refinements of technique. The
human eye is ill-adapted to sorting out
the components of a complex curve.
Sometimes different rhythms combine in
such a way as to give a completely false

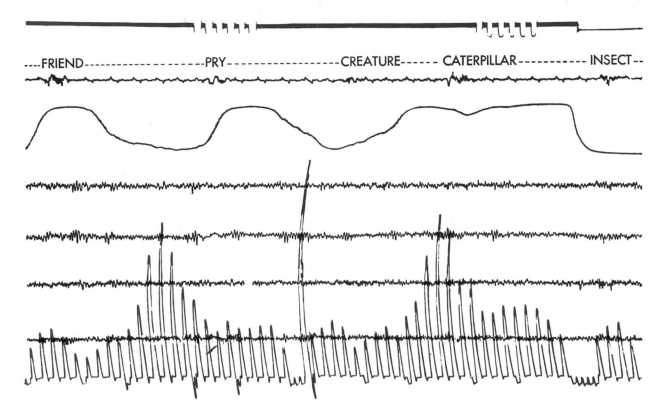

----FRIEND------------------PRY----------------CREATURE------CATERPILLAR----------INSECT--

at the bottom for the previous 40 seconds. While the record at the left was being made, the female subject rested; while the record at the right was being made, she spoke a series of words (*top of record*) which came into her mind spontaneously. The lack of variation in the wave analysis suggests low versatility. As she spoke the words, there were changes in her skin resistance indicating an emotional disturbance. This disturbance was reduced by the transition from thoughts about friendship to word "caterpillar."

impression. For example, during an examination in which a person becomes annoyed by something, the curve may change in a way which seems to indicate that the frequency of his alpha rhythm has dropped by one or two cycles per second. Actually the true change may be the breaking out of an entirely separate theta rhythm which is imposed on the alpha.

To unravel the situation many laboratories now employ special wave analyzers. These instruments deal with the complex electrical oscillations from the brain in rather the same way as a prism separates the colors in a beam of light. The components of the complex wave are isolated by electronic circuits tuned to the several frequencies. A moving pen automatically records the amount of activity at each frequency during a fixed interval, usually 10 seconds. The result is a set of curves giving the frequency spectrum of the brainprint. This process is repeated over and over, and other electronic circuits write out the statistical average of the spectrum readings every minute or so, so that the experimenter can measure not only the composition of the brain signals from time to time but also their variability over a longer period. From this can be assessed the versatility of the brain under investigation—an important measure of its repertoire of adaptive stratagems.

Frequency analysis by this means has proved a valuable tool, but like all tools it has its limitations. It cannot easily be applied to more than one part of the brain at once. Few laboratories can afford more than two analyzers, for they cost upward of $5,000 apiece. Furthermore, frequency analysis can be quite misleading unless it is used imaginatively; it can only suggest possible solutions to a problem, and the experimenter must then make further studies to decide which of the possible solutions is correct. Since the state of the brain is always changing, the fresh tactics suggested by frequency analysis may come too late to be of immediate value. Again, using the cipher comparison, frequency analysis will not give information about how the rapidly changing signals from different parts of the brain are related to one another, or which of the suggested meanings is the most likely one.

A State of Mind

Yet the sort of insight that frequency analysis is capable of providing is vividly illustrated by a recent laboratory experience. The investigator had just taken delivery of a new analyzer and had spent a Saturday morning tuning and calibrating his new treasure. By afternoon he was ready to try it, but the only test subject left in the laboratory was a technical assistant who had, by ordinary standards, rather a dull record. (Electroencephalographers mean no offense when they call a record "dull"—in fact, the best companions often give the dullest records. The reference is only to the lack of larger regular oscillations.) On this Saturday afternoon an international football match happened to be going on, and the subject listened to the radio while the test proceeded. After a few minutes the experimenter, who was not listening to the radio but was busily adjusting the settings of his new instrument and checking the consistency of its analysis, began to realize that he was unconsciously following the progress of the football game as it affected his subject. At first, when the home side was in the lead and the play was relatively uninteresting, the subject's alpha rhythm droned on at nine cycles per second, and there was only a trace of theta activity. Then the game livened up; the analyzer promptly showed an alpha rise to 10 cycles per second. When the visiting team scored a goal, the theta rhythms suddenly increased to the size of the alpha rhythms. This complex spectrum of theta and rapid alpha activity

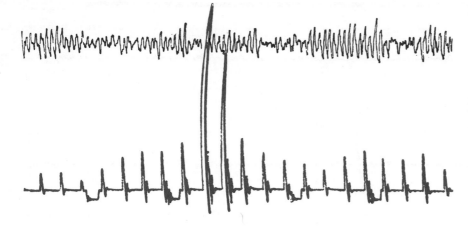

HOME TEAM LED at this point on the record of a man listening to a football match on the radio. The tallest spike of frequency analysis (*color*) represents nine cycles per second

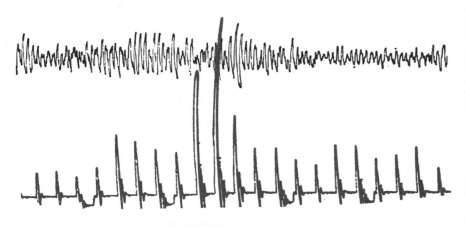

HOME TEAM SCORED at this point. The tallest spike of the frequency analysis represents 10 cycles per second, indicating that the amplitude of that frequency has increased.

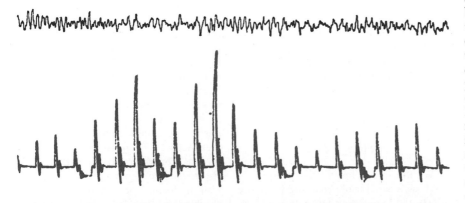

VISITORS TIED the home team at this point. The tallest spike of the analysis represents 10 cycles, but there is now a six-cycle spike associated with the annoyance of the subject.

persisted with only minor fluctuations until the game ended with the defeat of the home team. One may say that, knowing the score, one could tell the nationality of the subject from his brainprint, or knowing the subject, one could infer the state of the game. Testing a roomful of people, the instrument could show which of them were interested in football and whether an individual's interest was mainly in the niceties of play or in which side won.

Prolonged and detailed analysis of records from normal subjects has shown that the spectrum of alpha rhythms is far more complex than was at first supposed. When a person is performing a task—*e.g.*, trying to recognize an object by its feel—the various components in the alpha band wax and wane in a manner absolutely characteristic of that person. One component may be linked with the attempt to visualize what has been felt, another with a search for verbal expression, another with the recall of visual impressions, another with the effort to imagine a color, and so forth. For each person there are typical combinations and permutations of rhythmic change, associated with the way that person prefers to solve problems and handle the model of the world his head contains.

Decoding the Messages

To watch the unfolding brainprints of a friend is an absorbing experience, particularly if you have some idea of his state of mind and interests of the moment. You have the impression, however, of listening to a muttered soliloquy through a keyhole. You itch to ask a leading question, but only rarely can you frame a question simple enough to evoke an intelligible change in the brainprint. In 1945 there was introduced a method of stimulation, simpler than ordinary language, which has vastly extended the scope of electroencephalography. It is based on a principle well known to cryptographers. If you are trying to break a code, a useful trick is to force the enemy to send a message of your own selection: *e.g.*, "100 bombers approaching." When you pick up this known message in his code, you have the key in your hand. Radar, which obtains information from a reflected radio pulse of predetermined frequency, is another aspect of much the same principle. The idea was applied to the study of the brain by stimulating the eyes with very short flashes of light at controlled intervals.

The way this method developed is an interesting example of interplay between clinical needs and scientific conjecture. When frequency analysis was first applied to brainprints from epileptics, it was discovered that in many the rhythms had a tendency to appear in distinct bands with an almost arithmetical relationship to one another. For example, there might be activity at the frequencies of 3, 6, 9 and 24 cycles per second. During an epileptic fit these highly distinctive patterns became pronounced. This suggested that a seizure might be induced by electrical stimulation which accentuated the "harmonic" relation between these rhythms in different parts of the brain, or which synchronized the rhythms and supplied missing links in the harmonic series—12, 15, 18 or 21 in the example given. This sounds cruel, but the diagnosis of epilepsy is never sure until an attack has been seen by an experienced observer, and all kinds of disagreeable methods have been suggested for inducing an attack in unfortunate people who may be epileptic. The flicker method of synchronizing the inherent brain rhythms seemed to be relatively gentle and promised to be scientifically illuminating. Almost the first time the method was tried on a known epileptic, a dramatic success was achieved; the moment a certain combination of light flashes was established, the patient underwent one of his characteristic attacks. The success of this clinical stratagem naturally encouraged more detailed study of the way normal brains responded to flickering lights, and it was soon found that in most people stimulation of this sort evoked in the brain extraordinarily complicated and widespread responses.

Among other discoveries, it was found possible to make the brain stimulate itself by positive feedback. The electric impulses from the brain were connected through the recording machine to the electronic gadget that produced the flashes of light. In this way a brain response to a flash triggered a new flash and so on. This method of self-excitement is particularly effective for revealing a hidden tendency to epileptic seizures. It resembles very closely the way an engineer may test the stability of a transmission system: he applies positive feedback to disturb the system and observes how effectively the system's inherent negative feedback operates to damp the disturbance and restore equilibrium. A normal brain contains an automatic gain control which prevents overexcitement even during positive-feedback flicker experiments.

The importance of these discoveries is that they demonstrate the dynamic and personal response of the brain to a stimulus. When it receives a light signal, it sends a coded message to nearly every part of the brain. Usually messages arriving in brain regions far from the visual receiving department evoke no action; they are "to whom it may concern, for information only." But the administrative rules, so to say, are not watertight; the signaling procedure has certain weaknesses. In many epileptics and even in one normal person in 20, the relayed message is acted upon immediately by the executive part of the brain and something like an epileptic fit results. It is as though all the officials in a government office were to reply in exhaustive detail to instructions intended only for a single department. The reason flicker stimuli are so potent seems to be that they overwhelm the brain's channels of communication with their barrage of rapid, repetitive impulses. You cannot drive a nail into a piece of wood with your finger however hard you push, but the same amount of energy applied in repeated hammer blows will do the trick.

The Meaning of Flickers

An encouraging feature of the flicker stimulation method is that anyone looking at the flickering light sees more than just flicker. There is always a sensation of movement, pattern and color, though the stimulus is stationary, featureless and without distinctive hue. Margiad Evans, a novelist who underwent this experience, described her sensations as follows:

"Lights like comets dangled before me, slow at first and then gaining a furious speed and change, whirling color into color, angle into angle. They were all pure, ultra-unearthly colors, mental colors, not deep visual ones. There was no glow in them, but only activity and revolution."

Red flickers are more effective than those of any other color. Some people develop exaggerated electrical responses and sensations only with red flicker. Conversely, it has been found that some epileptics have fewer spontaneous fits when they wear spectacles that screen out the red wavelengths of light.

The cause of these visual illusions during flicker has intrigued us considerably. The intricate moving patterns may be subjective evidence for the scanning process outlined above; we have found that brief, intermittent stationary signals applied to a space-time converter or scanner will always produce an illusion of pattern or movement, just as such signals applied to a moving system can provide an illusion that the system is stationary—the stroboscopic effect. A person contemplating the illusions of "activity and revolution" is, in effect, examining the sweep of his own brain, raking and sifting the clutter of signals for anything which may have meaning or value.

From the experimental standpoint the outstanding virtue of the flicker method is that the stimulus is "tagged" with the frequency at which the light is flashing, so that frequency analysis can be used to particular advantage. Brainprints contain a great deal of confusing information—activity unconnected with the particular experiment. These interfering signals cannot be eliminated, because they are an essential part of brain functions—the sign of continuous active adaptation in the organ of adaptation. In searching for the response to an experimental stimulus against this background we are rather in the position of someone who has an appointment to meet a strange lady at a busy terminus: how to pick her out of the throng of passersby? The usual solution is to arrange to wear a flower of a certain color and wait at a certain place at a certain time. The combination of flicker and frequency analysis has the same effect. The stimulus has a known frequency and the amount of spontaneous activity at that frequency in the various parts of the brain can easily be measured beforehand. Any increase in the activity at that frequency during the stimulation period can be seen quite clearly in the analysis, even when it is completely hidden in the busy crowd of other rhythms and discharges. A regular response only one millionth of a volt in size can be measured even when the interfering signals are 20 times as big. Viewed in this way, the strange, remote responses to flicker are rather as though, having arranged to recognize a blind date by her red carnation, one came upon all her uncles and aunts in every corner of the rendezvous, wearing flowers of similar shades and with mysterious assignations.

Meeting under the clock has romantic associations, but the comparison with frequency analysis is not quite accurate; though we can recognize very small rhythmic signals by their frequency, the time and place of their occurrence are indeterminate. The ordinary written record could supply this information, but to interpret the multiple responses in detail is like listening to half a dozen witnesses all giving their testimony at once and chattering to one another as well. We wanted something that would give evidence in a curt, formal way, would be content to answer "yes" or "no" to leading questions, and would indicate when there was general agreement about the responses in different parts of the brain. We dreamed of developing a combination of expert witness, learned counsel and impartial jury.

The Enchanted Loom

In 1947 we began to work out an entirely new method of displaying brain signals which we hoped would enable us to eliminate the interference from irrelevant signals—to cloak with invisibility the crowd of strangers milling around our dear unknown. The machine that has "just growed" in our laboratory is called the Toposcope—Topsy for short—because it was originally intended to show the topography (space pattern) of the brain activity. Like the Taj Mahal, which it faintly resembles, the conception has grown in scope by marriage to four other instruments (each with its technical and pet name) so that it is now much more than merely an indicator of the topography.

In principle Topsy is rather like 22 small television or radar sets. Twenty-two little cathode-ray tubes, each connected by an electrode to a different region of the subject's head, translate into visual form, as pictures of changing brightness, the activity of the respective parts of the brain; they bring the brain signals, amplified, to their screens. When no signals are present, there is nothing to see; but when the brain is active, the tubes light up, and the display becomes "an enchanted loom where flashing shuttles weave a dissolving pattern: always a meaningful pattern but never an abiding one." Sir Charles Sherrington's poetic image describes exactly the impression these scopes give. An automatic camera records snapshots of these scenes, transforming into frozen vectors the procession of illuminated butterflies which recalls the passionate Psyche of the classic Mind.

The display tubes are arranged behind a plastic screen mapping the head as seen from above [*photograph on opposite page*]. Each tube is a sort of clock face too, for in each the electron beam which the brain signals turn on and off is formed by special circuits into a rotating line or spoke, like the sweep hand of a radar receiver. All these electronic clock hands turn at the same speed, and the speed is controlled either by the experimenter or by the subject's brain itself. When the operator controls the speed,

the time scale is ordinary clock time; when the subject's brain controls it, the time is "local" time—the time scale of that part of the brain at that moment. The varying relation between brain time and standard time shows as a blurring of the needle on a meter which records the time of each revolution of the hand. Thus parts of the brain that keep the same time can be picked out quite easily, and the signals they exchange can be distinguished from the gossip and backchat of bystanders and the welter of routine traffic. Since the instrument can also deliver stimuli in various patterns at selected times, the marriages of new sensations to pre-existing activity can be watched as an electric concordance of great variety and beauty.

When we began to use this machine, we found the time maps hard to understand. But gradually the new code has begun to penetrate our thick heads, and much of what was quite bewildering in the ordinary brainprints now seems to be taking on a new form and luster. When the brain is receiving a time pattern of visual signals (for example, a series, or group, of flashes, then an interval, then another group and so on), the pattern often is "dissected"; adjacent areas respond to selected parts of the pattern in sequence, as if some scanning process is "turning on" one part of the brain after another. In areas distant from the visual region, the responses are recombined in an arrangement resembling the original pattern.

Learning

These two effects—dissection and remote resynthesis—seem to solve partly two of the main mysteries posed by the brainprints, namely, the function of the alpha rhythms and the widespread effects of flicker stimulation. In most normal subjects activity appears in the temporal or the frontal lobes, which are remote from the visual projective area, mainly when the visual pattern is novel or interesting. There the pattern may be complete again, sometimes simplified or even abstracted, as it were, shorn of irrelevant variations and inconsistencies. In the temporal lobes, when the stimulation ceases the pattern hangs on—a phantom of meaning which as the seconds pass dwindles into the nothingness of all forgotten things. In subjects too experienced in these trials no hint of these strange processes is seen. The processes are not the well-worn trade routes of automatic life; rather they are the speculative, adventurous machinery

that guides the living brain to matching within itself the indifferent or hostile change and chance of the world it must manipulate.

This great problem of how a brain can decide that an association or coincidence of events is not mere chance was considered in a previous article ["A Machine That Learns," by W. Grey Walter; SCIENTIFIC AMERICAN, August, 1951]. The suggestion made there was that for even the most rudimentary learning by association seven distinct operations must be performed to decide whether one series of events implies another. The implications of this hypothesis were illustrated by the simple electronic learning circuit named *Machina docilis*, which was developed in the hope of explaining, or at least describing more coherently, the features of brain function which the Toposcope was beginning to illuminate. *M. docilis* can learn only one simple lesson. In the human brain no bounds can yet be set for learning, but on the lowest level we are beginning to have some confidence that the mechanisms of understanding are not unimaginably beyond our understanding.

The pictures of brain response produced by the Toposcope indicate that, as required by theory, signals entering the brain are subjected to considerable processing before they reach the primary receiving areas. Somewhere in the middle of the head is a diffuse foliage of nerve cells and tendrils that picks up from the stream of incoming messages a series of hints that "something has happened." This information, crude, unspecific but emphatic, is broadcast to many distant regions. The effect is to alert the whole brain. When the situation is novel and the intensity of the signals high, the widespread responses are almost in the nature of an alarm—"anything may happen." But, as we have seen, familiarity breeds indifference; the brain learns to assess the message and to file it away unless in fact it turns out to signal some important event. In the course of time, after many trials and rehearsals, the brain establishes the meaning and importance of new messages.

In the article on *M. docilis* it was suggested that this assessment of importance can be accurate only if the brain operates as a statistical computer. We conjecture that the living brains we are examining with our recording machine are engaged in working out as best they can the chances that what we are doing may have some meaning—some relevance to the problem of their survival. When, in moments of relatively lucid experimentation, we hit upon a message which apparently does convey some meaning, then the texture of the electric fabric woven before our eyes acquires indeed a meaningful pattern. In those of our subjects who suffer from seizures or disorders of consciousness during flicker, the "pari-mutuel" within the brain jumps the lines and throws out a wild and vulgar guess, as though everything meant anything. This conclusion is so utterly inconsistent with the continuation of life that only a general shutdown can avert catastrophe, and the patient lapses into a daze.

Topsy's Promise

The application of these methods and theories to clinical problems is becoming a serious preoccupation. Mental or nervous disorders which are undetectible in conventional brainprints often show up markedly when studied with the Toposcope during stimulation or excitement. One significant clue is the length of persistence of an electrical pattern after the stimulus is terminated. In some people whose thinking is confused and incoherent this "memory" time seems to be 10 times as long as in ordinary folk. When a succession of different patterns is presented to them, the brain activity shows a "double-exposure" effect—a pastiche of surrealistic phantoms and grotesques.

In a few cases we have been able to probe with the Toposcope some of the deeper levels of the brain, when surgeons have had to remove the upper part of the brain of a patient who has suffered some serious brain injury or disease. As we should expect from theory, the activity from the deep brain is simpler, more urgent, more evanescent than that from the upper regions. Most important of all, there is almost no trace of "memory" or persistence of a stimulated pattern when the upper crust of the brain is missing.

With the united efforts of the many laboratories now mobilized for these studies we can plan our campaign for investigation of the living brain with more confidence than ever before. The tactics and strategy of this great effort toward self-understanding were discussed in Boston last summer at the Third International Congress of Electroencephalography, where several hundred enthusiasts gathered to dispute such observations and theories as have been outlined here. No doubt in a few years both our machines and our notions will seem as crude and as incoherent as Berger's first articles did a generation ago.

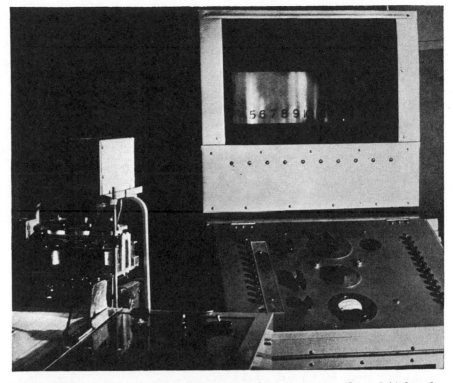

WAVE ANALYZER of the Burden Institute not only traces a curve (*lower left*) but also projects a luminous image (*upper right*). The vertical bands on the screen indicate the frequency components. This image indicates that a beat of 10 cycles per second is strongest.

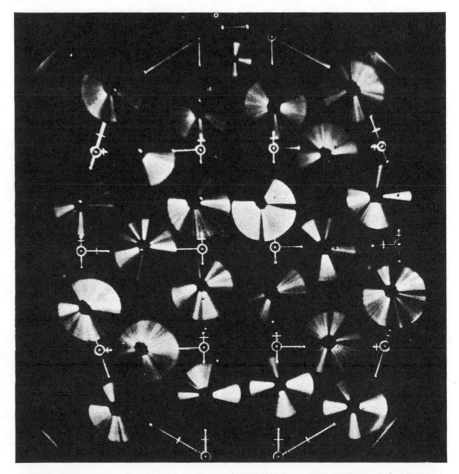

TOPOSCOPE DISPLAY is an array of cathode-ray tubes. The lines on the transparent screen in front of the tubes indicate the linkage of each tube to the electrodes on the head of the subject. The image on each tube is made by a luminous line sweeping like the hand of a clock.

2

THE ANALYSIS OF BRAIN WAVES

MARY A. B. BRAZIER
June 1962

The electrical activity that can be recorded from the surface of the human head is probably the most baffling cryptogram to be found in nature. It is therefore not surprising that electrophysiologists have turned to electronic computers for help. First observed in animals by the English physiologist Richard Caton in 1875, the surface waves reflect the rich and constantly changing electrical activity of the brain. The first recordings from the human brain were made in 1924 by Hans Berger, a German psychiatrist who, because of his oddly secretive nature, withheld publication of his "electroencephalograms" until 1929. The reception was at first skeptical, but the electroencephalogram, or EEG, soon demonstrated its value in the diagnosis of epilepsy and other brain damage. Now, within the past 20 years, physiologists have made a start at decoding the EEG and have begun to show how it is related to the functioning of the nervous system.

For analyzing the electrical activity of the brain the electronic computer has emerged as an instrument of great power and versatility. One of the principal uses of the computer is to extract meaningful signals from the background electrical noise generated by the brain, which normally makes any single recording undecipherable. Although analyses of this sort are usually performed with magnetic-tape records of the brain's activity, the computer becomes even more useful when it is designed to make its analyses in "real" time, while the subject is still connected to the recording apparatus and while the investigator is still able to manipulate the experimental variables. Employed in this way, the computer becomes a subtle new tool for the studies of neurophysiology.

In man the fluctuating potential dif-ference between leads on the unshaved scalp is commonly between 50 and 100 millionths of a volt, or about a tenth the magnitude of electrocardiographic potentials. These waves are most prominent at the back of the head over the visual-association areas of the brain; waves recorded there are called alpha waves. The alpha rhythm, which has a frequency of between eight and 13 per second in adult subjects, is most conspicuous when the eyes are closed. The alpha waves disappear momentarily when the eyes are opened.

Because of the regularity of the alpha rhythm, its frequency characteristics received most of the attention in the early days of electroencephalography. Physi-

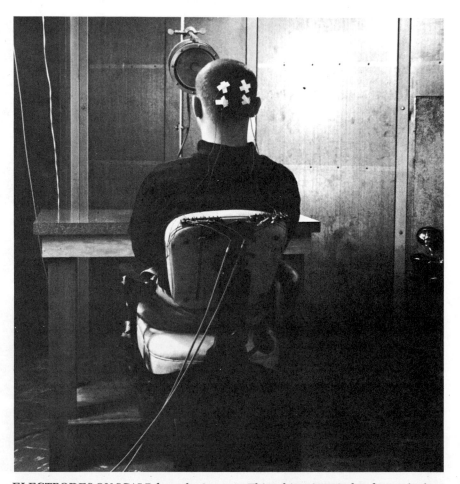

ELECTRODES ON SCALP detect brain waves. This subject, in an isolated room, is viewing brief flashes of light at regular intervals. A special computer simultaneously analyzes the brain waves from the visual region in back of head, producing the record seen in illustration on page 22. The photograph was made at the Massachusetts Institute of Technology.

ologists reasoned that if these waves were analyzed mathematically, using the technique known as Fourier analysis, components might be uncovered that were hidden to the unaided eye. The principle behind Fourier analysis is that any periodic wave form, however complex, can be resolved into elementary sine-wave components. Unfortunately the brain emits so many irregular and nonperiodic potential changes that the usefulness of this well-known principle is open to challenge.

During World War II W. Grey Walter of the Burden Neurological Institute in England spearheaded the development of the first practical instrument for making an automatic frequency analysis of consecutive short segments—each arbitrarily limited to 10 seconds—of an EEG trace. The Walter analyzer reports the mean relative amplitude at each frequency over the whole period being integrated but cannot indicate the time sequence in which the frequencies occur. A short wave train of high amplitude has the same effect on the integrating device as a long train of low amplitude.

Also lost is all information about phase relations between trains of waves.

This type of analysis proved especially valuable when coupled with the finding that the frequency characteristics of the human EEG can often be controlled by having the subject look at a flashing light; the technique, called photic driving, was discovered in the early 1940's. Subsequently it was found that flashes of specific frequency will induce epileptic seizures in some epileptic patients. This is an example of a physiological finding reaching over into medicine to become a clinical diagnostic test. The Walter analyzer, which can be regarded as an early form of computer, still provides the simplest and most practical method for obtaining the average frequency spectrum of an EEG trace.

The rapid development of high-speed general-purpose and special-purpose computers in the past decade has opened up many new ways of analyzing the brain's electrical activity. At the same time techniques have been perfected for recording from electrodes implanted

within the unanesthetized brain and left in place for weeks or months. Although used primarily with animals, the technique has been extended to man for diagnostic and therapeutic purposes.

It is therefore now possible to study the relation of the brain's electrical activity to behavioral performance and, in the case of man, to subjective experience. After a long period of concentrating on the rhythm observable when the subject was at rest with the eyes closed, electroencephalographers began to divert their attention from "the engine when idling" to the "engine at work," thereby examining how the brain responds to various stimuli.

Many types of stimulation can be used —sounds, odors, flashes of light, touch and so on—and their effect can be traced in brain recordings made both at the surface and deep within the brain. When such studies were first attempted in unanesthetized animals and man, it was soon discovered that the specific responses were largely masked, in the unanalyzed trace, by the ongoing EEG activity of the normal brain, activity that

AVERAGE RESPONSE COMPUTER (ARC) was designed by W. A. Clark, Jr., of the Lincoln Laboratory of M.I.T. It samples the brain waves for a prescribed interval after each stimulus, adding and averaging the samples. Oscilloscope face on computer (*left*) displays trace of average as the experiment proceeds. Reels of magnetic tape (*center, rear*) permanently record all the raw data. In the foreground, beside the laboratory technician, is an "X-Y plotter," which makes pen tracings of the averaged data.

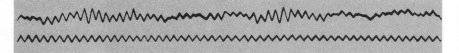

FIRST PUBLISHED ELECTROENCEPHALOGRAM (EEG) of man appeared in 1929. The recording was made by the German psychiatrist Hans Berger from the scalp of his young son. Upper channel is the EEG, lower one an artificial sine wave used as a marker.

had been conveniently depressed by the anesthetic agents in the earlier studies. Since the electrodes used must be small enough to discriminate between neuronal structures less than a millimeter apart, appropriate computer techniques are essential for detecting the faint signals that are all but lost in the roar of biological noise that is the normal milieu of the active brain.

The principal means for increasing the signal-to-noise ratio is simply to have the computer add up a large number of responses—anywhere from a few dozen to a few hundred—and calculate an average response. One can then regard this average response, or certain features of it, as the characteristic "signal" elicited by a given stimulus. In applying this technique the neurophysiologist must necessarily make certain assumptions about the character of the biological phenomena he regards as signal and that which he chooses to call noise.

In the usual averaging procedure the brain's potential changes, as picked up by several electrodes, are recorded on multichannel magnetic tape, in which one channel carries a pulse coincident with delivery of the stimulus. Since the stimulus may be presented at irregular intervals, a pulse is needed as a time marker from which the responses are "lined up" for averaging. In the averaging process only those potential changes that occur with a constant time relation to the pulse are preserved and emphasized. Those unrelated in time cancel out in the averaging process, even though in any single record they may be of higher amplitude. In this way responses never before detectable at the surface of the human skull not only can be found but also can be correlated with the subject's report of his sensations.

For example, the lightest of taps on the back of the hand is found to evoke a clear-cut response in one special area on the opposite side of the head [see illustrations on page 20]. Other computer analyses show that a click in the ear gives a decipherable response in another location on the scalp. A flash of light not only evokes an immediate sharp response in the visual area at the back of the head but also gives rise to a long-lasting train of waves, all time-locked to the flash [see illustration on page 22]. It has been shown, moreover, that clinical patients who report a disturbance in their subjective sensation of touch, hearing or sight produce EEG traces that reveal distortions when analyzed by computer.

The long-lasting train of waves evoked by a flash of light raises a number of questions. Is this the electrical sign of further processing of the initial message received by the eye? Is it the sign that the experience is being passed into storage, initiating in its passage the cellular changes that underlie memory? There is already evidence that under conditions that retain the initial sharp response but obliterate the subsequent wave train all memory of the experience is expunged. Two such conditions, which support this suggestion in human experiments, are anesthesia and hypnotically induced blindness.

Valuable though computers can be for averaging taped EEG records, they still leave the investigator feeling somewhat frustrated. Hours, and sometimes days, may elapse between the experiment and the completed analysis of the recordings. When he sees the results, the investigator often wishes he could have changed the experimental conditions slightly, perhaps to accentuate a trend of some sort that seemed to be developing, but it is too late. The experimental material of the biologist, and particularly of the electrophysiologist studying the brain, is living, changing material from which he must seize the opportunity to extract all possible information before the passage of time introduces new variables. The computers familiar to business and industry have not been designed with this problem in mind.

To meet the needs of the neurophysiologist a few computers have now been built that process brain recordings virtually as fast as data is fed in from the electrodes. The investigator can observe the results of his manipulations on the face of a cathode-ray tube or other display device and can modify his experiment at will. One of the first machines built to operate in this way is the Average Response Computer (ARC), designed by W. A. Clark, Jr., of the Lincoln Laboratory of the Massachusetts Institute of Technology [see illustration on preceding page]. ARC is a simple-to-operate, special-purpose digital computer that requires no programmer as a middleman between the biologist and the machine.

When searching for an evoked response, Clark's computer samples the EEG at a prescribed interval after the stimulus, converts it into a seven-digit binary number proportional to the amplitude and sends the number into one of the many memory registers. This particular register receives and adds all further numbers obtained at the same interval after each stimulus. ARC is equipped to sample the EEG at 254 different time intervals and to store thousands of samples at each interval. Only rarely, however, is the full capacity of the register required. The cumulative sums in each register are displayed on an oscilloscope after each stimulus [see illustration on page 18]. The investigator watches the cumulative display and stops the stimulation when he sees that he has enough signal-to-noise discrimination to satisfy the needs of the experiment. He can then photograph the face of the oscilloscope or have the cumulative wave form printed out graphically by a plotter.

What might one see if one were to watch the build-up of summed re-

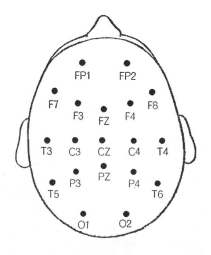

TYPICAL MODERN EEG shows that different regions of cortex give rhythms that differ widely. Berger thought the whole brain

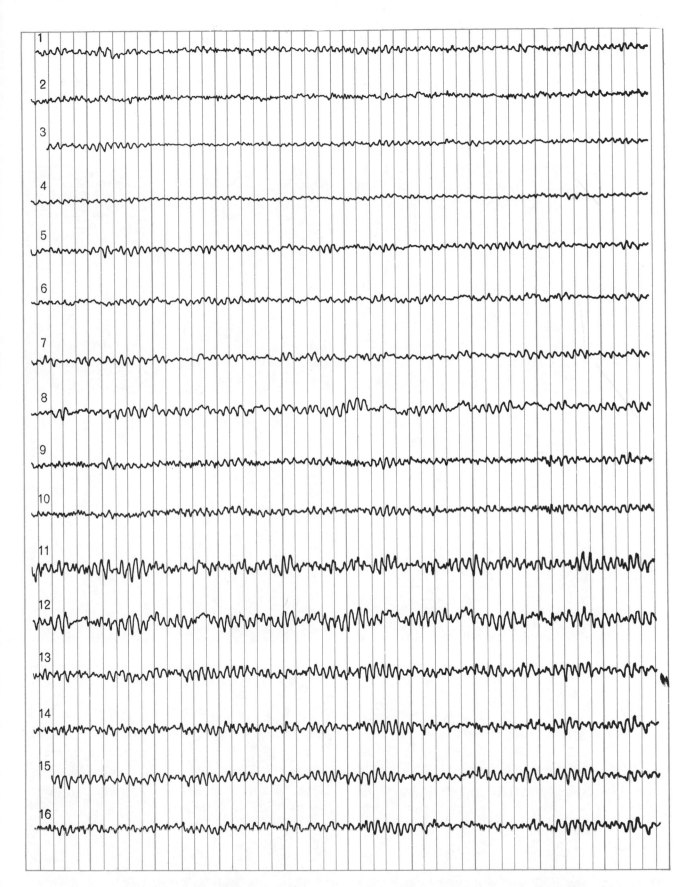

emitted only one rhythm. Today as many as 16, 24 and even 32 channels can be used. The great complexity obviously makes computer analysis desirable. Each EEG trace records changes in electric potential between two electrodes. Thus line 1 came from electrodes FP1 and F7 on head as diagramed at left, while line 10 came from FP2 and C4. This data has not been processed by a computer.

sponses? If the man or animal being studied were anesthetized, the response would be markedly stereotyped; the averaged sum of 100 responses would look very much like the average of 50 responses. This is not so if the subject is unanesthetized. Responses to a series of clicks or flashes of light may show great variation, both in wave shape and in amplitude, and may require many samples before the characteristic signal emerges clearly from the background noise.

Operating in another of its modes, ARC can give an amplitude histogram, or profile, at any chosen interval after the stimulus. Such histograms indicate the degree of fluctuation of the response and its complexity. They supply the investigator with important clues to the behavioral state of the subject, to his level of wakefulness, to the degree of attention he is paying to the stimulus and to the feelings the stimulus arouses.

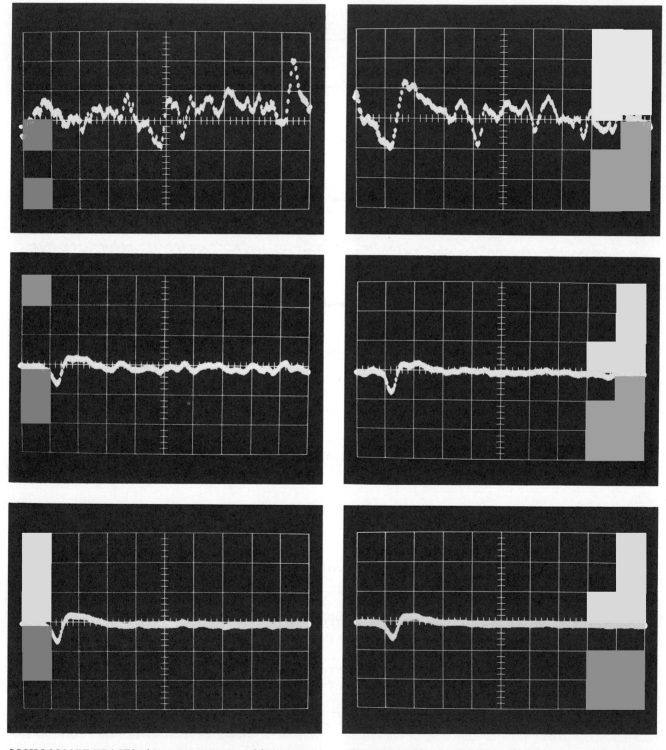

OSCILLOSCOPE TRACES of responses as averaged by computer appear while experiment is in progress, enabling experimenter to observe in "real time." As a result he can change conditions and stop when he has enough data. The traces (*left to right, top to bot-* *tom*) are averages of 1, 2, 32, 64, 128 and 512 responses. These traces appeared during an experiment by Nelson Kiang of the Eaton-Peabody Laboratory of the Massachusetts Eye and Ear Infirmary in Boston. The subject was responding to a long series of clicks.

When ARC is operated in the histogram mode, the memory registers are set to count the number of times the amplitude, or voltage, of the EEG falls within a certain preset range. Each register is set for a different range and the results are finally written out as a histogram for the chosen interval [*see top illustration on this page*]. By analyzing other intervals similarly one can put together a composite survey.

The study of such records may reveal little dispersion of amplitude at some particular interval after the stimulus and a much greater dispersion at some other interval. This may be a clue that the neuronal message in the first case has traveled over a nerve pathway containing few synapses, or relays, and thus has been subject to little dispersion, whereas in the second case the message has reached the recording site after traveling through multiple paths that finally converge. The complex wave train evoked by a single flash of light is susceptible to this interpretation. The initial deflection is caused by impulses that have traveled through a few synapses only and by means of the large, rapidly conducting fibers of the specific visual system. The subsequent shallower waves—so clearly revealed by the computer—reach the cortex through the more slowly conducting, indirect, nonspecific system with its many relay stations. The histogram of the earlier event, being more stereotyped, shows less dispersion around the median than does the histogram of the later events. Still more elaborate processing of histograms can show whether the amplitudes follow a normal, bell-shaped distribution pattern or are skewed in some manner.

If a physicist were to analyze the results of a series of complex experiments in his field, he would normally expect to find the results to be invariant. The biologist, working with an unanesthetized animal or man, can search in vain for an invariant response. It is precisely this subtlety of variation that electrophysiologists have recently identified as the concomitant of behavioral change. One such change is known as habituation. Early workers in electrophysiology could perceive, in their unanalyzed records, subtle changes in the shape of an EEG trace when the subject had been repeatedly exposed to the same stimulus. Computer analyses have now revealed clearly that under such conditions significant changes take place not only in the EEG as recorded outside the skull but even more markedly in

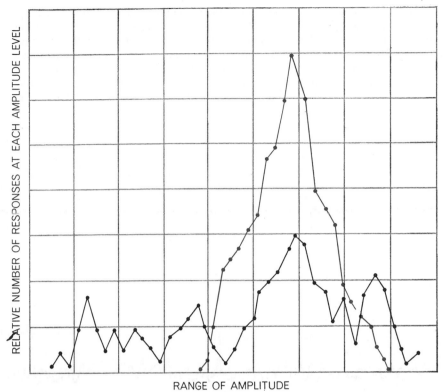

RANGE OF AMPLITUDE

STEREOTYPED RESPONSE of brain of anesthetized animal to flash of light (*colored curve*) shows plainly when computer is programed to give information on amplitude variation. Unanesthetized animal gives widely fluctuating response (*black curve*). In each case the computer analyzed point in time at which response reached its maximum amplitude.

recordings made deep within the brain.

For example, the Average Response Computer has been used to analyze the electrical activity recorded from a particular relay station in a nucleus located deep in the mid-line region of an animal's brain. The nucleus, in turn, lies within the portion of the brain called the thalamus. Until a dozen years ago

little except its anatomy was known about this mid-line region of the thalamus and its inflow from the portion of the brain stem called the reticular formation. The thalamic region and the reticular formation together constitute the nonspecific sensory system mentioned earlier.

In 1949 H. W. Magoun (now at the

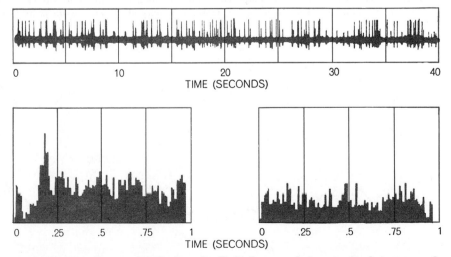

HISTOGRAMS showing distribution of cell discharges relative to stimulus were made by George L. Gerstein at M.I.T. Upper line shows a short section of raw data consisting of cell discharges in the auditory part of a cat's brain in response to one-per-second clicks. The histogram at left shows number of cell discharges at fractional-second intervals after clicks. The histogram at right shows same analysis of cell discharges when no click occurred.

University of California in Los Angeles) and G. Moruzzi (now at the University of Pisa) jointly discovered that the reticular system is crucially concerned with the organism's state of alertness and with the behavioral nuances that lie in the continuum between vigilant attention and the oblivion of sleep. Later work has revealed further nuances that can be discerned in the electrical record only with the fine-grained analyses that a computer can provide.

Computer analyses of records from one of the mid-line nuclei of this non-specific sensory system in an unanesthetized animal have detected many unsuspected details. For example, when a light, flashing at a constant rate, is directed into the animal's eye, the ARC oscilloscope reveals that the averaged response is not at all simple but contains

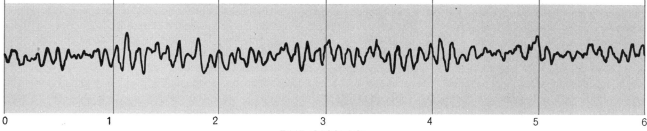

TAP RECORD

4,6 RECORD

6,8 RECORD

0   1   2   3   4   5   6

TIME (SECONDS)

REGULAR TAPS ON LEFT HAND, indicated by top trace, do not show up in standard EEG (*next two traces*). Ongoing activity of brain drowns signal even though electrode 4 (*see diagram of head on opposite page*) is over area that receives nerve inflow from hand.

4,6 RECORD

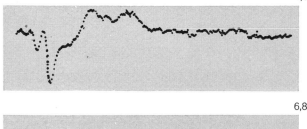

6,8 RECORD

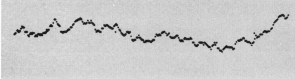

AVERAGED RESPONSE after 90 taps, however, tells a different story. Upper trace at left, from electrodes 4 and 6, shows that the brain definitely reacts to the taps. The computer also detects a faint response when the right hand, which is on the same side of the body as the electrodes, is tapped. (Nerves on the left side of the body are connected with the right side of the brain and vice versa.)

three distinct components and that, as time passes, one of these components gradually fades out. If the computer's mode of operation is then changed so as to produce amplitude histograms, the third component is found to have a greater dispersion than the other two and a skewed distribution.

A hypothesis suggests itself. One of the relatively constant components may pass on to the visual cortex, thereby signifying to the animal that the stimulus is visual and not, say, olfactory or auditory. Perhaps the second component indicates that the stimulus is a recurrent one. The third and waning component may be signaling "unexpectedness" and, by dropping out, may carry the message that the stimulus is simply repeating over and over without change. It may be saying, in effect, that the stimulus is devoid of novelty (or information) and can be safely ignored.

The experimenter, still watching the computer's oscilloscope, can then proceed to test this hypothesis by introducing novelty into the stimulus. For example, he can change the strength of the flash, its wavelength or its repetition rate, and watch for the reappearance of the third component. In this way the three-way interlocution between investigator, subject and machine proceeds.

The questions the investigator asks are not exhausted by those outlined above. He may want to know what the individual cells of the brain are doing. It has been known for many years that the frequency of action "spikes" in a nerve fiber is related to the intensity of the stimulus. As a rule the more intense the stimulus, the higher the firing rate. But how wasteful of "channel capacity"

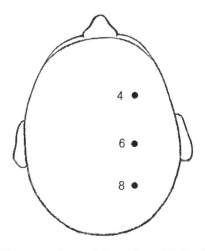

The averaged record from electrodes 6 and 8, which are not over the "hand area" of the brain, shows no response to the taps.

(to use the language of information theory) it would be if the only information conveyed by the action spikes were limited to stimulus intensity.

This has led investigators to consider the fluctuations in the groupings of these unit discharges. The unanalyzed record is bewildering, because different kinds of cell give different patterns of response to a given stimulus. Some that were busily active stop firing when the stimulus is given; others wake from idleness and burst into activity; still others signal their response by a change in the pattern of discharge.

Computers are invaluable for this type of analysis. The Average Response Computer, as one example, has a special mode of operation that helps to clarify this patterning of activity in individual brain cells. It does this by giving a histogram of the time intervals between successive cell discharges. Each of its memory registers is allotted a different interspike interval. Whenever a cell fires, the interval since the last firing is established and a digit is added to the appropriate register. On command, the digits accumulated in the different registers are written out as a histogram [see bottom illustration on page 19]. Analyses of this kind, pioneered by George L. Gerstein with the TX-O computer at the Massachusetts Institute of Technology, have revealed a differentiation of response mechanisms among cortical cells that indicates a far greater degree of discriminatory capability than the old frequency-intensity rule would suggest.

Among other computer techniques under development are those for identification of temporal patterns in the EEG. These techniques should relieve the electroencephalographer of the tedium of searching many yards of records for meaningful changes. For example, Belmont Farley of the Lincoln Laboratory of M.I.T. has worked out programs for analyzing the trains of alpha rhythm that come and go in the EEG of man and provide clues to his level of consciousness and to the normality of his brain.

Farley's program specifies the range of amplitude, frequency and duration of the pattern known as an alpha burst. The program allows the investigator to make a statistical examination of the EEG of the same individual, as recorded under different experimental circumstances. The investigator may be interested in the effect of drugs or the changes brought about by conditioning of behavior. The degree of variation in the EEG can be accurately and objectively assessed, removing the hazards of subjective judgment. It is obvious that

such objective methods of appraisal can be of great value in the clinical use of the EEG.

The rhythmicity of the EEG, as exemplified in the alpha rhythm, continues to be a mystery. It was first thought that brain waves were merely the envelopes of the spike discharges of the underlying neurons. But this view had to be abandoned when microelectrodes, reporting from inside the brain, showed the hypothesis untenable. It is now thought that the EEG waves reflect the waxing and waning of excitability in what are called the dendritic layers of the cortex. (Dendrites are hairlike processes that extend from the body of a nerve cell.) Quite unlike the explosive discharge of the nerve cell itself, the finely graded changes in dendritic activity seem to modulate cortical excitability.

In the common laboratory animals, with their comparatively small association cortexes, the simple, almost sinusoidal oscillation of the alpha rhythm is hard to find, if it exists at all. It is therefore tempting to relate rhythmic waves to the large volume of association cortex possessed by man. These rhythmic waves usually signify that the brain is not under bombardment by stimuli, and their stability may reflect the homeostatic, or self-stabilizing, processes of the association cortex when undisturbed by the processing of transmitted messages.

In the course of evolution homeostatic processes throughout the body, largely under the control of the brain stem, have provided the higher animals with a remarkably constant internal environment. The constancy of this milieu intérieur, as the French physiologist Claude Bernard pointed out, is "la condition de la vie libre." Conceivably it is the stabilizing effect of the brain stem that frees the cortex of man for its highest achievements.

Whatever the case, it has been discovered by the statistical method of autocorrelation analysis that EEG recordings from man often show a long-persisting phase constancy that has not been found in lower animals. There are also individual differences. In some people phase-locking of oscillations is, for long periods, nearly as predictable as a clock. In others (a minority) there is little, if any, stability of phase. Are the people who lack a stable phase-locked oscillation unable to clear their association cortex of interfering activity? Have they not yet attained the "free life" of Claude Bernard?

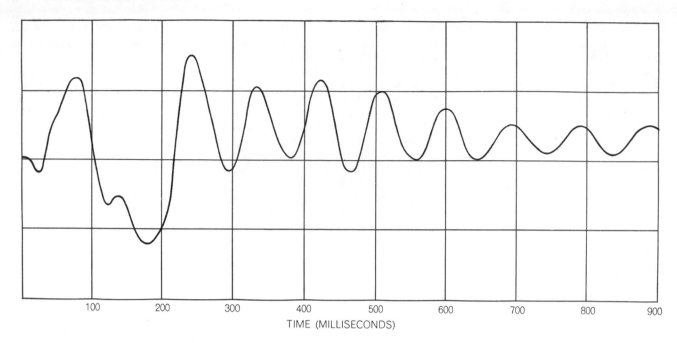

TIME (MILLISECONDS)

LONG-LASTING TRAIN OF WAVES can be recorded from scalp following flash of light. This, of course, is an averaged record of many responses to many flashes. It emphasizes only the changes in electric potential time-locked to the flash and washes out the "noisy" background activity, which is actually of much higher amplitude. The flashes were all synchronized with beginning of trace.

One of the earliest workers to encourage electroencephalographers to explore this approach was the M.I.T. mathematician Norbert Wiener. His strong influence lies behind much of the computer work in this area, and especially that which has come from the laboratory of Walter A. Rosenblith of M.I.T.'s Research Laboratory for Electronics.

No account of the electroencephalographer's use of computers should omit their recent use in seeking information about the correlations between deep and superficial activity in various parts of the brain. What is the correlation between the waves recorded from the outside of man's skull and activity in the depths? With what confidence can one say that an EEG is "normal" when only scalp recordings can be made?

The first answers to these and many other questions are just emerging as computer analyses of electrical potentials from inside man's head are being correlated with those simultaneously recorded from his scalp. As more and more clinical investigators adopt computer techniques it should be possible to build up for the electroencephalographer, who can record only from the surface of the unopened scalp, a reference library of correlations to use in assessing the probability of events in the hidden depths of the brain.

Nearly all the applications of the computer described here have involved averaging. This is not only because the average is an empirically useful statistic but also because many brain investigators suspect that the brain may work on a probabilistic basis rather than a deterministic one. To analyze the myriad complexities of the brain's function by nonstatistical description is too gigantic a task to be conceived, but exploration in terms of probability theory is both practical and rational. In characterizing nervous activity one would not therefore attempt the precise definition that arithmetic demands but would seek the statistical characteristics of the phenomena that appear to be relevant.

The margin of safety that the brain has for acting appropriately on a probabilistic basis would be much greater than that which would be imposed by a deterministic, arithmetically precise operation. Chaos would result from the least slip up of the latter, whereas only a major divergence from the mean would disturb a system working on a probability basis. The rigidity of arithmetic is not for the brain, and a search for a deterministic code based on arithmetical precision is surely doomed to disappointment.

One can speculate how a brain might work on statistical principles. Incoming sensory messages would be compared with the statistical distribution of nerve cell characteristics that have developed as functions of the past activities of these cells. Significance of the message would then be evaluated and, according to the odds, its message could

be appropriately acted on or ignored. The brain, with its wealth of interconnections, has an enormous capacity for storage, and one can observe the development of appropriate responses by watching the limited capacity of the child grow to the superior capacity of the man.

One might ask why it is the brain investigator, among biological scientists, who has reached out most eagerly to the computer for help. A likely answer is that within man's skull—a not very large, rigidly limited space—a greater number of transactions are taking place simultaneously than in any other known system of its size. The multiplicity of signals that these transactions emit and the truly formidable complexity of codes that they may use have proved beyond the capabilities of analysis by the methods of an earlier age.

The neurophysiologist cannot hope to study a single variable in isolation. The living brain will not still its busy activity so that the investigator can control whatever he wishes; neither will it forget its past. Every stimulus, however "constant" the experimenter may succeed in making it, enters a nervous system that is in an ever changing state. The "stimulus-response" experiment of an earlier day is no longer adequate. Experiment has to enter a phase of greater sophistication that may well prove out of reach without the help of the computer.

3

THE RETICULAR FORMATION

J. D. FRENCH
May 1957

The title "reticular formation" might suggest various things—a football line-up, a chess gambit, a geological structure or whatnot—but as readers of SCIENTIFIC AMERICAN well know, it is actually a part of the brain, a once mysterious part which has re-cently come in for a great deal of attention from biologists. The reticular formation is a tiny nerve network in the central part of the brain stem. Investigators have discovered that this bit of nerve tissue, no bigger than your little finger, is a far more important structure than anyone had dreamed. It underlies our awareness of the world and our ability to think, to learn and to act. Without it, an individual is reduced to a helpless, senseless, paralyzed blob of protoplasm.

The actual seat of the power to think,

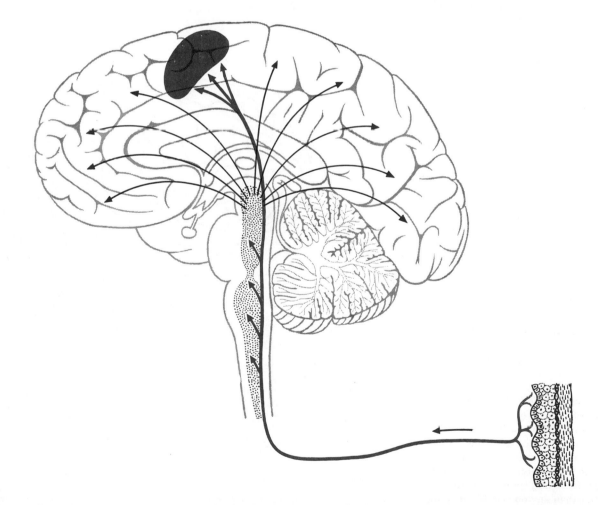

THE RETICULAR FORMATION is the area stippled with red in this cross section of the brain. A sense organ (*lower right*) is connected to a sensory area in the brain (*upper left*) by a path-way extending up the spinal cord. This pathway branches into the reticular formation. When a stimulus travels along the pathway, the reticular formation may "awaken" the entire brain (*black arrows*)

to perceive, indeed to respond to a stimulus with anything more than a reflex
reaction, lies in the cortex of the brain.
But the cortex cannot perceive or think
unless it is "awake." Consider the alarm
ring that awakens you in the morning:
several seconds pass before you recognize the disturbance and can respond to
stop the painful jangle. A sensory signal
arriving at the cortex while it is asleep
goes unrecognized. Experiments on
anesthetized individuals have shown further that stimulation of the cortex alone
is not sufficient to awaken the brain.
Something else must arouse the cortex:
that something is the reticular formation.

It was only about eight years ago that
two eminent physiologists, H. W. Magoun of the U. S. and Giuseppe Moruzzi
of Italy, working together at Northwestern University, discovered this fact.
They were exploring the mystery of the
reticular formation's functions by means
of an electrode planted in this area in
the brain of a cat. They found that stimulation of the area with a small electric
current would awaken a drowsing cat as
peacefully as a scratch on the head. The
animal's behavior, and recordings of
changes in its brain waves with the electroencephalograph, showed all the signs
of a normal arousal from sleep. Magoun
and Moruzzi decided that the reticular
formation acted as a kind of sentinel
which aroused the cortex, and they
named it the RAS (reticular activating
system).

Now mysteries began to clear—not
only with regard to the function of the
reticular formation but also as to some
previously puzzling features of the nervous system's anatomy. All the great sensory nerve trunks in the body have
brush-like branches which stream into
the reticular formation. Sensory signals
from all parts of the body go to the cortex by direct pathways, but on the way
through the brain stem they also feed
into the reticular formation. Evidently
the reticular formation, when so stimulated, sends arousing signals to the cortex. The awakened cortex can then interpret the sensory signals it is receiving
directly.

The RAS is a kind of general alarm:
that is to say, it responds in the same
way to any sensory stimulus, whether
from the organs of hearing, seeing, touch
or whatever. Its response is simply to
arouse the brain, not to relay any specific
message. Its signals spray the entire cortex rather than any one center of sensation. A noise, a flash of light, a pinch on
the hand, the smell of burning wood, a

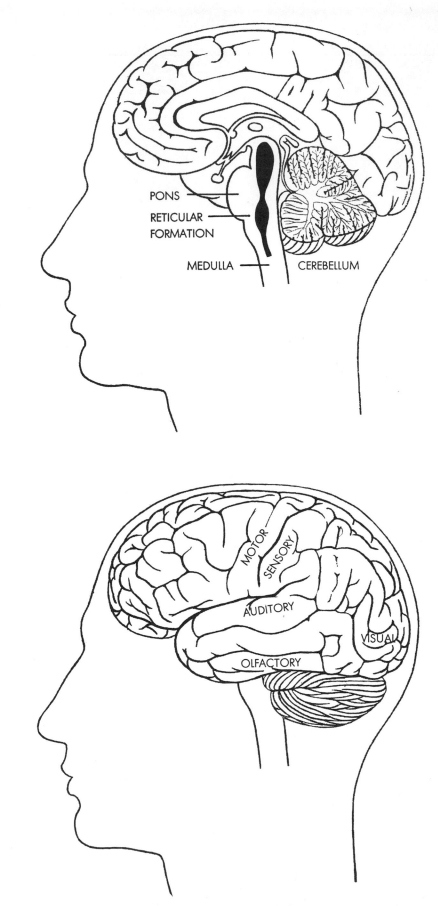

RELATIONSHIP OF THE RETICULAR FORMATION (*black area*) **to various parts
of the brain is indicated at the top. The functional areas of the brain are outlined at bottom.**

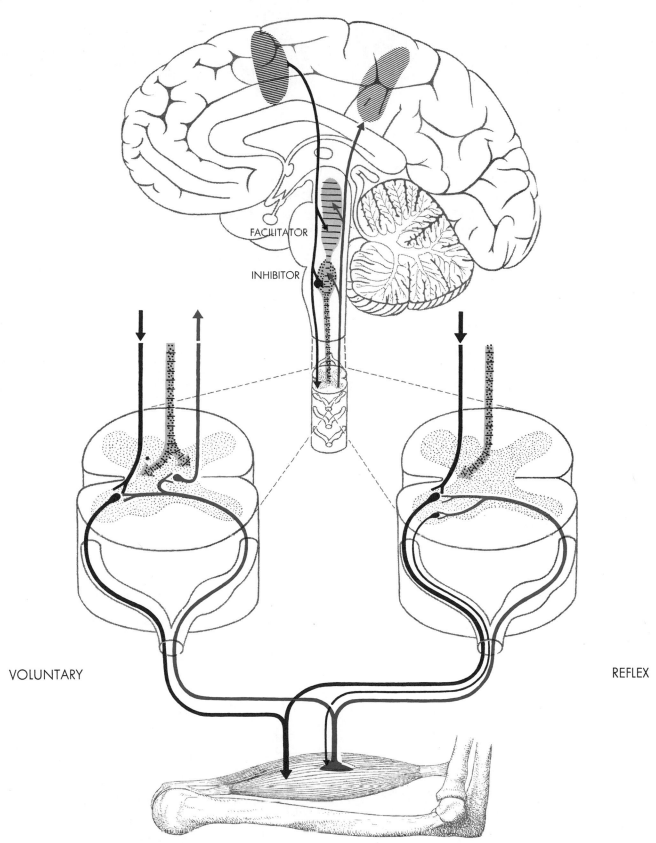

FACILITATOR

INHIBITOR

VOLUNTARY

REFLEX

MOVEMENTS ARE MODIFIED by the RAS. In voluntary movement sensory nerves (*red*) conduct impulses from the muscle spindle (*bottom*) to a sensory area in the brain (*red hatching*). Motor nerves (*black*) conduct impulses from the motor area (*black hatching*) to the muscle. Both nerve systems branch into the RAS. The RAS sends down impulses (*heavy red arrows*) that facilitate or inhibit the response. In reflex movement sensory impulses are passed on immediately to motor nerves in the spinal cord. One nerve activates the muscle and maintains its "tone." The other (*thin black line*) sensitizes the spindle. The RAS controls both.

pain in the stomach—any of these excites the reticular formation to alert the cortex to a state of wakefulness, so that when the specific stimulus arrives at the appropriate center in the cortex, the brain can identify it.

Apparently the RAS learns to be selective in its sensitivity to particular stimuli. A mother may be instantly awakened by the faintest whimper of her baby. Father, on the other hand, may sleep through baby's fiercest bellowings but be aroused by a faint smell of smoke. A city dweller may sleep peacefully in the midst of the riotous din of traffic while his visitor from the country spends a sleepless night wishing he were elsewhere. It is as if the RAS becomes endowed by experience with the ability to discriminate among stimuli, disregarding those it has found unimportant and responding to those that are helpful. Happily so. Imagine how unbearable life would be if you could not shut out most of the environment from consciousness and were at the mercy of the thousands of sights and sounds simultaneously clamoring for attention.

The RAS, like the starter in an automobile, starts the brain engine running, but this is by no means the end of its job. It goes on functioning to keep the individual in a conscious state. ("Consciousness" is a controversial word among psychologists, but for our purposes its meaning is clear enough.) If the RAS cannot function normally, consciousness is impossible. A person whose reticular formation has been permanently injured or destroyed falls into a coma from which he can never recover. He may live on for a year or more, but he remains as helpless and shut off from communication as a vegetable.

If uninjured, the RAS can maintain a wakeful state (but not consciousness) even in the absence of the cortex. In a newborn baby the cortex has not yet begun to function, but the infant nevertheless has short periods of wakefulness throughout the day. The same is true of the tragic creatures born without any cortex at all (called anencephalic monsters). Such a child (sometimes kept alive for three or four years) never achieves any understanding or real contact with its surroundings, but it has periods of wakefulness during which it swallows and digests food, smiles and coos when fondled and cries when treated roughly. We must conclude, therefore, that wakefulness of a very crude sort is possible without the cortex, so long as the RAS can function.

For sustained wakefulness, however,

ASLEEP

CAT IS AWAKENED by the sound of a bell. The sound stimuli (*incoming red arrows*) reach the reticular activating system, or RAS, and the auditory area of the brain. The RAS acts (*black arrows*) to awaken the cortex so that it can "hear" signals arriving in the auditory

CORTEX IS STIMULATED by passing an electric current to the brain surface of a sleeping monkey. Six recording electrodes show the RAS has been activated to awaken the brain.

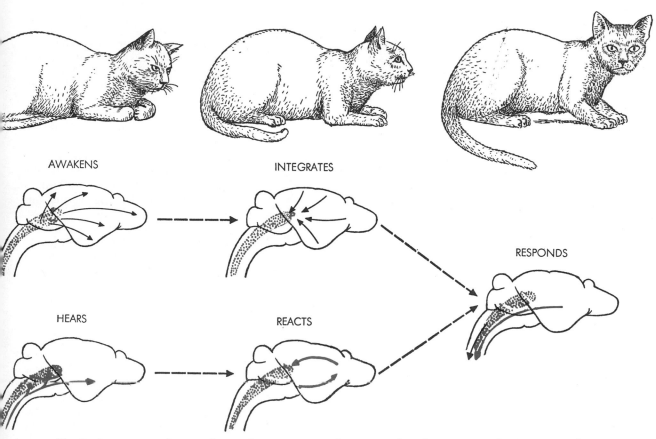

AWAKENS   INTEGRATES   RESPONDS

HEARS   REACTS

area. The brain waves at the top change from a pattern of sleep to one of wakefulness. The RAS then integrates the brain's activity so that the brain can react as a whole. The cat finally responds with a motor impulse (*outgoing red arrow*) that is regulated by the RAS. The cat then jumps to its feet and runs away. The entire process takes place in a matter of a few seconds.

RAS IS STIMULATED by passing an electric current into the brain stem of a sleeping monkey. Recording electrodes show a more abrupt transition from sleep to wakefulness. The waves become sharp, short and more frequent. This is a typical waking pattern.

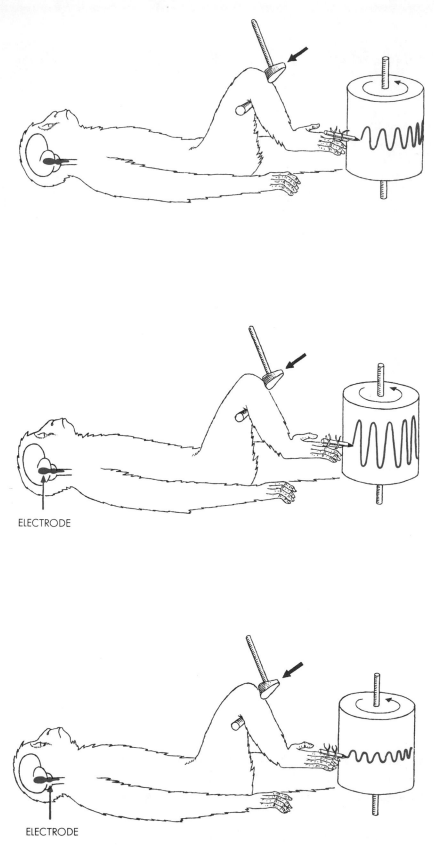

ELECTRODE

ELECTRODE

CONTROL OF REFLEX MOTOR REACTIONS by the reticular formation was demonstrated by this experiment on an anesthetized monkey. When the monkey's knee is tapped regularly, its knee jerks record a series of regular curves on a rotating drum (*top*). When the upper part of the monkey's reticular formation is stimulated, the jerks are larger (*middle*). When the lower part of the formation is stimulated, the jerks are smaller (*bottom*).

the cortex certainly is essential. The alert state seems to depend upon an interplay between the cortex and the RAS. The reticular formation is stimulated not only by the sensory nerves but also by impulses from some parts of the cortex. This has been demonstrated by electrical stimulation of certain areas of the cortex in monkeys: such stimulation will awaken a sleeping monkey. When the experiment is tried on a monkey that is awake, it evokes a dramatic response. The monkey instantly stops whatever it is doing and looks about intently and slightly puzzled, as if to say: "What was that?" It does not seem distressed or agitated—only warily alert. So it would seem that in the waking state the RAS plays a part, in combination with the cortex, in focusing attention and probably in many other mental processes.

All this raises the possibility that the RAS may be importantly involved in mental disorders. Investigations of this possibility have already begun by means of experiments with drugs. It is natural to start with anesthetic and sleep-inducing drugs, to see how they affect the RAS. The results of these experiments are illuminating but not surprising. They show that the drug blocks the flow of nerve impulses in the reticular formation but has little effect on the flow along the direct pathways from sense organs to the cortex. As the anesthesia wears off, the flow in the RAS returns to normal. A stimulating drug, on the other hand, has the opposite effect: it enhances the conduction of impulses in the RAS. It will be interesting to extend these experiments to the new tranquilizing drugs and the substances that produce experimental psychoses. Already there is evidence that these drugs do affect the functioning of the RAS.

Still another domain is under the control of this amazingly cogent bit of tissue in the brain. The RAS apparently has a hand in regulating all the motor activities of the body. It can modify muscle movements of both the voluntary type (controlled by the brain) and the reflex type (controlled in the spinal cord).

Just as the brain cortex has specific centers of sensation, it also has specific motor centers which generate muscle contractions. If one stimulates a motor center with an electric current, the appropriate muscles will respond, but the resulting body movements are jerky and uncontrolled. These powerful movements are normally controlled and polished by other motor centers of the cortex, acting through the reticular formation. If the RAS is not stimulated or does not function properly, the movements will be jerky.

More surprising is the fact that the RAS can also act on the reflexes, centered in the spinal cord. The reflex apparatus has two functions. First, it generates automatic muscle movements. When signals from a sudden and alarming sensory stimulus (*e.g.*, touching something hot) arrive at the spinal cord, they are passed on immediately to an adjacent motor nerve and travel right back to the affected part of the body to jerk it away. In general, the automatic, reflex activities are protective—responses to danger or sudden challenges in the surroundings. But some of them can be tricked into action by suddenly stretching a muscle: for example, a tap on the knee elicits the well-known knee jerk.

The second function of the reflex system is to keep the muscles ready for action by maintaining "tone"—that is, a state of partial contraction. Just as a violin string must be stretched to a certain tension before it can emit music, so a muscle must be maintained at a certain tension to respond efficiently to a stimulus. The mechanism that regulates its resting tension, or "tone," is a small structure within the muscle called a "spindle." When a muscle contracts, it squeezes the spindle; when it relaxes, the pressure on the spindle loosens. Either departure from normal tone causes

the spindle to send signals by way of a sensory nerve to the spinal cord; there they excite a motor nerve to correct the contraction or relaxation of the muscle. This feedback system automatically keeps each muscle at precisely the right tone. And the appropriate tone itself is adjusted to suit the needs of the moment by nerve impulses which regulate the sensitivity of the spindle.

Now experiments have clearly demonstrated that the RAS exerts some control over voluntary and reflex motor reactions. Let us take for illustration an experiment on the reflex knee jerk, which is easy and convenient to perform. A monkey is anesthetized and a pen is tied to its toe to record the size of its knee kicks on a rotating drum. We keep tapping its knee and we get a uniform response, recorded as a nice series of regular curves on the drum. Then we suddenly stimulate the reticular formation electrically. The knee jerks immediately become larger: the RAS has enhanced them. When we stop stimulating it, the kicks return to normal size. Now in the course of exploratory experiments along the reticular formation a new fact emerges. If we stimulate the formation at a point toward its lower end in the brain stem, the kicks are not enhanced but instead are inhibited!

Following up this finding, we discover that these centers can enhance or inhibit sensory as well as motor impulses. In short, the RAS acts as a kind

of traffic control center, facilitating or inhibiting the flow of signals in the nervous system.

The astonishing generality of the RAS gives us a new outlook on the nervous system. Neurologists have tended to think of the nervous system as a collection of more or less separate circuits, each doing a particular job. It now appears that the system is much more closely integrated than had been thought. This should hardly surprise us. A simple organism such as the amoeba reacts with totality toward stimuli: the whole cell is occupied in the act of finding, engulfing and digesting food. Man, even with his 10 billion nerve cells, is not radically different. He must focus his sensory and motor systems on the problem in hand, and for this he obviously must be equipped with some integrating machine.

The RAS seems to be such a machine. It awakens the brain to consciousness and keeps it alert; it directs the traffic of messages in the nervous system; it monitors the myriads of stimuli that beat upon our senses, accepting what we need to perceive and rejecting what is irrelevant; it tempers and refines our muscular activity and bodily movements. We can go even further and say that it contributes in an important way to the highest mental processes– the focusing of attention, introspection and doubtless all forms of reasoning.

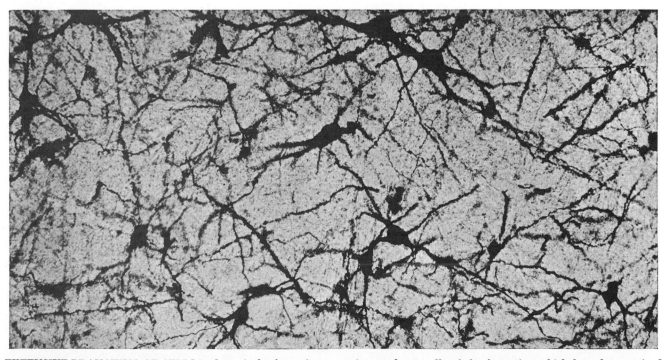

EXTENSIVE BRANCHING OF CELLS in the reticular formation is depicted by this photomicrograph of a section of the reticular formation in the brain of a dog. The dark areas in the photo- micrograph are cells of the formation which have been stained with silver. The section was lent by Drs. M. and A. Scheibel of the Medical School of the University of California at Los Angeles.

4

THE PHYSIOLOGY OF IMAGINATION

JOHN C. ECCLES
September 1958

Imagination—the synthesis of new ideas and images from elements of past experiences and perceptions—is a process that goes on in the sheet of gray matter, .1 inch thick and 400 square inches in area, which forms the deeply folded surface of the two great hemispheres of the brain. This statement contains a premise that is best made explicit. It says all mental activity, including the supreme activity of creative imagination, arises somehow from the activity of the brain. Few would deny this premise, though a wealth of philosophical disputation lies concealed in that noncommittal word "somehow." Our task here is to see how far our present ideas on the working of the brain can be related to the experiences of mind. The way to the imagination, the highest level of mental experience, lies through the lower levels of sensory experience, imagery, hallucination and memory, and

that is the path we shall traverse. All that we shall learn must itself, of course, be the product of perceiving, reasoning and imagining by our brains!

By the early part of this century, investigators had established the still-reasonable likeness of the brain to a complex telephone exchange, with lines of communication bringing electrical impulses in from sense organs and carrying impulses out to effector organs such as muscles or glands. They showed that the lines from the different sense organs ended in well-defined regions of the cerebral cortex: those from the eye at the back of the brain, those from the ear low down on each side, and those from the skin to a band running downwards from the midline over the side of the cerebral hemispheres. Just in front of the area associated with skin sensation they located a band for the control of movement: the

motor cortex. Since then workers with more refined techniques have confirmed the outlines of the map and filled in significant detail.

The switchboard analogy is further supported by the nature of the working units of the cortex, the individual nerve cells, or neurons. Functionally they are similar to simple relays in man-made circuits. Just as the relay has two states, either off or on, so the neuron fires an impulse or remains quiescent.

Beyond this point, however, the analogy fails. Study of the densely packed fine structure of the cortex has generated an immense literature on the various neuron types and their arrangement and interconnection in the half-dozen layers in which the cortex is divided [*see illustration below*]. We do not even begin to comprehend the functional significance of this richly com-

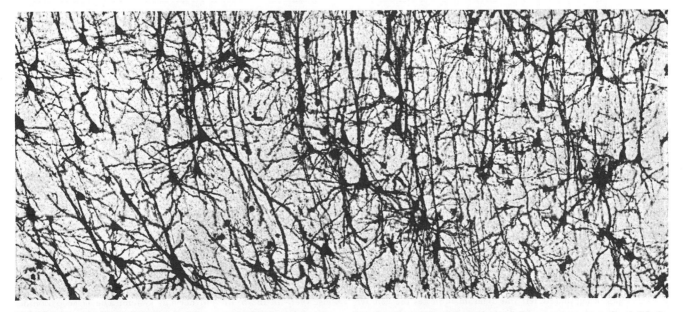

CEREBRAL CORTEX, a layer of cells .1 inch thick, appears in cross-section photomicrograph by D. A. Sholl of University College London. Only 1.5 per cent of the neurons are made visible by staining; their fibers make rich interconnection among them.

plex design. It is enough, however, to count the number of neurons—some 10 billion—and to see that each receives connections from perhaps 100 other neurons and connects to still 100 more. The profusion of interconnections among the cells of the gray matter is beyond all imagination; it is ultimately so comprehensive that the whole cortex can be thought of as one great unit of integrated activity. If we now persist in regarding the brain as a machine, then we must say that it is by far the most complicated machine in existence. We are tempted to say that it is infinitely more complicated than the most complex man-made machines: the electrical computers.

For the purposes of this consideration of brain activity in relation to imagination we may regard the cortex simply as a sheet of richly interconnected neurons. We must, however, consider briefly the design and behavior of the individual

cell and the character of its interconnection with others.

Each neuron is an independent living unit. It receives impulses from other cells through intricately branching dendrite fibers which sprout from its central body; it discharges impulses to other cells via a single slender fiber, the axon, which branches profusely to make contact with numerous receiving cells via their dendrites or directly to their central bodies.

Connections between cells are established by the synapses, specialized junctions where the cell membranes are separated by a cleft only 200 angstrom units across. At these synapses the transmitting cell secretes highly specific chemical substances whose high-speed reaction carries the signal from one cell to the next. The whole of this all-important life process occurs on an exquisitely small scale. A neuron operates on a power of about a thousand-millionth of a

watt (hence the entire brain operates on about 10 watts). At some synapses the transmitter substance is liberated in quanta of a few thousand molecules. The vesicles on the axon side of the synapse which apparently contain the transmitter substance are so tiny that, in accordance with the Heisenberg uncertainty principle, there is a relatively large uncertainty as to their location over a period as brief as a millisecond.

The neuron is characteristically an "all-or-nothing" relay. An impulse arriving across a synapse produces a very small and transient electrical effect, equivalent to .001 volt and lasting .01 to .02 second. It requires an excitation of about 10 times this voltage to cause the neuron to fire its discharge [see illustration on page 39]. Some of the incoming impulses on the surface of a neuron, however, come from a special inhibitory system of nerve cells and generate the reverse electrical change. Thus, under a

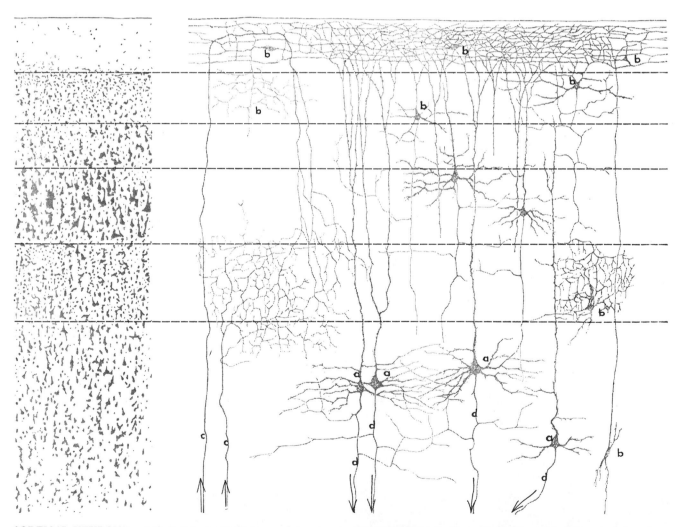

CORTICAL NEURONS and their interconnections are shown in this schematic diagram. At left the diagram indicates the relative density of the various types of cells in the six layers of the cortex. At right the diagram suggests the interconnections between cells established by their fibers. Input fibers (c) deliver impulses from elsewhere in the brain and nervous system. The large pyramidal cells (a), which are outnumbered by smaller cells (b), provide the axonal fibers (d) that carry the outgoing impulses from the cortex.

barrage of incoming impulses, a neuron must sum the opposing synaptic effects and can fire only when its net excitation exceeds the critical level. The time interval between the synaptic activation of a neuron and its own synaptic activation of the neuron next in sequence may nonetheless be no more than a millisecond. After firing, however, a neuron will resist activation for several milliseconds; its alternate states of refractoriness and excitability are probably reflected in the brain as a whole in the rhythm of the brain waves.

Since convergence of many impulses on any one neuron is required to make it discharge, chains of single neurons cannot propagate a wave of activity through the cortex. Rather the propagation resembles an advancing front of multilane traffic, with many cells activated in parallel at each synaptic linkage in the chain. Since it is difficult to visualize the operation of such a chain, let us study the properties of a much simpler network [*see illustration on page 34*]. Here simplification has been achieved by neglecting inhibitory action, by reducing the number of excitatory synapses made by each axon to no more than three, and by requiring the activation of only two synapses to excite a cell to discharge. By tracing the pathways of waves through this scheme we can get a faint glimpse of the way in which actual neuronal networks develop their virtuosity and plasticity.

We can see immediately the explanation for one remarkable property of a neuronal network: how two completely different inputs (one to cells A_1 and A_2, the other to A_3 and A_4) can be transmitted through the same pattern of cell connections, crossing each other and emerging as completely different outputs (D_3-D_4 and D_1-D_2). Naturally there would have to be an interval of at least several milliseconds between the two wavefronts, else there would be interference at the crossing by summation of synaptic excitations or by the postsynaptic refractoriness of the cells. Note that cells C_2 and C_3 each receive an excess of excitation (by three synapses); this helps the wave to withstand the effects of inhibition or the extinction of an excitatory line. Note also that some neurons along the fringe of an advancing wavefront receive a less than critical single excitation; such subliminally excited neurons give opportunity for growth of a wave should fringe impulses flow in from other sources.

On closer inspection we can see how

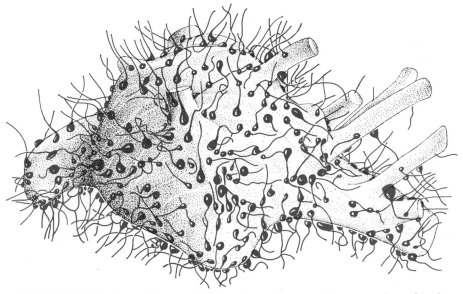

SINGLE NEURON, the working unit of the cortex, is diagrammed to suggest the multitude of interconnections with other cells. Axon fibers from other cells (*in color*) make synaptic junctions with the cell body and with its dendrites, of which only truncated stumps are shown. Impulses go out from the neuron via its axon, the stump of which appears at left.

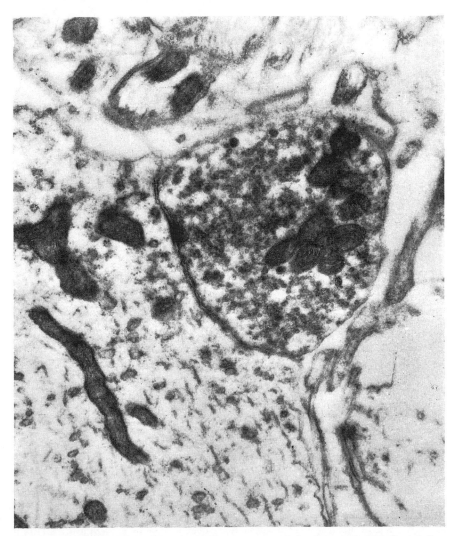

SYNAPTIC JUNCTION is shown in electron micrograph by George E. Palade and Sanford L. Palay of the Rockefeller Institute. A portion of the receiving cell fills the lower left quadrant, and the synaptic ending of the transmitting cell forms the rough triangle at center. In synaptic ending can be seen vesicles which may contain "transmitter substance."

34

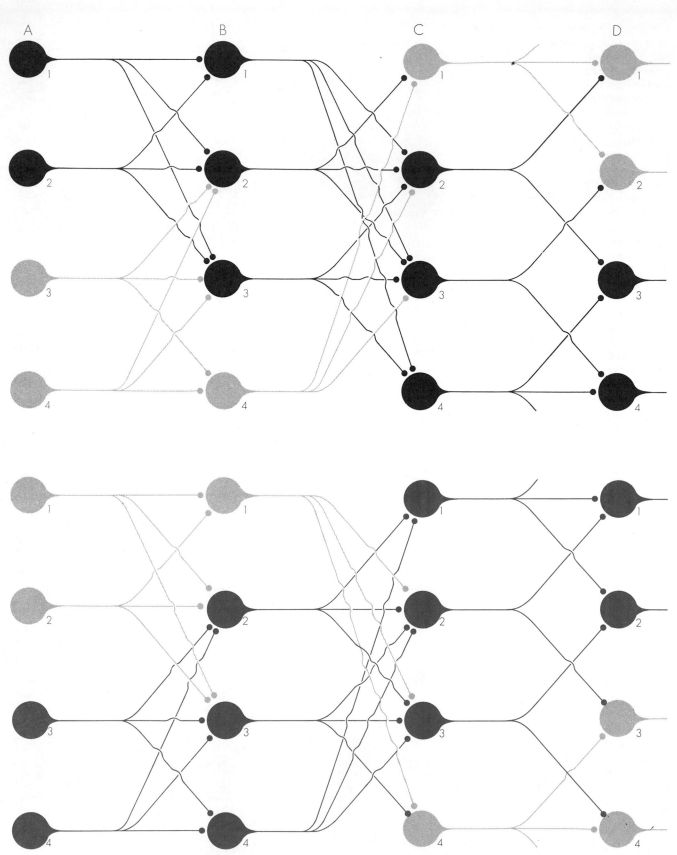

NEURONAL NETWORK, in highly schematic representation, shows how waves may be propagated along multilane pathways in cerebral cortex. In this scheme each cell body puts out an axon to the right, with as many as three branches, which carry impulses to the cell bodies in the next column; activation of at least two synapses is necessary to cause a cell to fire and relay the impulse. Activated cells and fibers are shown in black at top and in color at bottom; inactive cells and fibers are shown in gray. The diagram shows how two different incoming waves (*A1-A2 in the black pattern and A3-A4 in the colored pattern*) can propagate through the same cell connections, emerging as two different outputs (*D3-D4 in the black pattern and D1-D2 in the colored pattern*). The reader may trace out other patterns of operation. For example, it can be seen that a wave entering at A1 and A3 would fade out at column C.

a wave may be extinguished when there is inadequate convergence of impulses at any stage of the advancing wavefront; for example, a wave starting at cells A_1 and A_3 or A_2 and A_4, would necessarily fade out at the stage of synaptic relay from C to D. Our simple model suggests further that two wavefronts propagating at the same time into the same pool of neurons may coalesce and give an onwardly propagating wave having features derived from both, with additional features due to the summation. Thus activation of the two pathways leading to A_1-A_2 and to A_3-A_4 would cause all four neurons at the D stage to discharge. In addition neurons outside the diagram fringing C_1 and C_4 would be activated, creating opportunities for further interaction beyond the D neurons. Conversely we can visualize how a wavefront moving into neuronal pathways of suitable configuration may bifurcate into two waves propagating independently.

The transmission of a wavefront in the cortex is, of course, a much more complicated matter. With as many as 100 neurons involved at each relay stage, an advancing wave may sweep over 100,000 neurons in a single second. Such a wave has much richer potentiality than the simple case we have been considering. The diagram on the opposite page suggests a few of the configurations it may exhibit, branching at intervals, often abortively, reconverging, and coalescing with other waves.

Of particular interest are the closed loops that appear along the main pathways of the waves. Delisle Burns of McGill University and other investigators working with isolated slabs of cortex have found that rhythmical waves of several seconds' duration may be evoked by brief electrical stimulation. Such reverberatory activity implies the existence of closed self–re-exciting chains, in which waves recirculate again and again. These reverberatory waves need not follow stereotyped paths through the neuronal multilane channels, but may open new paths in the same vicinity on each rhythmic cycle, depending upon the convergence of excitatory impulses on each neuron.

It is important to realize that a wave is not restricted to advance through immediately adjacent neurons. The key pyramidal cells of the cortex operate not only on nearby cells, reached by short branches from their axons, but also upon cells in remote parts of the cortex. Via their very long branches which pass

through the massive bridge of nerve fibers in the corpus callosum, the pyramidal cells in one hemisphere of the brain may activate the symmetrical region of the other hemisphere. Thus part of an advancing wavefront may dip through the white matter to start up a new excitatory focus at a distant point in the cortex, or even perhaps in the thalamus or other large masses of nerve cells at the base of the brain. It may even return to reinforce the activity close to its zone of origin, so completing an immense reverberatory circuit.

Here we have come upon a mechanism to explain the brain waves made familiar by electroencephalography. During inattentive, but waking, states the predominating wave is that of the 10-a-second "alpha" rhythm. Its frequency is readily explained by the circulation of impulses in reverberatory circuits with a circuit time of about .1 second, which corresponds approximately to the post-synaptic refractory time of the pyramidal cell. To maintain even the low activity giving rise to the alpha rhythm the cortex must be subjected to continuous excitation by impulses from lower centers. Otherwise the activity of

the cortex virtually ceases, and it lapses into deep sleep.

When the brain is active, the alpha wave gives way to fast, small irregular waves. Visual experience, for example, brings an immense barrage of impulses into the cortical neurons which disrupts their tendency to settle into the phased activation of the alpha rhythm; concentration on a problem or on a task involving skill stirs up similarly heightened neuronal activity over a large area of the cortex. At such times the massive synaptic bombardment of the neurons must evoke discharges at intervals much shorter than the .1 second needed for a virtually full recovery of excitability. It is apparent, moreover, that specific local patterns of activity replace the diffuse random activation indicated by the alpha rhythm. The relatively high voltage of the alpha waves is evidence that large numbers of neurons are activated in phase, while the negligibly small potential of the fast waves suggests an intense and finely patterned activity. This interpretation is supported by an interesting experiment: A flickering light on the retina will drive

INTERSECTION OF PATHWAYS in schematic neuronal network corresponds to the intersection diagrammed in larger scale on the opposite page. Each dot represents a neuron, the black and colored dots being activated and the gray dots inactive. The two pathways utilize the same group of neurons, each entering the group from a different direction and leaving it in a different direction. The waves may have to be separated by an interval of time in order not to lose or merge their identity; the black wave occupies most of the intersection at the moment shown. Isolated black and colored dots represent "fringe" neurons excited by waves.

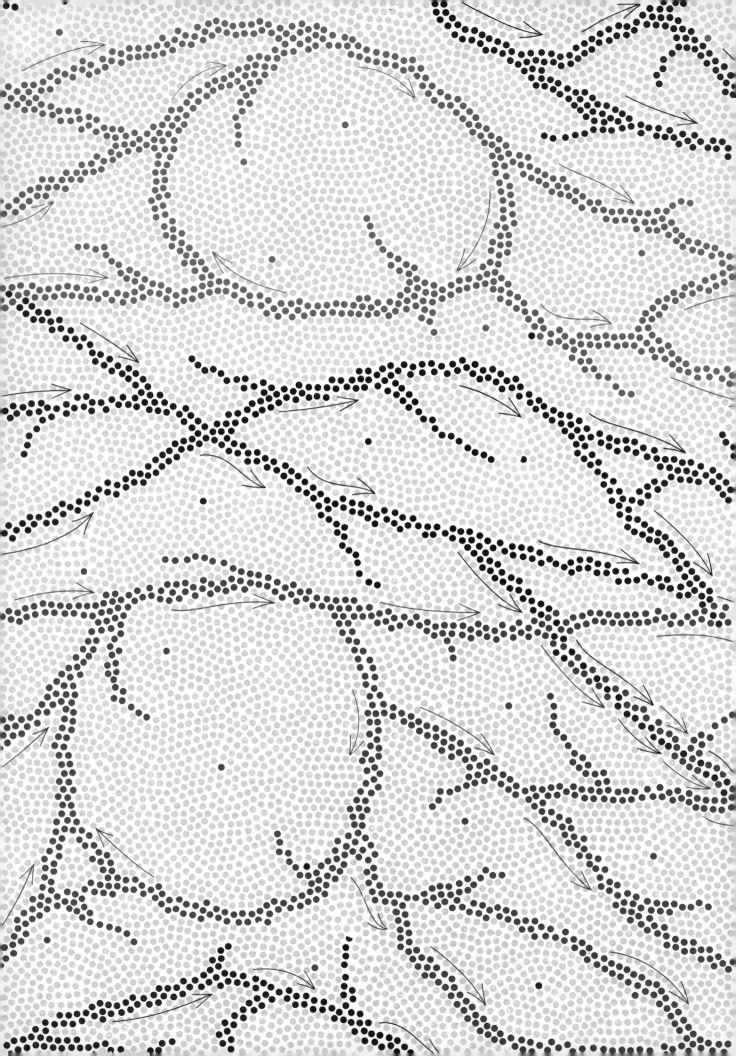

large-amplitude brain waves at frequencies up to 20 a second. Here the powerful visual pathway becomes a channel for the input of synchronous bursts of discharges rather than the fine pattern of activation of ordinary visual experience.

We are now ready to attempt a picture of the patterns in the cortex that attend simple sensory experience, the raw material on which in the end the imagination acts. As will be seen, our picture must be largely speculative. But it is based upon secure evidence which answers the primary question of how it is that information is conveyed to the cortex with a sufficient degree of specificity to make subsequent interpretation possible. As the well-established map of the cortex shows, each of the sense organs reports on its own lines to specific regions in the cortex. Vernon Mountcastle of Johns Hopkins University has found, moreover, that the sensory receptors of each different type, e.g., touch, pressure or joint movement, initially activate neurons in narrow vertical columns that are arranged as an interdigitated mosaic in the cortical map. At the receptors the intensity of stimulus from instant to instant is encoded in impulses of varying frequency, like a Morse system of dots only. This specificity of discharge is preserved through the sensory pathways up to the cortex, where it can be observed in the responses of single neurons. Sensory information thus comes into the brain as a specific signal to a sharply defined point in the cortex.

Beyond this stage virtually nothing is known about the evolving patterns of cortical activity. But we may speculate that a wavefront initiated by the arrival of a sensory signal in the cortex preserves the specificity of that signal as it propagates through the neuronal network. We may further assume that the interaction of wavefronts originating at different sites in the cortex effects the integration and synthesis of the information relayed from different sensory receptors. For example, a wavefront initiated by the sensation of pressure on a certain area of

skin, interacting with wavefronts signaling muscle sensation and cold, would integrate in an assembled wave form characteristic of a smooth, cold object of a certain shape and mass—perhaps a stone. If this line of speculation is valid, then integration must occur between wavefronts generated by the most diverse receptor-organ discharges from eye and hand, or from eye and ear, or, to take the more complicated example of the interpretation of the visual field, discharges from the retina, the eye muscles, the neck and body musculature, and the apparatus of the inner ear which signals the orientation of the head. In fact, information from any sense organ must potentially be capable of integration with that from any other.

In the light of these speculations it is significant that electrical stimuli applied to the sensory zones of the cortex evoke only chaotic sensations: tingling or numbness in the skin zones; lights and colors in the visual zone; noises in the auditory zone. Such chaotic responses are to be expected, since electrical stimulation of the cortex must directly excite tens of thousands of neurons regardless of their functional relationships, and so initiate a widely spreading amorphous field of neuronal activation quite unlike the fine and specific patterns that must be set up by input to the cortex from the sensory organs. A familiar chaotic sensation, involving elements of touch, heat, cold and pain, arises for similar reasons when a sensory nerve is directly stimulated, as when the ulnar nerve in the elbow (the "funny bone") is injured.

From the cortical patterns that mirror sensory experience we proceed next to consider what mechanism may account for the recall of some sensory experience. Here we come to imagery or memory and so to the simplest level of imagination. Memory must be dependent on some enduring change that has been produced in the cortex by its previous activation. Theory and even some experimental evidence favor the hypothesis that the initial activation of the synapses in a network brings about a

lasting improvement in the efficacy of these junctions. As yet no one knows just how. One suggestion is that the synaptic knobs grow in size, another is that the synaptic transmitter substance becomes available in increased volume. For the present it is sufficient to consider the increased synaptic function as giving a "congealed" neuronal pattern or "engram" ready to be replayed by an appropriate input.

Experiments on the synapses at simpler levels of the nervous system lend considerable support to this postulate; they suggest that usage enhances synaptic efficacy for periods of days or weeks. Investigators have also found that the conditioned reflex is attended by changes in the electroencephalogram of experimental animals, indicating that specific patterns of neuronal activation are laid down during the conditioning. D. O. Hebb of McGill University has surmised that significant synaptic change requires reverberatory circulation of impulses many times around the pattern that is to be "remembered." In this connection it is relevant that an experience may not be remembered if a cerebral trauma (concussion or electric shock) is sustained as long as 20 minutes later. Such amnesia is much less pronounced, however, when cerebral activity is blocked by rapid anesthesia, suggesting that something other than recirculation of the impulses helps to establish the engram in the cortex.

The engram postulate accords well with the experience of remembered imagery. By far the most vivid memories are evoked by some closely similar experience. Here the new, evolving spatiotemporal pattern must tend to correspond closely to the old, congealed pattern; the impulses of the new pattern flow into a channel of the old and trigger its replaying. Such an intersection of patterns is suggested by the diagram on the facing page. In less favorable situations we call upon various devices or tricks of memory, deliberately choosing specific sensory inputs (trains of thought) that may trigger the memory.

Language, whether spoken or written, is overwhelmingly important to the function of memory and becomes increasingly so with education and cultural development. Thus we learn to experience vicariously the imagery of writers and artists. Poetry is a particularly effective medium for the transmission of imagery, transcending time and place and appealing to all who have educated themselves to have in their cortex engrams

NEURONAL PATHWAYS in this schematic diagram suggest the variety of configurations made possible by the rich interconnection of neurons in the cortex. Here a number of waves (shown in black, red and green dots, respectively) are shown traveling through a neuronal field, branching and coalescing and putting out abortive channels. An important feature in both the red and the green pathways is the reverberatory circuit, in which the wave travels repeatedly around the same closed loop of cells, as indicated by the arrows; such a reverberatory circuit can presumably maintain the excitation of the entire system of pathways in the direction of the arrows beyond. The abortive branches in a reverberatory circuit may develop into new functional pathways. In the black and red pathways at bottom two different waves are shown to propagate through the same chains of cells over portions of their lengths.

ready to be evoked by the reading—or better still the hearing—of some "pregnant" lines of poetry. The word "pregnant" is significant of our experience of the wealth of evoked imagery.

Karl S. Lashley, former director of the Yerkes Laboratories of Primate Biology, has convincingly argued that "the activity of literally millions of neurons" is involved in the recall of any memory. Furthermore, his experimental study of the effects of cortical lesions indicates that a particular engram has multiple representation in the cortex. With such a huge number of neurons involved in the fixing of a single memory in the cortex, one might think that the capacity of even 10 billion neurons would be quickly exhausted. Lashley concludes, however, that a cortical neuron need not belong exclusively to one engram, but on the contrary each neuron and even each synaptic junction can be built into many engrams. The diagram on page 36 shows how two separate patterns of activation can spread through the same assemblage of neurons and emerge therefrom each with its own identity. Such economical employment of neurons gives the brain capacity to hold a lifetime of memories.

Here a caveat should be entered against any too-literal reading of the diagrams that have illustrated this discussion. They bear the same relationship to the presumed real three-dimensional patterns of the cortex as chemical formulas to their molecules. In particular it must be emphasized that, because of continued replaying and interaction with intersecting patterns, the "congealed" engrams will be continuously changing, growing into new branches and shedding others. Correspondingly, successive recollections of the same past experience tend to undergo a gradual change.

Thus we have envisaged the working of the brain as a patterned activity formed by the curving and looping of wavefronts through a multitude of neurons, now sprouting, now coalescing with other wavefronts, now reverberating through the same path—all with a speed deriving from the millisecond relay time of the individual neuron, the whole wavefront advancing through perhaps one million neurons in a second. In the words of Sir Charles Sherrington, the brain appears as an "enchanted loom where millions of flashing shuttles [the nerve impulses] weave a dissolving pattern, always a meaningful pattern, though never an abiding one; a shifting harmony of sub-patterns."

But how does the working of the brain give us valid experience of the external world? The communication from sense organ to cerebral cortex is by a signal quite unlike the original stimulus, and the spatio-temporal pattern evoked in the cerebral cortex must again be different. Yet as a consequence of this cerebral pattern of activity we experience an impression which we project to somewhere outside the cortex—to the surface of the body or even within it, or, as sight, hearing or smell, to the outside world. On the other hand, as René Descartes first clearly saw, the only condition necessary for us to see colors, hear sounds or experience the existence of our own body is that appropriate patterns of neuronal activity shall occur in appropriate regions of our brain. It is immaterial whether these events are caused by local stimulation of the cerebral cortex or some part of the afferent nervous pathway, or whether they are, as is usual, generated by impulses discharged by sense organs.

Actually a long period of education is required before the brain events produced by the sensory organs can be interpreted as belonging to an external world and so be useful in sensing this world. This is impressively illustrated by the behavior of adults who gain sight for the first time upon the removal of congenital cataracts, and by chimpanzees reared in darkness.

But so far the key problem in perception has remained beyond this discussion. We may ask: How can some specific spatio-temporal pattern of neuronal

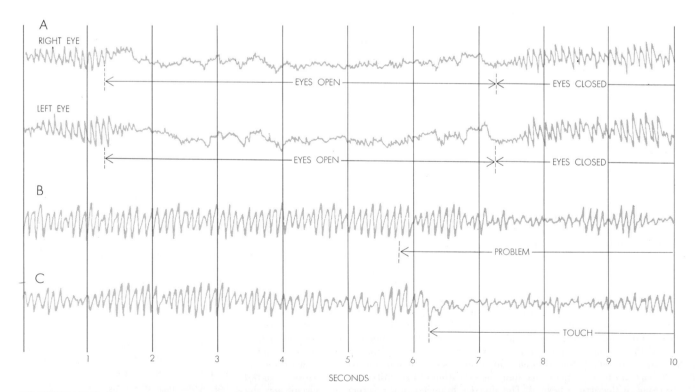

BRAIN WAVES show contrasting patterns of the active and inactive brain. The dominant pattern of the resting brain is the large-amplitude wave of approximately 10 cycles per second. When the eyes are open or when the brain responds to other sensory input or when it is engaged by a mental problem, these "alpha" waves give way to irregular waves of higher frequency and smaller amplitude.

activity in the cerebral cortex evoke a particular conscious experience? Furthermore, how does it happen that only when there is a moderate level of activity in the cerebral cortex does it come into liaison with mind to result in a conscious state? If our cortical activity is too low, we lapse into the unconsciousness of sleep or anesthesia or coma. If it becomes too intense, unconsciousness also supervenes, as during the convulsions of epilepsy or shock therapy.

Another problem relates to attention, for much organized cortical activity can be carried on at a subconscious level. How does it come about that our attention is diverted now to this patterned activity which then gives its unique conscious experience, now to that? Is the magnitude of the cortical activation significant in thus achieving conscious attention? These fundamental problems escape all but the vaguest formulation in fragmentary hypotheses.

Our speculation has covered only the simplest aspect of imagination: imagery or the re-experiencing of images. In passing beyond this stage let us first consider the peculiar tendency to association in imagery. The experience of one image is evocative of other images, and these of still more, and so on. When these images are of beauty and subtlety, blending in harmony, and are expressed in some language—verbal, musical or pictorial—to evoke transcendent experiences in others, we have artistic creation of a simple or lyrical kind. Alternatively, entrancing displays of imagery of great beauty and clarity can be experienced by ordinary people under the influence of hallucinogenic drugs such as mescaline. One may suspect that the cortex under these conditions tends to develop ever more complex and effectively interlocked patterns of neuronal activity involving large fractions of its neuron population. This would account for the withdrawal of the subject from ordinary activities during these experiences. Not unrelated to these states are the psychoses where the inner experiences of the patients also cause them to be withdrawn.

An entirely different order of image-forming is involved in creative imagination, the most profound of human activities. It provides the illumination that gives a new insight or understanding. In science that illumination takes the form of a new hypothesis which embraces and transcends the older hypotheses. Such a creation of the imagination has immediate esthetic appeal in its simplicity and scope; it must neverthe-

less be subjected to rigorous criticism and experimental testing. The illumination often has had the suddenness of a flash, as with Kekulé and the benzene ring, Darwin and the theory of evolution, Hamilton and his equations. But suddenness of illumination is no guarantee of the validity of a hypothesis. I have had only one such sudden illumination—the so-called Golgi-cell hypothesis of cerebral inhibition—and some years later it was proved false! Most of the great scientific hypotheses are the offspring of more labored births. They developed in stages, being perfected and shaped by critical reason, as with Planck and the quantum theory and with Einstein and the theory of relativity.

Before attempting to picture the brain activities that underlie innovation in science, let us recall that such illumination comes only to a mind that has been prepared by the assimilation and critical evaluation of the knowledge in its field. One can deliberately seek to experience some new imaginative insight by first pouring into one's mind hypotheses and the related experiments and then relaxing to give opportunity for the subconscious processes in the brain that

may lead to the conscious illumination of a new insight. Such illuminations are often fragmentary and require conscious modification, or are so erroneous as to invite immediate rejection by critical reason. Nevertheless they all give evidence of the creativeness of the subconscious mind.

It may now be asked: What activity in the brain corresponds to this creative activity of the subconscious mind, and how eventually does it flash into consciousness? Let us consider first the prerequisites for such cerebral action. The wealth and subtlety of stored memories and critical evaluations imply that in the neuronal network there is an enormous development of highly complex engrams whose permanency derives from the postulated increase in synaptic efficacy. We may say that these congealed patterns supply the know-how of the brain; when there is a great wealth of expert knowledge, the engrams may occupy the greater part of the cortex. One can speculate further that some failure in the synthesis of the engrams or some conflict in their inter-relationship is the neuronal counterpart of a problem that clamors for solution.

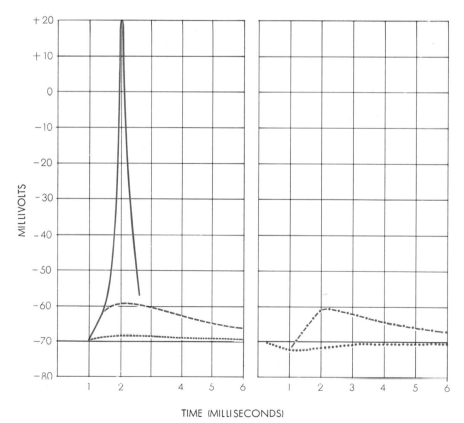

TIME (MILLISECONDS)

NEURONAL IMPULSE is triggered by an "all-or-nothing" excitation of the cell. In the diagram at left the lower broken line represents the change in potential induced by a single excitatory synaptic impulse; the upper broken line shows the summed action of a number of such impulses which triggers the spike potential, shown by the solid line. In the diagram at right the lower dotted line represents the change in potential induced by an inhibitory impulse, which depresses excitation of cell below the critical level for firing of impulse.

Such are the prerequisites leading to creative insight. We may surmise that the "subconscious operation of the mind" involves the intense and unimaginably complex interplay of the engrams. We have seen that on repeated activation there tends to be a progressive change in their congealed patterns resulting particularly from interaction with other patterns. Thus we can expect that new patterns will arise during the subconscious phase of the effort. Should an emergent pattern combine and transcend the existent patterns, we may expect some resonant-like intensification of activity in the cortex, which will bring this pattern to conscious attention. There it comes to light as a new idea.

Then begins the process of conscious criticism and evaluation, the deliberate effort to discover flaws in the new idea. This done, there comes the crucial stage of the designing and carrying out of experiments that test predictions derived from the new idea. From the point of view of science, a creative imagination is fruitful if it develops new hypotheses that are powerful in their generality and stand up to experimental test.

Finally we may ask: What are the characteristics of a brain that exhibits creative imagination? In attempting an answer we must venture more deeply than ever into the realm of speculation. Certain general statements can be made, but their inadequacy will be apparent. The creative brain must first of all possess an adequate number of neurons, having a wealth of synaptic connection between them. It must have, as it were, the structural basis for an immense range of patterns of activity. But even this obvious generalization must be hedged. There is poor correlation between brain size and intelligence, even assuming proportionality of brain size and neuron population: a chimpanzee brain has a neuron population 80 per cent as large as a human brain and displays little or no creative imagination. The synapses of the brain should also have a sensitive tendency to increase their function with usage, so that they may readily form and maintain memory patterns.

Such a brain will accumulate an immense wealth of engrams of highly specific character. If in addition this brain possesses a peculiar potency for unresting activity, weaving the spatio-temporal patterns of its engrams in continually novel and interacting forms, the stage is set for the deliverance of a "brain child" that is sired, as we say, by creative imagination.

II

ALTERED STATES OF AWARENESS: INTERNAL CONTROL

II

ALTERED STATES OF AWARENESS: INTERNAL CONTROL

INTRODUCTION

In this section, we will be concerned with those modulating influences on our states of awareness that can be said to have primarily internal or bodily origins. The perceptive reader will recognize that any attempt to make a strict separation of internal and external events is doomed to failure. The division employed here is one of convenience rather than absolute biological reality.

Many scientists shudder at the thought of dealing with the realm of subjective experience—studies of this aspect of human experience are fraught with experimental difficulties, and the history of such studies is somewhat less than satisfactory. Nathaniel Kleitman's article "Patterns of Dreaming," however, stands as testimony that investigations of the world of subjective experience, if properly approached, can yield great scientific insight. Kleitman and others have set out to study a decidedly subjective event—the dream. Dreaming is accompanied by a characteristic set of physiological changes in the brain and skeletal musculature. By taking advantage of these physiological correlates of an alteration in the state of awareness, investigators have been able to study many of the phenomena associated with dreams and dreaming.

Michel Jouvet, the author of the article "The States of Sleep," has extended the work of Kleitman and others to animal subjects. Jouvet has been able to study, in greater detail, the brain mechanisms that underlie these altered states of awareness. From electrodes buried deep in the brains of sleeping and waking cats, Jouvet has identified brain structures associated with the modulation of sleep and wakefulness. Sleep accompanied by rapid eye movements (REM sleep), which is associated, in man, with dreaming, has been observed in organisms ranging from chicks to chimps. Jouvet raises the question of the biological function of dreaming, and concludes that it is "one of the great mysteries of biology."

Whereas dreaming is a normal consequence of life and an accepted and "approved" distortion in awareness, the same is not true for hallucinations. Woodburn Heron, who wrote "The Pathology of Boredom," deprived human subjects of sensory stimulation by placing them in controlled, monotonous environments and observed that such deprivation produced profound distortions of awareness. Heron suggests that the brain's response to a lack of stimulation is to create activity in the form of hallucinations. It is of interest that these hallucinations are similar to those experienced by persons who have taken the psychotomimetic drug mescaline. This suggests that the brain is responding in the same, abnormal way to two totally different kinds of experiences.

In the article "On Telling Left from Right," Michael C. Corballis and Ivan L. Beale note that only in a man-made environment are there left–right assymetries, the natural environment being perceptually symmetrical. The authors note that our brains are basically symmetrical, which accounts for the difficulties that children often have in telling left from right. The authors maintain that it is with respect to the assymetrical nature of symbolic behavior in man that the human brain is lateralized. This ingenious line of reasoning holds considerable promise for an increased understanding of the brain processes that underlie experiences unique to man.

How can a yogi "stop his heart," thrust pins through his skin without bleeding, or walk on hot coals? Is it evidence of supernatural powers, or are yogis simply trained in a way that is unfamiliar to Westerners? The experiments cited by Leo V. DiCara in his article "Learning in the Autonomic Nervous System," wherein animals learned to alter their heart rate, blood pressure, intestinal contractions, blood-vessel diameter, and urine formation, suggest that yogis are similarly skilled in altering their own bodily processes. This pioneering work of DiCara and others is being applied, with promising results, to the problem of "training" individuals suffering from such problems as heart and circulatory dysfunctions and epilepsy to overcome their diseases.

5

PATTERNS OF DREAMING

NATHANIEL KLEITMAN
November 1960

Dreams have troubled the waking hours as well as the sleep of men since time immemorial. These hallucinatory experiences have inspired soothsayers and psychiatrists alike, and their bizarre contents, variously interpreted as prophetic insights and clues to personality, are the subject of a considerable body of literature. The scientific value of even the most recent contributions to this literature, however, is seriously qualified: The sole witness to the dream is the dreamer himself. The same limitation confronts the investigator who would inquire into the process of dreaming, as distinguished from the contents of dreams. Only the awakened sleeper can testify that he has dreamed. If he reports that he has not, it may be that he fails to recall his dreaming.

Nonetheless, in the course of our long-term investigation of sleep at the University of Chicago, we found ourselves venturing into research in the hitherto subjective realm of dreaming. We discovered an objective and apparently reliable way to determine whether a sleeper is dreaming—in the sense, of course, of his "reporting having dreamed" when he wakes up or is awakened. The objective indicator of dreaming makes it possible to chart the onset and duration of dreaming episodes throughout the night without disturbing the sleeper. One can also awaken and interrogate him at the beginning of a dream, in the middle, at the end, or at any measured interval after the end. By such means it has been determined that there is periodicity in dreaming, and the consequences of efforts to disturb this periodicity have been observed. The results indicate that dreaming as a fundamental physiological process is related to other rhythms of the body. As for the folklore that surrounds the process, this

work has answered such questions as: Does everyone dream? How often does one dream in the course of a night's sleep? Is the "plot" of a dream really compressed into a moment of dreaming? Do external and internal stimuli—light, noise, hunger or thirst—affect the content of dreams?

As so often happens in research, the objective indicator of dreaming was discovered by accident. During a study of the cyclic variations of sleep in infants, a graduate student named Eugene Aserinsky observed that the infant's eyes continued to move under its closed lids for some time after all major body movement had ceased with the onset of sleep. The eye movements would stop and then begin again from time to time, and were the first movements to be seen as the infant woke up. Aserinsky found that eye movements provided a more reliable means of distinguishing between the active and quiescent phases of sleep than did gross body movements.

These observations suggested that eye movements might be used to follow similar cycles in the depth of sleep in adults. Disturbance to the sleeper was minimized by monitoring the eye movements remotely with an electroencephalograph, a device that records the weak electrical signals generated continuously by the brain. A potential difference across the eyeball between the cornea and the retina makes it possible to detect movements of the eyes by means of electrodes taped to the skin above and below or on either side of one eye. Other channels of the electroencephalograph recorded the sleeper's brain waves, his pulse and respiration rates and the gross movements of his body.

The tracings of the electroencephalograph showed not only the slow move-

ments of the eyes that Aserinsky had observed in infants but also rapid eye-movements that came in clusters. Each individual eye-movement took a fraction of a second, but a cluster often lasted, with interruptions, as long as 50 minutes. The first rapid eye-movements usually began about an hour after the onset of sleep, and clusters appeared in cyclic fashion through the night [*see illustration on page 48*].

Coincident with this cycle of eye movement the electroencephalograph recorded a fluctuation in the brain-wave pattern. As each series of movements began, the brain waves changed from the pattern typical of deep sleep to one indicating lighter sleep. The pulse and respiration rates also increased, and the sleeper lay motionless.

Considered together, these observations suggested an emotionally charged cerebral activity—such as might occur in dreaming. This surmise was tested by the only possible means: arousing and questioning the sleepers. Those awakened in the midst of a cluster of rapid eye-movements testified they had been dreaming. Those awakened in the apparently deeper phases of sleep said they had not. Thus the objective indicator of dreaming came into use.

It is clear that such an indicator can reveal nothing about the content of dreams. But the process of dreaming is no more bound up with dream content than thinking is with what one is thinking about. The hallucinatory content of dreams would appear, in this light, to be nothing more than the expression of a crude type of activity carried on in the cerebral cortex during a certain phase of sleep. The contrast with the kind of cerebral activity that characterizes the waking state in healthy adults and older children is instructive. Responding to

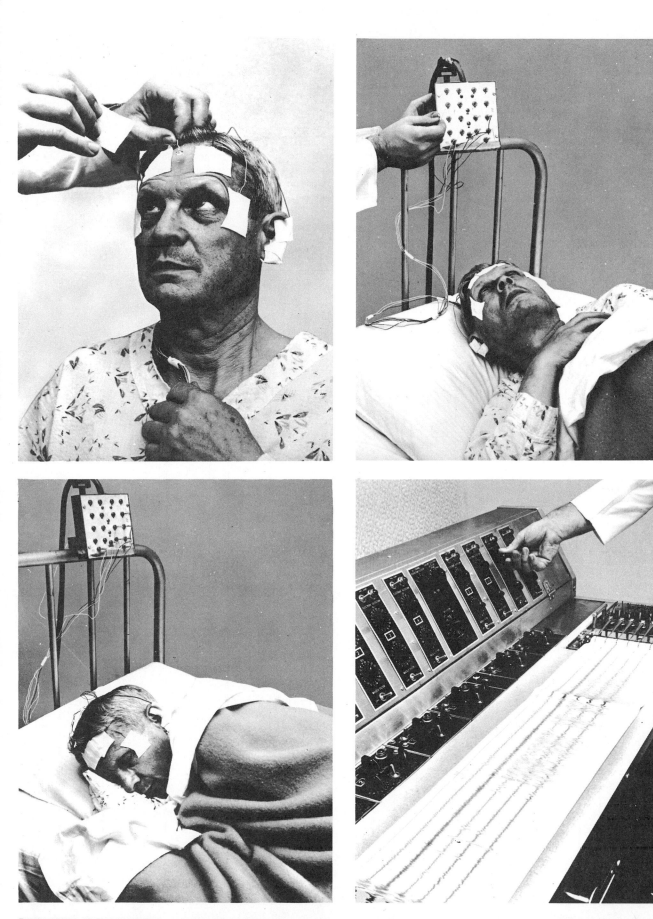

DREAMING IS DETECTED by attaching electrodes to the subject's scalp and to the skin at the corners of the eyes (*top left*). Leads are connected to cable (*top right*) that leads to electroencephalograph in another room. As the subject sleeps (*bottom left*), his brain waves and eye movements are recorded by pens of electroencephalograph (*bottom right*). The subject here is the author of this article.

the impulses that stream in from the various receptor organs of the sensory system, the cortex first subjects them to analysis. It refers the present moment of experience to its memory of the past and projects past and present into the future, weighing the consequences of action not yet taken. A decision is reached, and the cortex generates an integrated response. This is manifested in the action of the effector organs (mostly muscles) or in the deliberate inhibition of action. (A great deal of civilized behavior consists in not doing what comes naturally.) In dreaming, the same kind of cortical activity proceeds at a lower level of per-

formance. The analysis of events is faulty; the dreamer recognizes a deceased friend but accepts his presence without surprise. The memory is full of gaps and brings the past to the surface in confusion. In consequence the integration of the cortical response is incomplete, and the dreamer is often led into the phantom commission of antisocial acts. Fortunately the impulses from the sleeping cortex die out on the way to the effector organs, and no harm is done.

Such protoplasmic poisons as alcohol may reduce cortical activity to an equally low level of performance. A markedly

intoxicated person misjudges the situation, assumes unwarranted risks in action and later does not recall what happened. Even when quite drunk, however, some persons stop short of foolish and dangerous extremes of behavior. So, also, a dreamer will accept absurdities in the imaginary series of events until they become too painful and ludicrous; he then wakes up to the comforting discovery that he was dreaming. The fantasizing of very young children, senile aged people and of persons suffering certain disorders of the central nervous system may also be likened to dreaming. After sudden awakening, even normal people may

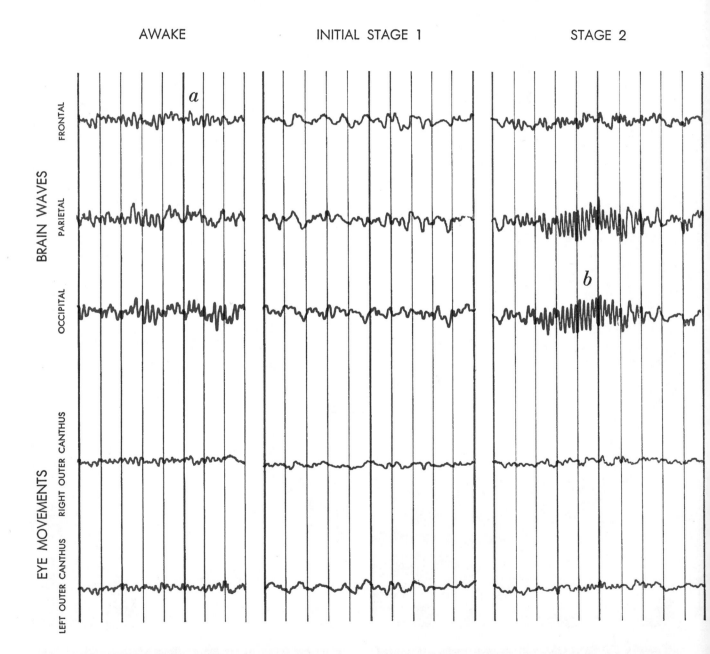

ELECTROENCEPHALOGRAMS show the patterns of brain waves (*top three tracings*) and eye-movement potentials (*bottom two tracings*) that are characteristic of each level of sleep. Labels at left indicate region of head to which recording electrodes are at-

tached. Vertical lines are time-scale; 10 lines represent an interval of four seconds. A subject who is awake but resting with his eyes closed shows the brain-wave pattern known as alpha rhythm (*a*). As sleep begins, pattern known as Initial Stage 1 electroen-

be bewildered and act in a deranged manner for some time. The content of dreams, explicit or hidden, may indeed have inherent interest. But for the purpose of an investigation of dreaming, it is sufficient to recognize the dream itself as a manifestation of low-grade thinking.

The objective indicator that a sleeper is dreaming, it must be admitted, is not infallible. Some subjects reported they had been dreaming during periods when they showed no rapid eye-movements. Others moved their bodies restlessly when the records on the other channels of the electroencephalograph indicated they were dreaming. Sometimes the heart and respiration rate slowed down instead of speeding up. Occasionally a subject claimed to have been dreaming when his brain waves indicated a deeper phase of sleep. William Dement, another student in our laboratory who is now at Mount Sinai Hospital in New York City, showed that of the four criteria the most reliable is the brain-wave pattern.

A person who is awake but resting with his eyes closed shows the so-called alpha rhythm—brain waves with a relatively large amplitude and a frequency of eight to 13 cycles per second [*see illustration on these two pages*]. As he falls asleep, the amplitude of the waves decreases, and the rhythm slows to four to six cycles per second. Dement called this pattern the Stage 1 electroencephalogram (Stage 1 EEG). Deeper sleep is characterized by the appearance of "sleep spindles"—short bursts of waves that progressively increase and decrease in amplitude and have a frequency of 14 to 16 cycles per second; Dement divided this level of sleep into two stages (Stage 2 and Stage 3 EEG). The deepest level of sleep is characterized by the appearance of large, slow waves (Stage 4 EEG). During a typical night of sleep,

STAGE 3   STAGE 4   EMERGENT STAGE 1 (DREAMING)

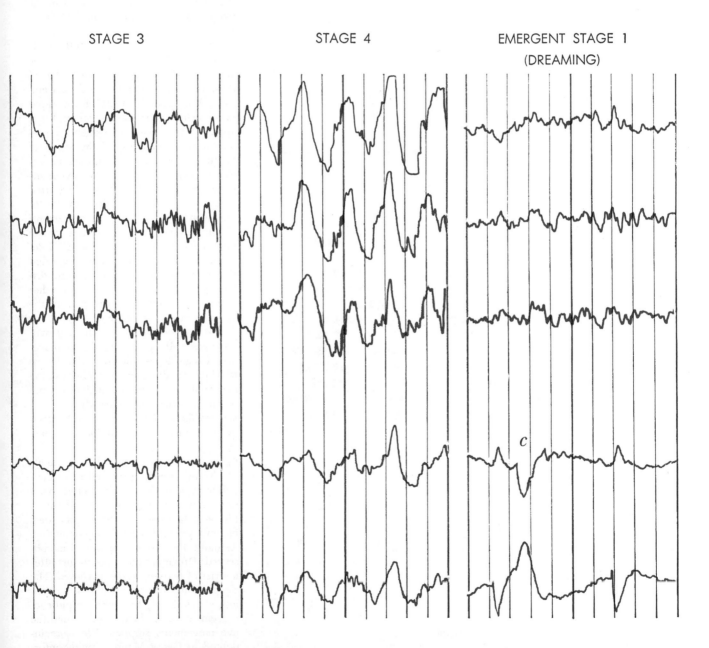

cephalogram (Initial Stage 1 EEG) appears. During deeper sleep subject shows short bursts of waves called sleep spindles (*b*). Deepest level of sleep (Stage 4 EEG) is characterized by the appearance of large, slow waves. EEG pattern changes from Stage 1 through Stage 4, then swings back to Stage 1. This "emergent" Stage 1 is accompanied by rapid eye-movements, as indicated by peaks in tracings of eye-movement potentials (*c*). Similar peaks during Stage 4 are not eye movements but brain waves that spread to eye electrodes.

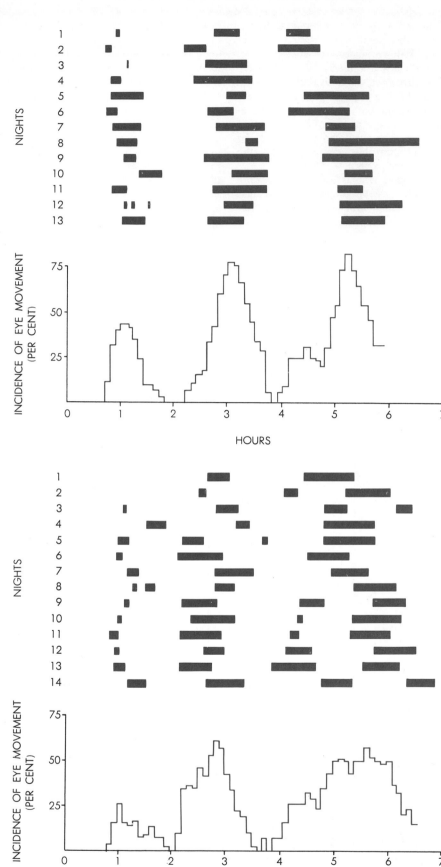

the depth of sleep fluctuates on a cycle lasting roughly 90 minutes. The EEG pattern passes from Stage 1 through Stage 4, then swings back to Stage 1. During later cycles the sleep may not be so deep; the EEG pattern may dip no farther than the intermediate stages before it returns to Stage 1 [*see illustration on opposite page*].

Dement found that dreaming occurs during the Stage 1 EEG, but not when this brain-wave pattern first appears at the onset of sleep. Only when the cycle returns to the Stage 1 EEG from a deeper EEG level does it mark a dreaming episode. During this "emergent" Stage 1 it is much more difficult to awaken the sleeper than during the "initial" Stage 1 EEG.

The inconsistencies between the EEG record and the other criteria may be largely explained by the relationship of these other activities to the dream episode. For example, most of the rapid eye-movements are horizontal, and it is apparent that these movements represent a busy scanning of the scene of dream action. On the infrequent occasions when the rapid eye-movements were vertical, the sleepers reported dreams that involved the upward or downward motion of objects or persons. When the record showed few or no rapid eye-movements, and the EEG denoted dreaming, the subjects reported that they had been watching some distant point in their dreams. In other words, the amount and direction of the eye movements correspond to what the dreamer is looking at or following with his eyes. Moreover, rapid eye-movements seem to be related to the degree to which the dreamer participates in the events of the dream. An "active" dream, in which the dreamer is greatly involved, is more likely to be accompanied by rapid eye-movements than is a "passive" one.

The absence of gross body movements during dreaming seemed more difficult to explain. One would assume that a sleeper would begin to move about as his sleep lightens and that a good deal of activity would occur during dreaming. Actually the exact opposite was observed. Dreaming often began just after a series of body movements ceased. The sleeper usually remained almost motionless, showing only the telltale rapid eye-movements, and stirred again when the eye movements stopped. We were indebted to Georg Mann, a public-information officer at the University of Chicago, for the metaphor that captured the essence of this situation. He compared the dreamer to a spectator at a theater:

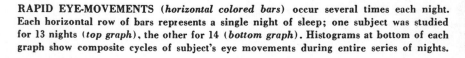

RAPID EYE-MOVEMENTS (*horizontal colored bars*) occur several times each night. Each horizontal row of bars represents a single night of sleep; one subject was studied for 13 nights (*top graph*), the other for 14 (*bottom graph*). Histograms at bottom of each graph show composite cycles of subject's eye movements during entire series of nights.

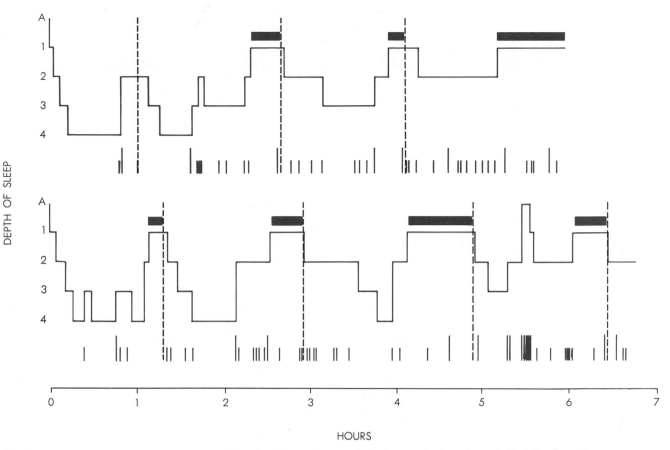

DEPTH OF SLEEP

HOURS

EEG STAGES of two subjects show a cyclic variation during typical night of sleep. Measured in terms of EEG stages, depth of sleep fluctuates on a 90-minute cycle. Cycle begins when subject who is awake (A) falls into light sleep (EEG Stage 1), then into successively deeper levels of sleep (EEG Stages 2, 3 and 4). Cycle ends with swing back to Stage 1. Periods of rapid eye-movement (*horizontal colored bars*) occur during this stage. Vertical broken lines indicate when next cycle begins. Vertical colored lines at bottom of each graph indicate when body movements occurred; longer lines represent major movements; shorter lines, minor ones.

fidgeting in his seat before the curtain goes up; then sitting quietly, often "spellbound" by the action, following the motions of the actors with his eyes; then stirring again when the curtain falls.

Some body movement may be related to dream content. Edward A. Wolpert of the University of Chicago attached electrodes to the limbs of sleeping subjects and recorded the electrical "action" potentials of the muscles. The record of one of his subjects showed a sequence of motor activity first in the right hand, then in the left, and finally in one leg (only one leg was wired for recording). When aroused immediately thereafter, the sleeper reported dreaming that he lifted a bucket with his right hand, transferred it to his left, and then started to walk. Sleepwalking may be an extreme expression of such motor outflow to extremities. Occasionally a subject would vocalize when he stirred, mumbling and even talking distinctly, but such activity usually occurred between episodes of dreaming.

Some people assert that they seldom or never dream. But all of the subjects—and all of those observed in other laboratories that employ the objective indicator—reported dreaming upon being awakened at appropriate times. It can be stated with some assurance, therefore, that everybody dreams repeatedly every night. Donald R. Goodenough and his associates at the Downstate Medical Center of the State University of New York compared one group of subjects who said they never dreamed with another group who said they always dreamed. Certain unexplained differences showed up in the EEG records of the two groups, and the "dreamers" were more likely to report dreaming in correspondence with rapid eye-movements than the "nondreamers." Rapid eye-movements were observed with the same frequency, however, in both groups. The evidence is overwhelming that the two groups should be classified as "recallers" and "nonrecallers."

These studies have also upset the notion that a long series of events can be compressed into a moment of dreaming. Whether the subject was loquacious or laconic in recounting his dream, the time-span of the narrative was consistent with dreaming time as indicated by our objective criteria. It appears that the course of time in dreaming is about the same as in the waking state.

It is often said that external events in the sleeper's immediate environment may suggest or affect the content of dreams. To test this idea Dement and Wolpert exposed a number of subjects to the stimuli of sound, light and drops of water during periods of dreaming. Elements suggestive of such stimuli appeared in only a minority of the dreams recounted thereafter. Drops of water, falling on the skin, proved to be the most suggestive. Falling water showed up in six dream reports out of 15 that followed arousal by this stimulus, and water had a place in 14 narratives out of 33 when the sleepers were subjected to the stimulus but not awakened by it. An electric bell used routinely to awaken the subjects found its way into 20 out of 204 dreams, most commonly as the ringing of a telephone or doorbell.

Internal stimuli from the viscera have

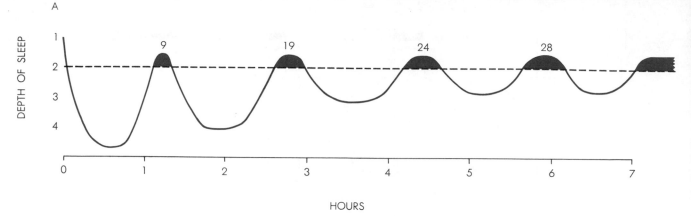

EPISODES OF DREAMING (*colored areas*) alternate with periods of deeper sleep. Dreaming and rapid eye-movements begin when sleeper emerges from deep sleep to level of EEG Stage 1. Numbers over colored areas show length of successive periods of dreaming.

been held to cause, or at least influence, dreams. Dreams about eating are said to be stimulated by contractions of an empty stomach. Dement and Wolpert had three subjects go without fluids for 24 hours on five occasions; only five of 15 dream narratives contained elements that could be related to thirst. In no case did the narrative involve an awareness of thirst or descriptions of drinking, although the subjects were very thirsty when they went to bed.

Most of the dream experience in normal sleep is never recalled. Recollection is best when the sleepers are awakened during the dreaming episode and becomes progressively poorer the longer they are permitted to sleep after a dream has ended. At the University of Chicago, Wolpert and Harry Trosman found that 25 out of 26 subjects had no memory of dreaming when they were roused for questioning more than 10 minutes after the Stage 2 EEG had superseded the Stage 1.

Once the objective indicator had shown itself to be a reliable measure of dreaming, it was employed to enact the pattern of dreaming through many nights of uninterrupted sleep. In a sampling of 71 nights of sleep, with 33 different subjects, the first emergent Stage 1 EEG—plus the accompanying rapid eye-movements and cardiac and respiratory changes—appeared a little over an hour after sleep had begun. This episode of dreaming lasted on the average less than 10 minutes. Three, four and even five dreaming periods followed at intervals of about 90 minutes. These lasted 20 to 35 minutes and added up to a total of one or two hours of dreaming for an average night's sleep. All of the subjects exhibited the cycle of alternate periods of dreaming and deeper sleep, some on

a more constant schedule than others.

The mechanism that spaces the episodes of dreaming is unknown, but it may be related to the cycle of rest and activity which Aserinsky found in infants. The mean length of that cycle is approximately an hour, and at the end of a cycle the infants stir, either to awaken fully or to go back to sleep for another cycle. In infants on a self-demand feeding schedule, the duration of the period between feedings tends to be roughly whole multiples of the length of this cycle. Apparently the cycle lengthens with age, extending to the 90-minute dreaming cycles observed in adults. A similar increase occurs in the length of the cardiac, respiratory and gastric cycles, indicating that the dream cycle is in line with the basic physiological rhythms of the body.

What happens if the dreaming cycle is disturbed? This interesting question has been taken up by Dement and his associates. Monitoring the subject's cycle, they awaken him as soon as he starts to dream and thus keep him from dreaming. Since one must be certain that dreaming has started before attempting to stop it, such interference cannot completely deprive the subject of his dreaming, but total dreaming time can be reduced by 75 to 80 per cent. Dement established that the mean normal dreaming time of his eight male subjects was 20 per cent, or about 82 minutes in about seven hours of sleep. Attempts to curtail their dreaming in the course of three to seven consecutive nights required in each case a progressively larger number of awakenings—in some cases three times as many. During the "recovery" period after this ordeal, the dreaming time of five of the subjects went up to 112 minutes, or 27 per cent of the sleeping time,

on the first night and gradually fell back to normal on succeeding nights. In six of the subjects arousal in the midst of nondreaming periods during "control" nights of sleep had no effect on dreaming during the recovery nights that followed. The curtailment of dreaming time produced anxiety, irritability, a greater appetite and a gain in body weight; the control awakenings had no such effects. As soon as the subjects of the experiment were allowed their usual dreaming time, they regained their emotional composure.

Dement tentatively interprets his findings as indicating that "a certain amount of dreaming is a necessity." Charles Fisher, a psychiatrist at Mount Sinai Hospital in New York, adds that "the dream is the normal psychosis and dreaming permits each and every one of us to be quietly and safely insane every night of our lives."

From the same evidence, however, one may equally well argue that the curtailment of dreaming engenders irritability and anxiety simply because it interferes with an acquired habit. Animals (and some people) that have acquired a "sweet tooth" may be similarly upset by deprivation of sugar. They will also consume excessive quantities of sugar after the supply is restored, just as Dement's subjects sought to make up for "missed" dreaming. In other words, the low-grade cerebral activity that is dreaming may serve no significant function whatever.

Further observation and experiment will have to decide which of these conflicting views is sound. The objective indicator is now available to help investigators find the answer to this and other questions about the nature and meaning of dreaming.

6

THE STATES OF SLEEP

MICHEL JOUVET
February 1967

Early philosophers recognized that there are two distinctly different levels of sleep. An ancient Hindu tale described three states of mind in man: (1) wakefulness (*vaiswanara*), in which a person "is conscious only of external objects [and] is the enjoyer of the pleasures of sense"; (2) dreaming sleep (*taijasa*), in which one "is conscious only of his dreams [and] is the enjoyer of the subtle impressions in the mind of the deeds he has done in the past," and (3) dreamless sleep (*prajna*), a "blissful" state in which "the veil of unconsciousness envelops his thought and knowledge, and the subtle impressions of his mind apparently vanish."

States 2 and 3 obviously are rather difficult to investigate objectively, and until very recently the phases of sleep remained a subject of vague speculation. Within the past few years, however, studies with the aid of the electroencephalograph have begun to lift the veil. By recording brain waves, eye movements and other activities of the nervous system during the different sleep states neurophysiologists are beginning to identify the specific nervous-system structures involved, and we are now in a position to analyze some of the mechanisms responsible.

Brain Activities in Sleep

Lucretius, that remarkably inquisitive and shrewd observer of nature, surmised that the fidgetings of animals during sleep were linked to dreaming. Some 30 years ago a German investigator, R. Klaue, made a significant discovery with the electroencephalograph. He found that sleep progressed in a characteristic sequence: a period of light sleep, during which the brain cortex produced slow brain waves, followed by a period of deep sleep, in which the cortical activity speeded up. Klaue's report was completely overlooked at the time. In the 1950's, however, Nathaniel Kleitman and his students at the University of Chicago took up this line of investigation. Kleitman and Eugene Aserinsky found (in studies of infants) that periods of "active" sleep, alternating with quiescent periods, were marked by rapid eye movements under the closed lids. Later Kleitman and William C. Dement, in studies of adults, correlated the eye movements with certain brain-wave patterns and definitely linked these activities and patterns to periods of dreaming [see the article beginning on page 44, "Patterns of Dreaming," by Nathaniel Kleitman]. In 1958 Dement showed that cats may have periods of sleep similarly marked by rapid eye movement and fast cortical activity. He called such periods "activated sleep."

Meanwhile at the University of Lyons, François Michel and I had been conducting a series of experiments with cats. In the cat, which spends about two-thirds of its time sleeping, the process of falling asleep follows a characteristic course, signaled by easily observable external signs. Typically the animal curls up in a ball with its neck bent. The flexing of the nape of its neck is a clear sign that the muscles there retain some tonus, that is, they are not completely relaxed. In this position the cat lapses into a light sleep from which it is easily awakened.

After about 10 to 20 minutes there comes a constellation of changes that mark passage over the brink into deep sleep. The cat's neck and back relax their curvature, showing that the muscles have completely lost tonus: they are now altogether slack. At the same time there

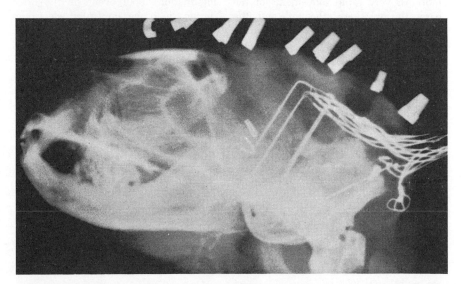

X RAY OF CAT'S HEAD shows a cluster of electrodes with which the author obtained a record of the electrical signals from various parts of the cat's brain. The cat's mouth is at the left; one electrode at far right measures the changes in the animal's neck-muscle tension.

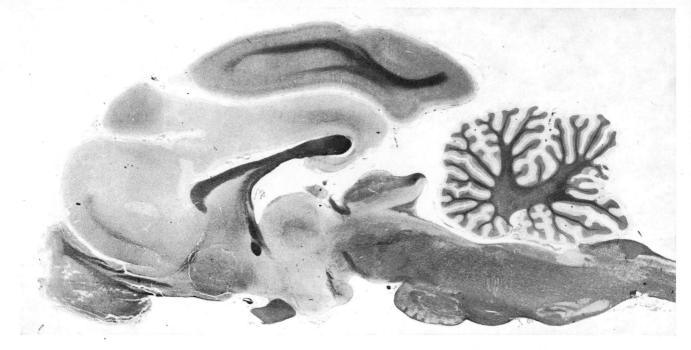

CAT'S BRAIN, seen in front-to-back section, has a number of segments. Some of the principal ones are identified in the illustration at the top of the opposite page. Many segments of the cat's brain, such as the cerebellum (*top right*), have no role to play in sleep.

are bursts of rapid eye movements (eight to 30 movements in each burst) in either the side-to-side or the up-and-down direction, like the movements in visual use of the eyes. Occasionally these eyeball movements behind the closed eyelids are accompanied by a sudden dilation of the pupils, which in the main are tightly constricted during sleep. Along with the eye movements go events involving many other parts of the body: small tremors of muscles at the ends of the extremities, causing rapid flexing of the digits and now and then small scratching motions; very rapid movements of the ears, the whiskers, the tail and the tongue, and an episode of fast and irregular breathing.

It is somewhat startling to realize that all this activity goes on during a period in which the animal's muscular system is totally atonic (lacking in tension). The activities are also the accompaniment of deep sleep, as is indicated by the fact that it takes an unusually high level of sound or electrical stimulation to arouse the cat during this phase. The state of deep sleep lasts about six or seven minutes and alternates with periods of lighter sleep that last for an average of about 25 minutes.

To obtain more objective and specific information about events in the brain during sleep we implanted electrodes in the muscles of the neck and in the midbrain of cats. We used animals that were deprived of the brain cortex, since we wished to study the subcortical activities. In the course of extended recordings of the electrical events we were surprised to find that the electrical activity of the neck muscles disappeared completely for regular periods (six minutes long), and the condition persisted when sharp spikes of high voltage showed up now and then in the pontine reticular formation, situated just behind the "arousal center" of the midbrain. These electrical signs were correlated with eye movements of the sleeping animal. Further, we noted that in cats with intact brains both the abolition of muscle tonus and the sharp high-voltage spikes were strikingly correlated with the rapid eye

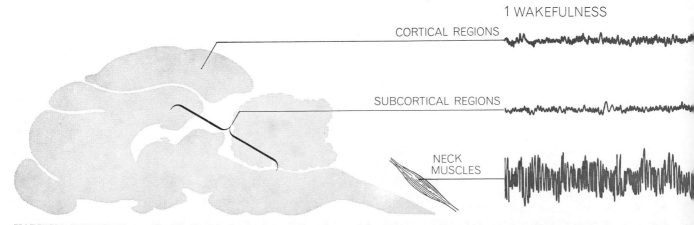

VARYING RHYTHMS are identified with the various states of sleep. From left to right, a wakeful cat (*1*) shows high-speed alternations in electric potential in both cortical and subcortical regions of the brain, as well as neck-muscle tension. In light sleep (*2*) the cat shows a slower rhythm in the traces from the cortical and subcortical regions, but neck-muscle tension continues. The phasic, or

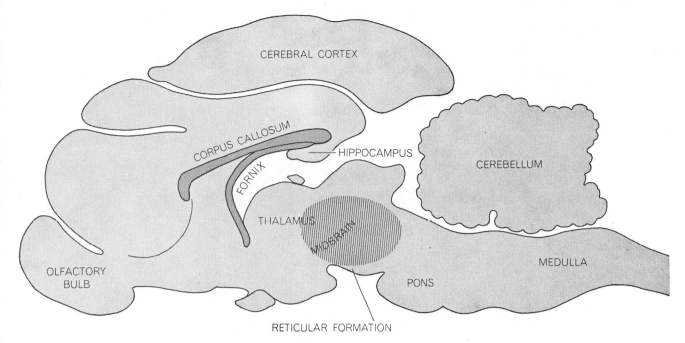

BRAIN SEGMENTS associated with sleep include the reticular formation, which controls wakefulness. This region is under the control of an area in the lower brain. When the control is blocked by making a cut through the pons, a normal cat becomes insomniac.

movement and fast cortical activity Dement had described. These findings presented a paradox. It was surely strange to find fast cortical activity (generally a sign of wakefulness) coupled with complete muscular atony (invariably a sign of deep sleep)!

The Two Sleep States

We named this strange state "paradoxical sleep." It is also called deep sleep, fast-wave sleep, rapid-eye-movement (REM) sleep and dreaming sleep, whereas the lighter sleep that precedes it is often called slow-wave sleep. We consider paradoxical sleep a qualitatively distinct state, not simply a deepened version of the first stage of sleep. Very schematically (for the cat) we can describe the three states—wakefulness, light sleep and paradoxical sleep—in the following physiological terms. Wakefulness is accompanied by fast, low-voltage electrical activity in the cortex and the subcortical structures of the brain and by a significant amount of tonus in the muscular system. The first stage of sleep, or light sleep, is characterized by a slackening of electrical activity in the cortex and subcortical structures, by the occurrence of "spindles," or groups of sharp jumps, in the brain waves and by retention of the muscular tension. Paradoxical sleep presents a more complex picture that we must consider in some detail.

We can classify the phenomena in paradoxical sleep under two heads: tonic (those having to do with continuous phenomena) and phasic (those of a periodic character). The principal tonic phenomena observed in the cat are fast electrical waves (almost like those of wakefulness) in the cortex and subcortical structures, very regular "theta" waves at the level of the hippocampus (a structure running from the front to the rear of the brain) and total disappearance of electrical activity in the muscles of the neck. The principal phasic phenomena are high-voltage spikes, isolated or grouped in volleys, that appear at the level of the pons and the rear part of the cortex (which is associated with the visual sys-

SLEEP

3 PARADOXICAL SLEEP (PHASIC)

4 PARADOXICAL SLEEP (TONIC)

PONS

HIPPOCAMPUS

periodic, aspects of paradoxical sleep (3) are marked by isolated spike discharges from the rear of the cortex and the pons, as well as by rapid eye movement and limb movements. Loss of neck-muscle tension is a tonic (4) rather than a phasic phenomenon. Other tonic, or continuous, aspects of paradoxical sleep are high-speed cortical rhythms and regular "theta" waves from hippocampus.

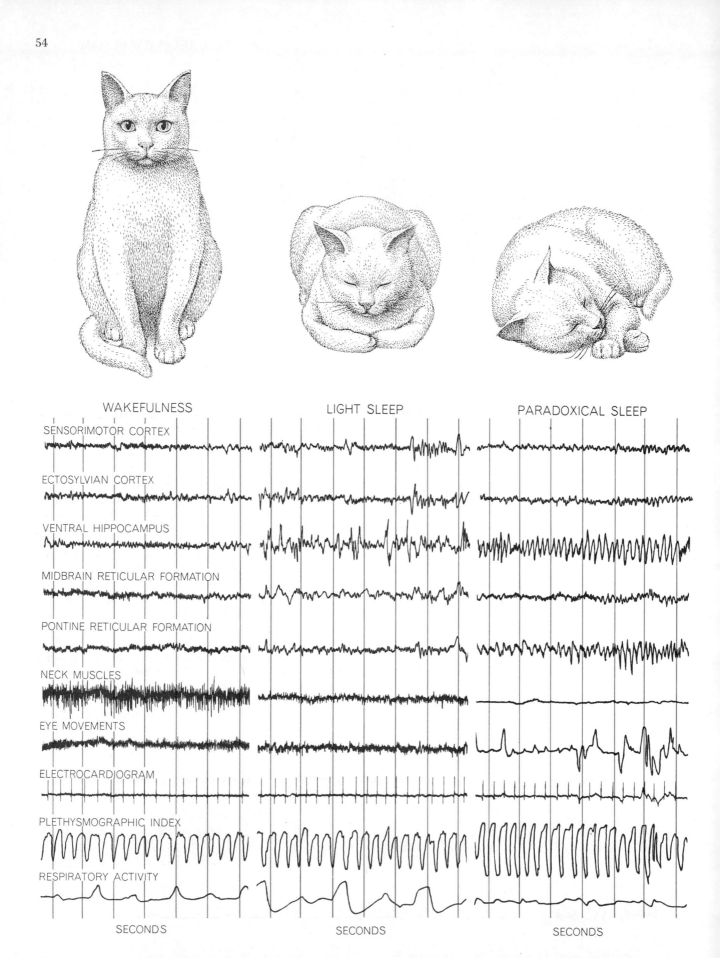

WAKEFULNESS	LIGHT SLEEP	PARADOXICAL SLEEP

SENSORIMOTOR CORTEX

ECTOSYLVIAN CORTEX

VENTRAL HIPPOCAMPUS

MIDBRAIN RETICULAR FORMATION

PONTINE RETICULAR FORMATION

NECK MUSCLES

EYE MOVEMENTS

ELECTROCARDIOGRAM

PLETHYSMOGRAPHIC INDEX

RESPIRATORY ACTIVITY

SECONDS   SECONDS   SECONDS

CHARACTERISTIC RHYTHMS associated with deep sleep in a cat (*group of traces at right*) are so much like those of wakefulness (*left group*) and so different from those of light sleep (*middle group*) that the author has applied the term "paradoxical" to deep sleep. Normal cats spend about two-thirds of the time sleeping. They usually begin each sleep period with 25 minutes of light sleep, followed by six or seven minutes of paradoxical sleep. In the latter state they are hard to wake and their muscles are relaxed.

tem). These spikes make their appearance about a minute before the tonic phenomena. Just as the latter show up, the peripheral phasic phenomena come into evidence: rapid eye movements, clawing movements of the paws and so on. The high-voltage spikes during paradoxical sleep in the cat come at a remarkably constant rate: about 60 to 70 per minute.

Our continuous recordings around the clock in a soundproofed cage have shown that cats spend about 35 percent of the time (in the 24-hour day) in the state of wakefulness, 50 percent in light sleep and 15 percent in paradoxical sleep. In most cases the three states follow a regular cycle from wakefulness to light sleep to paradoxical sleep to wakefulness again. An adult cat never goes directly from wakefulness into paradoxical sleep.

Thus we find that the two states of sleep have well-defined and clearly distinct electrical signatures. Equipped with this information, we are better prepared to search for the nervous structures and mechanisms that are responsible for sleep and dreaming.

The Suppression of Wakefulness

The first and most important question we must answer is this: Does the nervous system possess a specific sleep-producing mechanism? In other words, should we not rather confine our research to the operations of the mechanism that keeps us awake? Kleitman has put the issue very clearly; he observes that to say one falls asleep or is put to sleep is not the same as saying one ceases to stay awake. The first statement implies that an active mechanism suppresses the state of wakefulness—a mechanism analogous to applying the brakes in an automobile The second statement implies that the wakefulness-producing mechanism simply stops operating—a situation analogous to removing the foot from the accelerator. Thus the mechanism responsible for sleep would be negative or passive, not active.

Now, it has been known for nearly two decades that the brain contains a center specifically responsible for maintaining wakefulness. This was discovered by H. W. Magoun of the U.S. and Giuseppe Moruzzi of Italy, working together at Northwestern University [see the article beginning on page 23, "The Reticular Formation," by J. D. French]. They named this center, located in the midbrain, the reticular activating system (RAS). Stimulation of the RAS center in a slumbering animal arouses the animal; conversely, destruction of the center

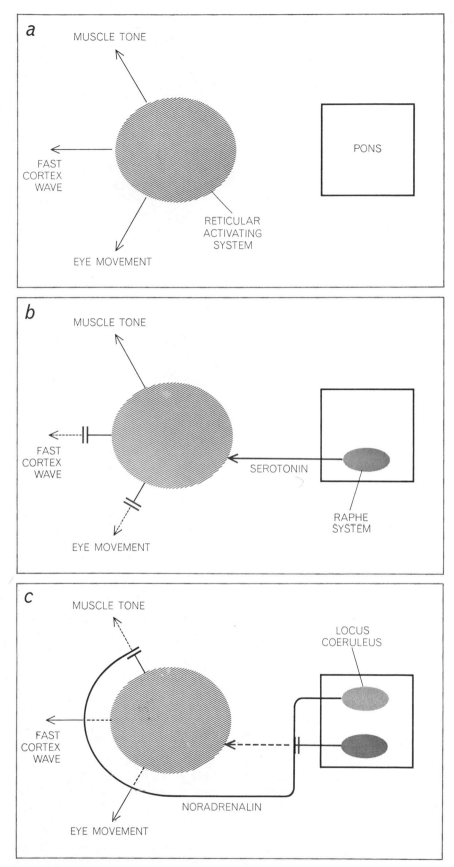

WORKING HYPOTHESIS, proposed by the author to provide a bridge between the neurophysiology and the biochemistry of sleep, suggests that the normal state of wakefulness (a) is transformed into light sleep (b) when a secretion produced by the nuclei of raphe modifies many effects of the reticular activating system. Paradoxical sleep follows (c) when a second secretion, produced by the locus coeruleus, supplants the raphe secretion and produces effects that resemble normal wakefulness except for the loss of muscle tension.

a

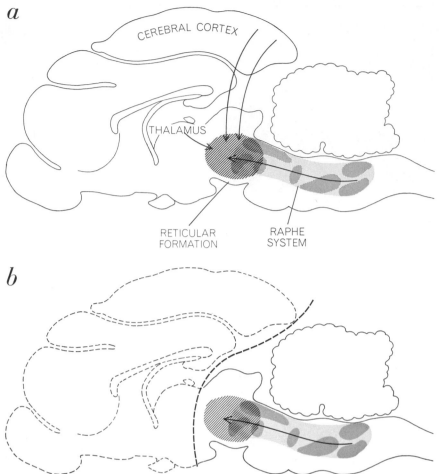

CEREBRAL CORTEX

THALAMUS

RETICULAR
FORMATION

RAPHE
SYSTEM

b

BRAIN STRUCTURES involved in light sleep include the raphe system, which, by producing the monoamine serotonin, serves to counteract the alerting effects of the brain's reticular formation ("*a*," color at left). The author suggests that raphe system structures act to modulate the fast wave pattern of the alert cortex into the slower pattern typical of light sleep. Such slow activity, however, depends on higher as well as lower brain structures (*b*); when a cat is deprived of its cerebral cortex and thalamus, the brain stem wave pattern characteristic of light sleep disappears. The reason for this is not yet understood.

causes the animal to go into a permanent coma. To explain normal sleep, then, we must find out what process or mechanism brings about a deactivation of the RAS for the period of sleep.

On the basis of the known facts about the RAS there seemed at first no need to invoke the idea of a braking mechanism to account for deactivation of the system. The Belgian neurophysiologist Frédéric Bremer suggested that the RAS could simply lapse into quiescence as a result of a decline of stimuli (such as disturbing noise) from the surroundings [see "Sleep," by Nathaniel Kleitman; SCIENTIFIC AMERICAN Offprint 431].

Several years ago, however, explorations of the brain by the Swiss neurophysiologist W. R. Hess and others began to produce indications that the brain might contain centers that could suppress the activity of the RAS. In these experiments, conducted with cats, the cats fell asleep after electrical stimula-

tion of various regions in the thalamus and elsewhere or after the injection of chemicals into the cerebrum. Interesting as these findings were, they were not very convincing on the question at issue. After all, since a cat normally sleeps about two-thirds of the time anyway, how could one be sure that the applied treatments acted through specific sleep-inducing centers? Moreover, the experiments seemed to implicate nearly all the nerve structures surrounding the RAS, from the cerebral cortex all the way down to the spinal cord, as being capable of inducing sleep. It was implausible that a sleep-inducing system could be so diffuse. Nevertheless, in spite of all these doubts, the experiments at least pointed to the possibility that the RAS might be influenced by other brain centers.

Moruzzi and his group in Italy proceeded to more definitive experiments. Seeking to pin down the location of a center capable of opposing the action of

the RAS, they focused their search on the lower part of the brainstem. They chose a site at the middle of the pons in front of the trigeminal nerve, and with cats as subjects they cut completely through the brainstem at that point. The outcome of this operation was that the cats became insomniac: they slept only 20 percent of the time instead of 65 percent! The brain cortex showed the characteristic electrical activity of wakefulness (fast, low-voltage activity), and the eye movements also were those of a wakeful animal pursuing moving objects. The experiments left no doubt that the cut had disconnected the RAS from some structure in the lower part of the brainstem that normally exercised control over the waking center. It was as if a brake had been removed, so that the RAS was essentially unrestricted and kept the animal awake most of the time.

The new evidence leads, therefore, to the conclusion that sleeping is subject to both active and passive controls. The active type of control consists in the application of a brake on the RAS by some other brain structure or structures; the passive type corresponds to a letup on the accelerator in the RAS itself.

Sleep Centers

What, and where, are the sleep-inducing centers that act on the RAS? Our suspicions are now focused on a collection of nerve cells at the midline of the brainstem that are known as the "nuclei of raphe" (from a Greek word meaning "seam" and signifying the juncture of the two halves of the brain). In Sweden, Annica Dahlström and Kzell Fuxe have shown that under ultraviolet light these cells emit a yellow fluorescence that shows they are rich in the hormone-like substance serotonin, which is known to have a wide spectrum of powerful effects on the brain and other organs of the body [see "Serotonin," by Irvine H. Page; SCIENTIFIC AMERICAN, December, 1957]. Suspecting from various preliminary pharmacological experiments that serotonin might play a role in sleep, we decided to test the effects of destroying the raphe cells, which are the principal source of the serotonin supply in the brain. We found that when we destroyed 80 percent of these cells at the level of the medulla in cats (the animals could not have survived destruction of a larger percentage), the cats became even more sleepless than those on which Moruzzi had performed his operation. In more than 100 hours of continuous observation with electrical recording instruments, our animals slept less than 10 percent of the time. Our results were closely related to those of Moruzzi's. His operation dividing the brainstem cut through the raphe system. We found that when we destroyed only the raphe cells on one side or the other of the site of his cut, our animals were reduced to the same amount of sleep (20 percent) as those on which he had performed his experiment. This gives us further reason to believe the raphe system may indeed be the main center responsible for bringing on sleep in cats.

These new developments bring serotonin into a prominent place in the research picture and offer an avenue for biochemical attack on the mysteries of sleep. The fact that the raphe cells are chiefly notable for their production of serotonin seems to nominate this substance for an important role in producing the onset of sleep. We have recently been able to demonstrate a significant correlation between the extent of the lesion of the raphe system, the decrease in sleep and the decrease in the amount of serotonin in the brain as measured by means of spectrofluorescent techniques.

In physiological terms we can begin to see the outlines of the system of brain structures involved in initiating the onset of sleep and maintaining the first stage of light slumber. At the level of the brainstem, probably within the raphe system, there are structures that apparently counteract the RAS and by their braking action cause the animal to fall asleep. Associated with these structures there presumably are nearby structures that account for the modulations of electrical activity (notably the slow brain waves) that have been observed to accompany light sleep. This slow activity seems to depend primarily, however, on the higher brain structures, particularly the cortex and the thalamus; in a decorticated animal the pattern characteristic of light sleep does not make its appearance. We must therefore conclude that the set of mechanisms brought into play during the process of falling asleep is a complicated one and that a number of steps in the process still remain to be discovered.

Paradoxical Sleep

In searching for the structures involved in paradoxical, or deep, sleep we are in a somewhat better position. When an animal is in that state, we have as clues to guide us not only the electrical activities in the brain but also conclusive and readily observable signs such as the disappearance of tonus in the muscles of the neck. This is the single most reliable

mark of paradoxical sleep. Furthermore, it enables us to study animals that have been subjected to drastic operations we cannot use in the study of light sleep because they obliterate the electrical activities that identify the falling-asleep stage.

A cat whose brainstem has been cut through at the level of the pons, so that essentially all the upper part of the brain has been removed, still exhibits the cycle of waking and deep sleep. Such an animal can be kept alive for several months, and with the regularity of a biological clock it oscillates between wakefulness and the state of paradoxical sleep, in which it spends only about 10 percent of the time. This state is signaled, as in normal animals, by the typical slackness of the neck muscles, by the electroencephalographic spikes denoting electrical activity in the pons structures and by lateral movements of the eyeballs.

When, however, we sever the brainstem at a lower level, in the lower part

of the pons just ahead of the medulla, the animal no longer falls into paradoxical sleep. The sign that marks this cyclical state—periodic loss of muscle tonus—disappears. It seems, therefore, that the onset of paradoxical sleep must be triggered by the action of structures somewhere in the middle portion of the pons. Further experiments have made it possible for us to locate these structures rather precisely. We have found that paradoxical sleep can be abolished by destroying certain nerve cells in a dorsal area of the pons known as the locus coeruleus. Dahlström and Fuxe have shown that these cells have a green fluorescence under ultraviolet light and that they contain noradrenalin. Hence it seems that noradrenalin may play a role in producing paradoxical sleep similar to the one serotonin apparently plays in bringing about light sleep.

What mechanism is responsible for the elimination of muscular tonus that accompanies paradoxical sleep? It seems

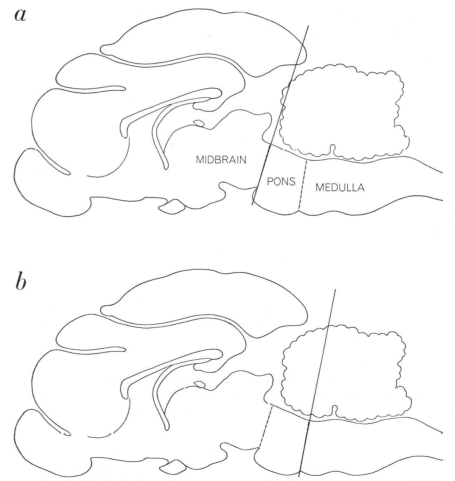

a

MIDBRAIN   PONS   MEDULLA

b

PARADOXICAL-SLEEP STRUCTURES evidently lie far back along the brainstem. A cat deprived of all its higher brain function by means of a cut through the pons (*a*) will live for months, alternately awake and in paradoxical sleep. If a cut is made lower (*b*) along the brainstem, however, the cat will no longer fall into paradoxical sleep, because the cut destroys some brain cells in that region, which produce another monoamine, noradrenalin.

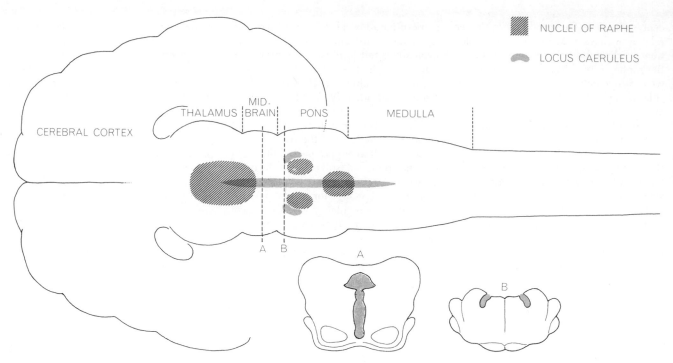

NUCLEI OF RAPHE

LOCUS CAERULEUS

CAT'S BRAINSTEM is the site of the two groups of cells that produce the substances affecting light and paradoxical sleep. The nuclei of raphe (*color*) secrete serotonin; another cell group in the pons, known as the locus coeruleus (*gray*), secretes noradrenalin.

most likely that the source of this inhibition lies in the spinal cord, and Moruzzi and his colleague Ottavio Pompeiano are making a detailed investigation of this hypothesis.

The objective information about paradoxical sleep developed so far gives us some suggestions about the mechanisms involved in dreaming. The controlling structures apparently are located in the dorsal part of the pons. They give rise to spontaneous excitations that travel mainly to the brain's visual tracts, and it seems possible that this excitation is related to the formation of the images that one "sees" in dreams. Regardless of how strongly the brain is stimulated by these spontaneous impulses (as Edward V. Evarts of the National Institute of Mental Health and others have shown by means of microelectrode recordings of the visual system), during sleep the body's motor system remains inactive because a potent braking mechanism blocks electrical excitation of the motor nerves. This inhibitory mechanism seems to be controlled by the hormone-secreting nerves of the locus coeruleus structure. If this structure is destroyed, the animal may periodically exhibit a spasm of active behavior, which looks very much as if it is generated by the hallucinations of a dream. In such episodes the cat, although it evinces the unmistakable signs of deep sleep and does not respond to external stimuli, will sometimes perform bodily movements of rage,

fear or pursuit for a minute or two. The sleeping animal's behavior may even be so fierce as to make the experimenter recoil.

All in all the experimental evidence from mammals obliges us to conclude that sleep has a fundamental duality; deep sleep is distinctly different from light sleep, and the duality is founded on physiological mechanisms and probably on biochemical ones as well. Can we shed further light on the subject by examining animal evolution?

The Evolution of Sleep

Looking into this question systematically in our laboratory, we failed to find any evidence of paradoxical sleep in the tortoise and concluded that probably reptiles in general were capable only of light sleep. Among birds, however, we start to see a beginning of paradoxical sleep, albeit very brief. In our subjects—pigeons, chicks and other fowl—this state of sleep lasts no longer than 15 seconds at a time and makes up only .5 percent of the total sleeping time, contrasted with the higher mammals' 20 to 30 percent. In the mammalian order all the animals that have been studied, from the mouse to the chimpanzee, spend a substantial portion of their sleeping time in paradoxical sleep. We find a fairly strong indication that the hunting species (man, the cat, the dog) enjoy more deep sleep than the hunted (rabbits, ruminants). In

our tests the former average 20 percent of total sleep time in paradoxical sleep, whereas the latter average only 5 to 10 percent. Further studies are needed, however, to determine if what we found in our caged animals is also true of their sleep in their natural environments.

The evolutionary evidence shows, then, that the early vertebrates slept only lightly and deep sleep came as a rather late development in animal evolution. Curiously, however, it turns out that the opposite is true in the development of a young individual; in this case ontogeny does not follow phylogeny. In the mammals (cat or man) light sleep does not occur until the nervous system has acquired a certain amount of maturity. A newborn kitten in its first days of life spends half of its time in the waking state and half in paradoxical sleep, going directly from one state into the other, whereas in the adult cat there is almost invariably a transitional period of light sleep. By the end of the first month the kitten's time is divided equally among wakefulness, light sleep and paradoxical sleep (that is, a third in each); thereafter both wakefulness and light sleep increase until adulthood stabilizes the proportions of the three states at 35, 50 and 15 percent respectively.

Considering these facts of evolution and development, we are confronted with the question: What function does paradoxical sleep serve after all? As Kleitman reported in his article "Patterns of Dreaming," Dement found that when he repeatedly interrupted people's dreams by waking them, this had the effect of making them dream more during their subsequent sleep periods. These results indicated that dreaming fulfills some genuine need. What that need may be remains a mystery. Dement's subjects showed no detectable disturbances of any importance—emotional or physiological—as a result of their deprivation of dreaming.

We have found much the same thing to be true of the deprivation of paradoxical sleep in cats. For such a test we place a cat on a small pedestal in a pool of water with the pedestal barely topping the water surface. Each time the cat drops off into paradoxical sleep the relaxation of its neck muscles causes its head to droop into the water and this wakes the animal up. Cats that have been deprived of paradoxical sleep in this way for several weeks show no profound disturbances, aside from a modest speeding up of the heart rate. They do, however, have a characteristic pattern of aftereffects with respect to paradoxical sleep. For several days following their removal from the pedestal they spend much more than the usual amount of time (up to 60 percent) in paradoxical sleep, as if to catch up. After this rebound they gradually recover the normal rhythm (15 percent in deep sleep), and only then does the heart slow to the normal rate. The recovery period depends on the length of the deprivation period: a cat that has gone without paradoxical sleep for 20 days takes about 10 days to return to normal.

The Chemistry of Sleep

All of this suggests that some chemical process takes place during the recovery period. Let us suppose that the deprivation of paradoxical sleep causes a certain substance related to the nervous system to accumulate. The excess of paradoxical sleep during the recovery period will then be occupied with elimination of this "substance," presumably through the agency of "enzymatic" factors that act only during paradoxical sleep.

There is reason to believe that certain enzymes called monoamine oxidases, which oxidize substances having a single amine group, play a crucial role in bringing about the transition from light sleep to paradoxical sleep. We have found that drugs capable of inhibiting these enzymes can suppress paradoxical sleep in cats without affecting either light sleep or wakefulness. A single injection of the drug nialamide, for example, will

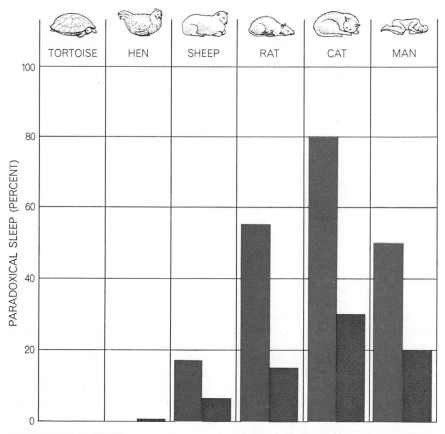

PARADOXICAL SLEEP among three vertebrate classes of increasing evolutionary complexity is shown as a percentage of each animal's time spent in light sleep. None is known in the case of the reptile, a tortoise; in the case of the hen it is only two-tenths of 1 percent of the total. In the case of each of the four mammal species shown, the newborn spend at least twice as much time in paradoxical sleep (*color*) as do their adult counterparts (*black*).

eliminate paradoxical sleep from the cycle for a period of hundreds of hours. We have also found that this potent drug can suppress paradoxical sleep in cats that have first been deprived of such sleep for a long period in the pool experiment.

The findings concerning the probable importance of the monoamine oxidases in the sleep mechanism raise the hope that it may soon be possible to build a bridge between neurophysiology and biochemistry in the investigation of sleep. If it is indeed a fact that these enzymes play an important role in sleep, this tends to strengthen the hypothesis that serotonin and noradrenalin, which are monoamines, are involved in the two states of sleep—serotonin in light sleep and noradrenalin in paradoxical sleep. There are other bits of chemical evidence that support the same view. For example, the drug reserpine, which is known to prevent the accumulation of monoamines at places where these compounds are usually deposited, has been found to be capable of producing some specific electrical signs of paradoxical sleep in experimental animals. Further, the injection of certain precursors in-

volved in the synthesis of serotonin in the brain can produce a state resembling light sleep, whereas drugs that selectively depress the serotonin level in the brain produce a state of permanent wakefulness.

We can put together a tentative working hypothesis about the brain mechanisms that control sleep. It seems that the raphe system is the seat responsible for the onset of light sleep, and that it operates through the secretion of serotonin. Similarly, the locus coeruleus harbors the system responsible for producing deep sleep, and this uses noradrenalin as its agent. In cyclic fashion these two systems apply brakes to the reticular activating system responsible for wakefulness and also influence all the other nerve systems in the brain, notably those involved in dreaming.

Dreaming itself, particularly the question of its evolutionary origin and what function it serves, is still one of the great mysteries of biology. With the discovery of its objective accompaniments and the intriguing phenomenon of paradoxical sleep, however, it seems that we have set foot on a new continent that holds promise of exciting explorations.

7

THE PATHOLOGY OF BOREDOM

WOODBURN HERON

January 1957

If you shake the surface on which a snail is resting, it withdraws into its shell. If you shake it repeatedly, the snail after a while fails to react. In the same way a sea anemone which is disturbed by a drop of water falling on the water surface above it ceases to be disturbed if drops continue to fall; a bird stops flying away from a rustling motion if the motion is steadily repeated. Most organisms stop responding to a stimulus repeated over and over again (unless the response is reinforced by reward or avoidance of punishment). Indeed, the higher organisms actively avoid a completely monotonous environment. A rat in a maze will use different routes to food, if they are available, rather than the same one all the time. It will tend to avoid areas in which it has spent considerable time and to explore the less familiar areas.

Monotony is an important and enduring human problem. Persons who have to work for long periods at repetitive tasks often complain of being bored and dissatisfied with their jobs, and frequently their performance declines. During the last war N. H. Mackworth of England made a series of researches for the Royal Air Force to find out why radar operators on antisubmarine patrol sometimes failed to detect U-boats. The operators usually worked in isolation, watching a radar screen hour after hour. Mackworth set up a comparable laboratory situation, requiring subjects to watch a pointer moving around a graduated dial and to press a button whenever the pointer made a double jump. The subjects' efficiency declined in the surprisingly short time of half an hour. As a result of this and other research the radar operators' tour of duty was shortened.

In this age of semi-automation, when not only military personnel but also many industrial workers have little to do but keep a constant watch on instruments, the problem of human behavior in monotonous situations is becoming acute. In 1951 the McGill University psychologist D. O. Hebb obtained a grant from the Defence Research Board of Canada to make a systematic study of the effects of exposure for prolonged periods to a rigidly monotonous environment. Hebb's collaborators in the project were B. K. Doane, T. H. Scott, W. H. Bexton and the writer of this article.

The aim of the project was to obtain basic information on how human beings would react in situations where

EXPERIMENTAL CUBICLE constructed at McGill University in Montreal to study the effects of perceptual isolation is at the right in this semischematic drawing from above. The subject lies on a bed 24 hours a day, with time out for meals and going to the bathroom. The room is always lighted. The visual perception of the subject is restricted by a translu-

nothing at all was happening. The purpose was not to cut individuals off from any sensory stimulation whatever, but to remove all patterned or perceptual stimulation, so far as we could arrange it.

The subjects were male college students, paid $20 a day to participate. They lay on a comfortable bed in a lighted cubicle 24 hours a day for as long as they cared to stay, with time out only for meals (which they usually ate sitting on the edge of the bed) and going to the toilet. They wore translucent plastic visors which transmitted diffuse light but prevented pattern vision. Cotton gloves and cardboard cuffs extending beyond the fingertips restricted perception by touch. Their auditory perception was limited by a U-shaped foam rubber pillow on which their heads lay and by a continuous hum of air-conditioning equipment which masked small sounds.

When we started the research we were not at all sure what aspects of behavior it would be most profitable to investigate. Accordingly we began with a preliminary run in which we merely observed the subjects' behavior and interviewed them afterward. Most of these subjects had planned to think about their work: some intended to review their studies, some to plan term papers, and one thought that he would organize a lecture he had to deliver. Nearly all of them reported that the most striking thing about the experience was that they were unable to think clearly about anything for any length of time and that their thought processes seemed to be affected in other ways. We therefore decided that the first thing to do was to test effects on mental performance.

We used three main methods of investigating this. One was a battery of oral tests involving simple arithmetic, anagrams, word association and so on. This battery was given before the experiment, at 12, 24 and 48 hours during the isolation and finally three days afterward. Another battery of tests, given two days before and immediately after the isolation period, included copying a design with blocks, speed of copying a prose paragraph, substituting symbols for numbers, picking out what was odd in each of a series of pictures (for instance, one picture showed a man in a canoe using a broom instead of a paddle) and recognizing patterns embedded in a complex background. The third test used a recording of a talk arguing for the reality of ghosts, poltergeists and other supernatural phenomena. It was played to each subject during his isolation. We examined the individual's attitude toward supernatural phenomena before he entered isolation and after he had emerged.

On almost every test the subjects' performance was impaired by their isolation in the monotonous environment (and was poorer than that of a control group of students). The isolation experience also tended to make the subjects susceptible to the argument for the existence of supernatural phenomena. Some of them reported that for several days after the experiment they were afraid that they were going to see ghosts.

As the subjects lay in isolation, cut off from stimulation, the content of their thought gradually changed. At first

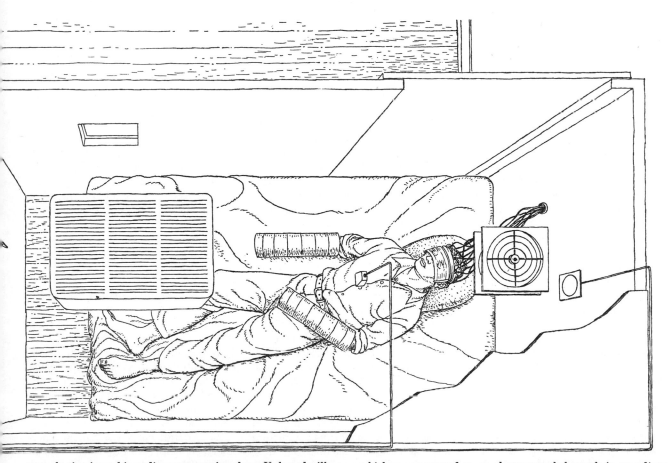

cent plastic visor; his auditory perception, by a U-shaped pillow covering his ears and by the noise of an air conditioner and a fan (*ceiling of cubicle*). In the experiment depicted here a flat pillow is used to leave room for the wires attached to the subject's scalp, which are connected to an electroencephalograph in an adjacent room. The subject's sense of touch is restricted by cotton gloves and long cardboard cuffs. The experimenter and the subject can communicate by means of a system of microphones and loud speakers.

they tended to think about their studies, about the experiment, about their personal problems. After a while they began to reminisce about past incidents, their families, their friends and so on. To pass the time some tried to remember in detail a motion picture they had seen; others thought about traveling from one familiar place to another and would try to imagine all the events of the journey; some counted numbers steadily into the thousands. (Incidentally, such experiences are commonly reported by persons who have been in solitary confinement for long periods.) Eventually some subjects reached a state in which it took too much effort to concentrate, and they became "content to let the mind drift," as one subject put it. Others said: "My mind just became full of sounds and colors, and I could not control it"; "I just ran out of things to think of"; "I couldn't think of anything to think about." Several subjects experienced "blank periods" when they did not seem to be thinking at all.

Not surprisingly, the subjects became markedly irritable as time went on and often expressed their irritation. Yet they also had spells when they were easily amused. In the interview afterward many of the subjects expressed surprise that their feelings could have oscillated so much, and that they could have behaved in such a childish way. They also said that they seemed to lose their "sense of perspective" while in the cubicle, and some subjects mentioned that at times they felt that the experimenters were against them, and were trying to make things exceptionally tough for them.

The subjects reported something else to which we at first paid no particular attention, but which was to emerge as the most striking result of the experiments. Many of them, after long isolation, began to see "images." One man repeatedly saw a vision of a rock shaded by a tree; another kept on seeing pictures of babies and could not get rid of them. Several subjects seemed to be "having dreams" while they were awake. Not until one of the experimenters himself went through the isolation experience for a long period did we realize the power and strangeness of the phenomenon. His report, and a review of the literature on other experiments in monotony, made clear that the experimental situation induced hallucinations.

The visual phenomena were similar to those experienced after taking the intoxicating drug of the mescal plant (mescal buttons), which is a ceremonial practice of some Indian tribes in the

Southwest. They have also been reported in experiments in which subjects were exposed for long periods to blank visual fields or flickering light.

Our subjects' hallucinations usually began with simple forms. They might start to "see" dots of light, lines or simple geometrical patterns. Then the visions became more complex, with abstract patterns repeated like a design on wallpaper, or recognizable figures, such as rows of little yellow men with black caps on and their mouths open. Finally there were integrated scenes: *e.g.*, a procession of squirrels with sacks over their shoulders marching "purposefully" across the visual field, prehistoric animals walking about in a jungle, processions of eyeglasses marching down a street. These scenes were frequently distorted, and were described as being like animated movie cartoons. Usually the subjects were at first surprised and amused by these phenomena, looked forward eagerly to see what was going to happen next and found that the "pictures" alleviated their boredom. But after a while the pictures became disturbing, and so vivid that they interfered with sleep. Some of the subjects complained that their eyes became tired from "focusing" on the pictures. They found sometimes that they could even scan the "scene," taking in new parts as they moved their eyes, as if they were looking at real pictures.

The subjects had little control over the content of the hallucinations. Some kept seeing the same type of picture no matter how hard they tried to change it. One man could see nothing but dogs, another nothing but eyeglasses of various types, and so on. Some subjects were able to realize visions of objects suggested by the experimenter, but not always in the way they were instructed. One man, trying to "get" a pen, saw first an inkblot on a white tablecloth, then a pencil, then a green horse, finally a pen.

The hallucinations were not confined to vision. Occasionally a subject heard people in the "scene" talking, and one man repeatedly heard a music box playing. Another saw the sun rising over a church and heard a choir singing "in full stereophonic sound." Several subjects reported sensations of movement or touch. One had a feeling of being hit in the arm by pellets fired from a miniature rocket ship he saw; another, reaching out to touch a doorknob in his vision, felt an electric shock. Some subjects reported that they felt as if another body were lying beside them in the cubicle;

in one case the two bodies overlapped, partly occupying the same space. Some reported feelings of "otherness" or "bodily strangeness"; trying to describe their sensations, they said, "my mind seemed to be a ball of cotton wool floating above my body," or "something seemed to be sucking my mind out through my eyes."

After emerging from isolation, our subjects frequently reported that "things looked curved," "near things looked large and far things looked small," "things seemed to move," and so on. We therefore made some systematic tests of their visual perception. The most striking finding was that when subjects emerged after several days of isolation, the whole room appeared to be in motion. In addition there was a tendency for surfaces to appear curved, and for objects to appear to be changing their size and shape. Asked to match a disk that was handed to them to one in a row of disks of various sizes 12 feet away, the subjects consistently chose a larger disk than did control subjects.

We recorded changes in the electrical activity of the brain in these subjects by means of electroencephalograms made before, during and after the isolation period. There was a tendency for some slow waves, which are normally present in sleep but not when an adult is awake, to appear after a period of isolation. In addition, the frequencies in the region of the principal brain rhythm slowed down [*see charts on opposite page*].

The overt behavior of the subjects during the experiment was, of course, carefully recorded. Most of the subjects went to sleep fairly soon after they had been placed in the cubicle. After waking they showed increasing signs of restlessness. This restlessness was not continuous but came in more and more intense spells, which were described as being very unpleasant. The subjects appeared eager for stimulation, and would talk to themselves, whistle, sing or recite poetry. When they came out for meals, they tended to be garrulous and attempted to draw the experimenters into conversation. In moving about, as when they were led to the toilet, they appeared dazed and confused, and had increasing difficulty in finding their way about the washroom.

As an outgrowth of the general experiment, we have begun some tests to find out the effects of restriction of just one sense. We tested six subjects who wore the frosted visors constantly but who otherwise were allowed to pursue

63

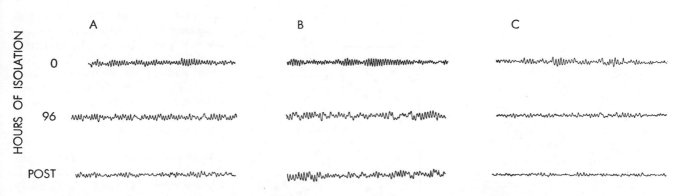

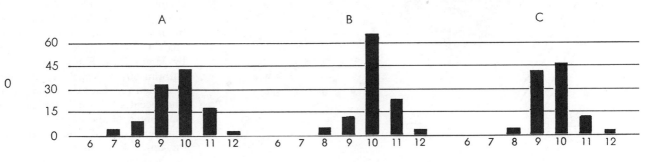

BRAIN WAVES from the occipital region of three subjects of the McGill University experiments (*above*) showed some change after 96 hours of isolation and three hours after the subject had emerged from isolation (POST). Similar changes in three other subjects are reflected in the bar charts (*bottom*). Below each bar is the number of waves counted in each one-second interval over a period of 300 seconds. The height of each bar is the percentage of all the waves during that period. Thus it indicates wave frequencies.

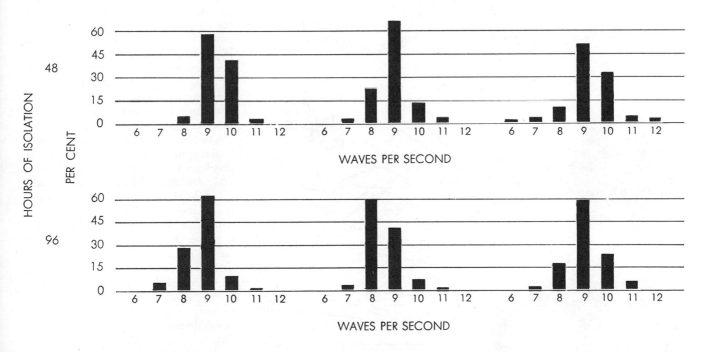

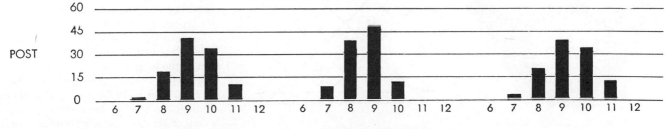

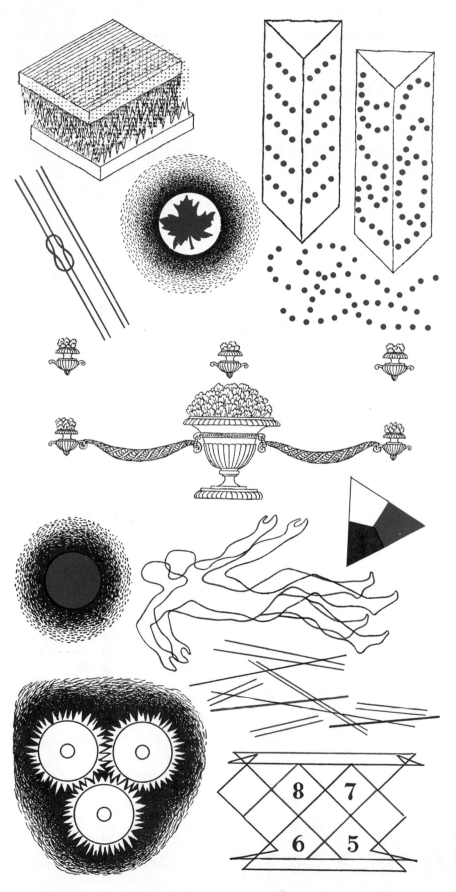

HALLUCINATIONS of isolated subjects are depicted. The drawings are based on descriptions by the subjects during the experiment and on sketches made after isolation period.

comparatively "normal" activities. Unfortunately the results of this experiment are not "pure," because the restriction of vision greatly restricted their movements and opportunity for other stimulation. These subjects developed visual hallucinations and also experienced some disorders of visual perception when the visors were removed.

Prolonged exposure to a monotonous environment, then, has definitely deleterious effects. The individual's thinking is impaired; he shows childish emotional responses; his visual perception becomes disturbed; he suffers from hallucinations; his brain-wave pattern changes. These findings are in line with recent studies of the brain, especially of the reticular formation in the midbrain [see "Pleasure Centers in the Brain," by James Olds; SCIENTIFIC AMERICAN Offprint 30]. In some way the reticular formation regulates the brain's activity. The recent studies indicate that normal functioning of the brain depends on a continuing arousal reaction generated in the reticular formation, which in turn depends on constant sensory bombardment. It appears that, aside from their specific functions, sensory stimuli have the general function of maintaining this arousal, and they rapidly lose their power to do so if they are restricted to the monotonously repeated stimulation of an unchanging environment. Under these circumstances the activity of the cortex may be impaired so that the brain behaves abnormally.

The results of our experiments seem to throw light on a number of practical problems. For instance, studies in France and at Harvard University have indicated that hallucinations are fairly common among long-distance truck drivers. After many hours on the road they may begin to see apparitions such as giant red spiders on the windshield and nonexistent animals running across the road, which frequently cause accidents. Similar phenomena have been reported by aviators on long flights: Charles Lindbergh described some in his autobiography. It is not improbable that some unexplained airplane and railroad accidents have been occasioned by effects of prolonged monotonous stimulation.

A changing sensory environment seems essential for human beings. Without it, the brain ceases to function in an adequate way, and abnormalities of behavior develop. In fact, as Christopher Burney observed in his remarkable account of his stay in solitary confinement: "Variety is not the spice of life; it is the very stuff of it."

8

ON TELLING LEFT FROM RIGHT

MICHAEL C. CORBALLIS AND IVAN L. BEALE
March 1971

Suppose that, like Alice passing through the looking glass, you have entered a world that is an exact reversal of the real world and yet you yourself have remained unreversed. (If, as some physicists believe, the effect of such a reversal would be to convert matter to antimatter, your stay would be short-lived, since the moment you made contact with antimatter you would be annihilated. Let us assume, however, that you have somehow been saved from this fate.) Living freely in the mirror world, you would soon notice some peculiar things. Printed words, for example, would look strange and unfamiliar. You might have some difficulty turning on a water faucet, using a corkscrew to open a bottle of wine, driving a car and writing words that would be intelligible to inhabitants of the reversed world. Yet not everything would appear strange. For the unreversed visitor the peculiarities and frustrations of the mirror world would be largely confined to those objects and symbols that are created by man. If you were to wander through a countryside where men had never lived, you might never know that you were in a reversed world [*see illustration on the next page*].

Next think of an animal with perfect bilateral symmetry that finds itself transported into such a mirror world. (Again we shall ignore possible subatomic considerations.) Will the animal be able to detect that it is in a world different from the real one? It will not. This conclusion is easily proved. Suppose that it was the animal that was mirror-reflected, and that the world remained the same. The process of reflection would leave a bilaterally symmetrical animal completely unaltered and so nothing would be different. Suppose now that it was the world that was reflected, and that the animal remained the same. In terms of

the animal's relation to the world—and therefore its perception of the world—the situation is exactly the same as it would be if the animal were changed and the world were not. In either case the world would appear quite unaltered.

All this is really to say that an animal with perfect bilateral symmetry could not tell left from right. That is essentially why the mirror world would appear the same to the animal as the real world. Now, most higher animals, including man, are in fact almost bilaterally symmetrical in terms of gross body structure and the anatomy of the nervous system. It is therefore of interest to inquire whether or not such animals have any fundamental difficulty telling left from right and, if so, whether or not the difficulty can be explicitly related to the approximate bilateral symmetry of the nervous system. We shall describe some of the evidence bearing on these questions. First, however, let us consider how one can determine if an animal other than man is able to distinguish left from right.

Two explicit tests are designed to provide an answer to that question. The first examines mirror-image stimulus discrimination: the ability of an animal subject to respond in two different ways that are *not* mirror images of each other when it is presented with two stimuli that *are* mirror images of each other. (For the purposes of this discussion the mirror image is understood to be a reflection with respect to the animal's plane of symmetry, that is, a left-right mirror image.)

It should be mentioned that the ability simply to give mirror-image responses to mirror-image stimuli does not prove the ability to tell left from right; in such cases the left-right information in the stimulus is simply copied in the response. If we are to be informed by an animal's behavior about the difference

between left and right, we need responses that differ in some regard other than left v. right. Examples of genuine mirror-image discrimination are provided by a dog that salivates when it is touched on the left flank but not when it is touched on the right, and a pigeon that pecks at a circular key displaying a line at an angle of 45 degrees to the horizontal but does not peck when the key displays a line at the mirror-image angle of 135 degrees.

An animal with perfect bilateral symmetry can only give mirror-image responses to mirror-image stimuli, because a symmetrical animal is not changed by reflection. If we watch such an animal in a mirror as it responds to an asymmetrical stimulus, what we see is essentially the same animal giving the mirror-image response to the mirror-image stimulus. (This argument is strictly true only if the laws of nature remain unaltered by mirror reflection. Physicists now suggest that the laws do not apply in the case of weak interactions at the subatomic level. We doubt, however, that such microcosmic interactions play a significant role in the neural processes involved in macrocosmic stimulus discrimination.)

Let us now relax the requirement that mirror-image discrimination involve only *exact* left-right mirror images. A bilaterally symmetrical animal need have no difficulty, for example, discriminating between up and down mirror images, such as telling the letter *b* from the letter *p*. Suppose, however, we consider mirror images that can appear in any orientation. The exact left-right mirror image of any particular manifestation of one image is at least a potential manifestation of the other, and so the perfectly symmetrical animal could not tell them apart. This is to say that a bilaterally symmetrical animal would not be able to give distinct, non-mirror-image labels to a left-

66

CONTRASTING SCENES demonstrate that most asymmetry is the work of man rather than of nature. Only an observer already familiar with the locale could recognize which is the actual image and which the mirror image of the natural landscape seen in the top pair of photographs. Anyone who knows the alphabet, however, can tell the actual from the mirror image in the bottom pair.

handed and a right-handed glove, to a corkscrew and its mirror image, or for that matter to any object and its counterpart through the looking glass. The animal might be able to recognize that the members of such a pair differed from each other, but it would have no basis for telling which was which.

The second test of the ability to tell left from right examines what can be called left-right response differentiation. The simplest version of this test requires an animal to make a "left" or "right" response in the absence of any consistent left-right information in the environment. An example would be the requirement to turn left in a symmetrical T-shaped maze. More elaborate tests of left-right response differentiation might require a dog to lift its left paw in response to a buzzer and its right paw in response to a bell, or a rat to turn into the left arm of a symmetrical T-maze when a light is on and into the right arm when the light is off. Such tests require that the animal make a left response to one stimulus and a right response to another when the stimuli are bilaterally symmetrical with respect to the animal, or at least when the stimuli exhibit no consistent left-right bias. A bilaterally symmetrical animal could not perform successfully in such a test, because there would be no information either in the environment or in the animal itself to indicate that it should make a left response or a right one. For example, a symmetrical "soldier," instructed to turn left or right on command, could not respond with consistent correctness if each command were as likely to be heard from one side as from the other.

These are the two kinds of question one might ask an animal or a man if one wished to discover whether or not the subject knew the difference between left and right. In a test of mirror-image stimulus discrimination we give examples of left and right orientation and the subject must indicate which is which. In left-right response differentiation we name left and right and ask the subject to exemplify which is which. This test essentially asks the subject to prove the ability to distinguish left from right by making a physical demonstration of it. Our query is not properly answered if the animal simply gives mirror-image responses to mirror-image stimuli. For example, an animal or a man does not need to "know" the difference between left and right in order to flick a fly from one ear, to follow a path that curves left and right or to move left or right to intercept a rolling ball. Nor need an animal with perfect bilateral symmetry have any difficulty performing these tasks.

The Austrian physicist and philosopher Ernst Mach, writing late in the 19th century, was perhaps the first to point out that the difficulty encountered with mirror-image discriminations could be attributed to bilateral symmetry. Mach had to rely on anecdotal evidence. Experimental studies since his time have shown that both animals and men often find it difficult to discriminate between left-right mirror images. The Russian physiologist I. P. Pavlov reported that it was impossible to condition a dog to salivate when it was touched on one side of its body and not to salivate when it was touched at the mirror-image point on its other side. N. S. Sutherland and his colleagues at the University of Sussex have found it virtually impossible to teach an octopus to discriminate between visually presented mirror-image patterns. The psychologist Karl S. Lashley reported that it was difficult, although not impossible, to teach rats to discriminate between visually presented left-right mirror images. Similar experimental findings have been reported for goldfish, cats, monkeys, chimpanzees and children. When children are learning to read, they have more difficulty discriminating between b and d and between p and q than they do discriminating between b and p and between d and q. Adults may also have trouble with left-right mirror images; for example, the great German investigator Hermann von Helmholtz is said to have been to a considerable degree "left-right blind."

Tests of left-right response differentiation are less widely documented than tests of mirror-image stimulus discrimination. It nonetheless seems to be fairly easy to teach an animal the simplest kind of left-right response differentiation. In such a test the animal must simply make a left or a right response in a situation where no left-right cues are provided. Rats can fairly readily learn to turn consistently into one arm of a symmetrical T-maze.

When one stimulus calls for a left response and another calls for a right response, the task may become much more difficult. The Polish physiologist Jerzy Konorski reports that he found it impossible to teach a dog to lift one paw at the sound of a buzzer and the other paw at the sound of a bell as long as both sounds came from the same direction. It is also a common observation that children may have difficulty learning to write letters in their correct left-right orientation or learning to turn left or right on command.

The experimental evidence we have been describing suggests that it is often difficult to learn to tell left from right; that is, animals apparently tend to behave according to their structural symmetry in spite of their asymmetrical training. One explanation for this fact is the possibility that the physical memory "traces" in the nervous system tend to become symmetrical. It may be that, as a memory trace for a given stimulus pattern is being established during learning, a second trace is simultaneously being established for the mirror image of the pattern even though the mirror image has not actually been presented. David R. Thomas and his colleagues at the University of Colorado have shown that pigeons trained to peck at a key when it displays a line slanted at, say, an angle of 60 degrees subsequently peck almost as much at a key that displays a line at the mirror-image angle of 120 degrees even though the birds have not seen a line at that angle before. They peck less frequently when the second line is oriented at some other angle.

A more complex example of mirror-image equivalence in pigeons has been demonstrated by Nancy K. Mello at the Harvard Medical School. In a series of studies she trained birds with one eye covered to peck at a key displaying a certain stimulus. When the birds were then tested with the covered eye open and the "trained" eye closed, they tended to peck at a key displaying the left-right mirror image of the stimulus. With respect to the midsagittal plane, which divides the pigeon's left side from its right, the mirror image of a pattern viewed through one eye is precisely the left-right reflection of the pattern viewed through the other eye. Mrs. Mello's pigeons were effectively treating these mirror-image stimuli as though they were identical, although the pigeons had been taught to peck in response to only one of them.

There are indications that humans also duplicate memory traces in mirror-image form. In his book *Remembering* the late Sir Frederic Bartlett reported an experiment in which subjects described pictures of various faces 30 minutes after having viewed them. In 82 cases the subjects volunteered that the face they had seen was a left profile or a right profile. The interesting thing is that in 30 instances the reported direction was wrong. Commenting on the remarkable ability of humans to remember pictures, Ralph Norman Haber of the University of Rochester noted that people recognize a picture during a test just as often

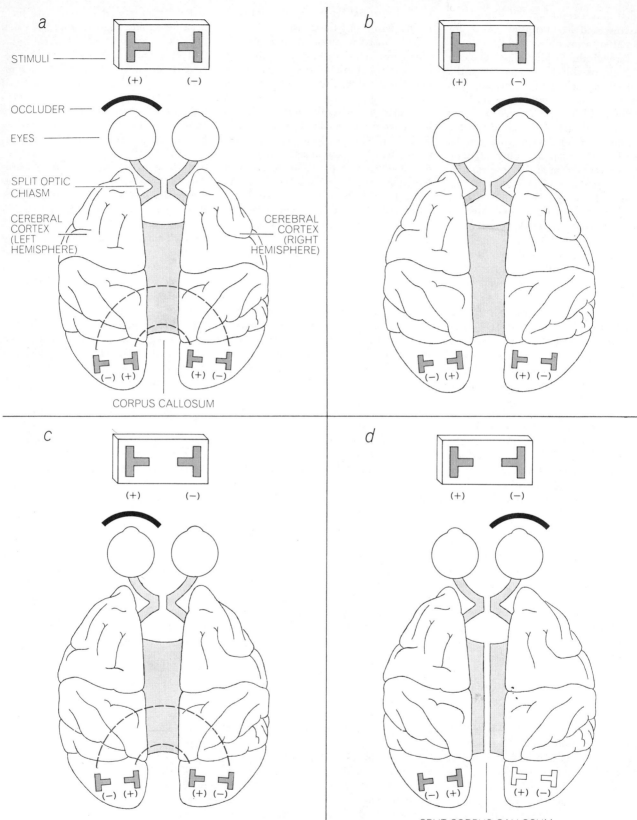

a

STIMULI

OCCLUDER

EYES

SPLIT OPTIC CHIASM

CEREBRAL CORTEX (LEFT HEMISPHERE)

CEREBRAL CORTEX (RIGHT HEMISPHERE)

(+) (−)

CORPUS CALLOSUM

b

(+) (−)

c

(+) (−)

d

(+) (−)

SPLIT CORPUS CALLOSUM

INFORMATION TRANSFER in mirror-image form from one hemisphere of the brain to the other was demonstrated by John Noble of the University of London, who used monkeys as subjects. In order to make sure that the rewarded and unrewarded visual cues were received by one hemisphere only, Noble blocked off the sight of one eye and severed the monkeys' optic chiasm before training (*a*). After training, the monkeys were tested with the sight of the trained eye (*b*) blocked off. They eventually showed a pref- erence for the cue that had gone unrewarded in training. Because the negative cue is a mirror image of the positive cue, Noble concluded that information was reversed during interhemispheric transfer but that the trained hemisphere influenced early choices. To test his conclusion he repeated the one-eyed training (*c*) but cut the main interhemispheric pathway, the corpus callosum, before testing the monkeys (*d*). With no way for the trained hemisphere to interfere, the monkeys selected the formerly negative cue at once.

when what is shown is a mirror image of the original as when the picture is correctly oriented. Moreover, even when they recognize the test picture as being familiar, they are often unable to state correctly whether it is in the original orientation or instead is a mirror image of the original. These observations are at least consistent with the interpretation that memory traces tend to be duplicated in mirror-image form.

The symmetry of such memory traces probably depends on the commissures: the tissue that connects the two hemispheres of the brain. We have mentioned that Pavlov reported that he was unable to condition a dog both to salivate when it was touched on one side of the body and not to salivate when it was touched on the other side. Pavlov went on to observe that there was no such mirror-image confusion when the corpus callosum, the main commissure between the two cerebral hemispheres, was cut. We find that mirror-image equivalence in pigeons is also abolished when the commissures are cut [*see illustration on this page*].

Anatomical and physiological evidence suggests that the commissures connect mirror-image points in at least some parts of the brain. Such connections would create a kind of neural mirror that serves to "reflect" neural activity across the midline. We believe the process might apply particularly to the transfer of memory traces between hemispheres: if a trace is established in one hemisphere, its mirror image will be established in the other.

This idea is not new. It was suggested in 1937 by Samuel Torrey Orton of Columbia University to explain the frequency with which mirror-image confusions and reversals occur among children who encounter problems in reading and writing. In some cases cited by Orton children were able to read reversed words as easily as normal words, even though they had previously been exposed only to normal words. Orton also gave some examples of children who found it difficult to learn to write normally but who were able to write better in the reverse direction without any practice or instruction. Here, somewhat paradoxically, the mirror-image memory appears to have been laid down more efficiently than the original one. According to Paul A. Kolers of the University of Toronto, when right-handed people are asked to write with their left hand, they are usually better at mirror writing than at normal writing. Leonardo da Vinci, who was left-handed, habitually wrote

a mirror-image script that has been mistakenly described as "secret writing." These observations lend some support to Orton's view that memory traces associated with reading and writing may be to some degree laid down in mirror-image form in the cerebral hemisphere opposite the hemisphere that is dominant for speech, and that in some cases the mirror-image representation may intrude to disrupt normal performance.

John Noble of the University of London has undertaken to assay the extent of the interhemispheric mirror-image reversal of memory traces in monkeys by teaching a mirror-image discrimination to one cerebral hemisphere and then testing the other hemisphere for mirror-image reversal. He restricts input to one hemisphere during learning by cutting the optic chiasm, the juncture of the two optic nerves that normally carries the nerve impulses from both eyes to both

hemispheres of the brain, and then presenting positive and negative stimuli to one eye only. When the discrimination has been learned, he assesses the degree of interhemispheric transfer by presenting the same stimuli to the "untrained" eye only. During the test trials the monkeys show some tendency to reverse the learned discrimination, favoring the stimulus that was "negative" during the original training over the stimulus that was "positive."

Noble found that the reversed preference did not appear at once but developed as the testing sessions continued, which implied that there may initially have been some conflict. He decided that the conflict may have arisen because in early test trials the discrimination was still controlled by the hemisphere that had been trained originally. In order to examine this possibility Noble carried out a further experiment. After the initial

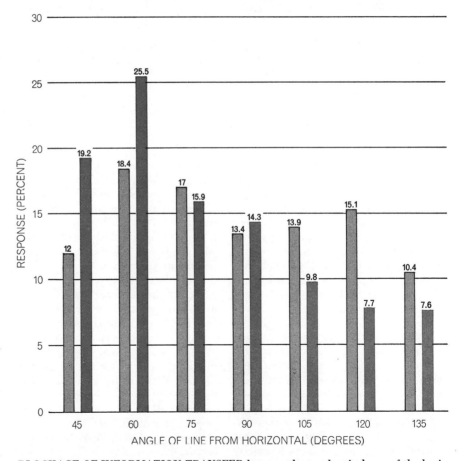

BLOCKAGE OF INFORMATION TRANSFER between the two hemispheres of the brain in pigeons was found to abolish information storage in mirror-image form. Two groups of pigeons were trained to peck a key for a food reward when the key displayed a line at an angle of 60 degrees to the horizontal on a green field, but not when the green key displayed no line. One group of birds had their interhemispheric connections surgically severed (*color*) but the brains of the other group were unaltered (*black*). The birds were next presented with keys that displayed lines at a number of angles ranging from 45 to 135 degrees. Both groups pecked most often at a key showing a 60-degree line. The birds with intact brains also tended to peck frequently at a 120-degree line, which is the mirror image of the 60-degree line. The altered birds' response, however, showed no mirror-image peak. Donald M. Webster and Robert J. Williams assisted the authors with the experiment.

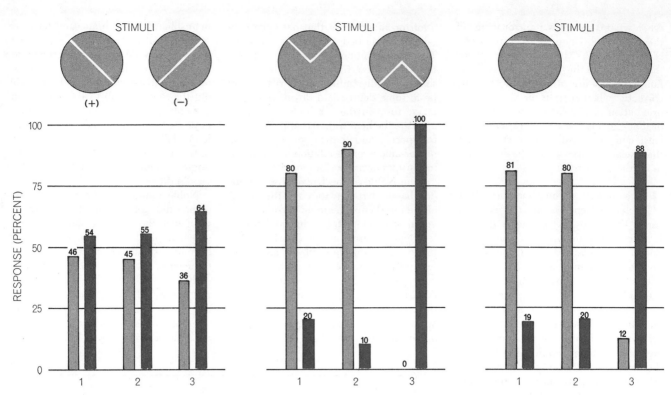

OSTENSIBLE REVERSAL of cues after interhemispheric transfer of information is shown to be the result, instead, of using only one eye while learning to discriminate between two cues. Three pigeons were trained to peck a key for a reward when it displayed a 135-degree line but not when it displayed a 45-degree line. The first two birds were trained with the left eye open and the third with the right eye open. Tested with the untrained eye open (*left*), all three pecked most frequently at the 45-degree mirror-image line. However, when the three used the trained eye to discriminate between other cues (*above bars at center and right*), their responses indicated that each had attended during training only to the part of the cue located on the bird's seeing-eye side. Instead of a mirror-image discrimination acquired as a result of interhemispheric transfer, the birds had learned discrimination between up and down.

training but before the test trials he cut the corpus callosum so that the stimuli were denied access to the originally trained hemisphere during testing with the untrained eye. If the animals were allowed a period of postoperative recovery to adapt to having the trained eye closed and the untrained eye open, Noble found that mirror-image reversal of the discrimination appeared at the time of the first test trials.

Noble's intricate and closely reasoned experiments provide convincing evidence of the role of the corpus callosum in producing symmetrical memory traces in monkeys. Nonetheless, they may not be conclusive. Mrs. Mello has also found interocular mirror-image reversal of discrimination learning in pigeons. In these birds the image from each eye is projected exclusively to only one hemisphere of the brain, so that her results are analogous to Noble's results with monkeys whose optic chiasm had been cut. We have conducted experiments, however, that suggest the mirror-image reversals demonstrated by Mrs. Mello may not have actually depended on interhemispheric reversal of memory traces. There is a simpler explanation.

In a typical experiment Mrs. Mello's pigeons would be taught, while one eye was open and one covered, to peck at a small circular key when it displayed one stimulus pattern but not to peck at it when the mirror image of the pattern was displayed. When the birds were tested with the trained eye covered and the untrained eye open, most of them pecked at the key more often when the mirror-image pattern was displayed. We have found that in the course of learning a mirror-image discrimination a pigeon with one covered eye attends to cues displayed on only one side of the key: the side of the seeing eye. This means that the bird may not really learn a mirror-image discrimination at all. For example, if the stimuli are lines at the angles of 45 and 135 degrees, the bird may be effectively learning an up-down discrimination. On the right side of the key, say, the 45-degree line occupies the upper portion, whereas the 135-degree line occupies the lower portion. Again, if one stimulus consists of a blue area on the left side of the key and a red one on the right and the other consists of a red area on the left and a blue one on the right, a pigeon restricted to the use of one eye and attending to only one side of the

key would learn a simple color discrimination.

If the pigeon now views the test key with its untrained eye and attends only to the other side of the key, the cues will clearly have been reversed. For example, on the left side of a key marked with a 45-degree line the line occupies the lower portion of the key; similarly, the left side of a key bearing a 135-degree line is marked in the upper portion. In the case of discrimination between blue-red and red-blue keys the color cues are likewise reversed between opposite sides of the key.

The same principle applies for any pair of stimuli that are mirror images with respect to a vertical division of the key. Therefore if a pigeon attends to one side of the key during training and to the other side during testing, its behavior will mimic mirror-image reversal even though what has been learned is not mirror-image discrimination at all [*see top illustration on page 72*].

We have generally failed to find such strong evidence for mirror-image reversal as Mrs. Mello has found. For instance, in one of our experiments we tested the ability of pigeons to discriminate between red-blue and blue-red keys. Four birds were trained with one eye covered. When the birds were tested with the other eye covered, two of them showed reversal and the other two did not. We believe that underlying this inconsistency is some conflict with respect to which side of the key the bird may attend to when the time comes for testing. On the one hand, there is a natural tendency for a bird restricted to the use of only one eye to attend to the side of the key on its own seeing-eye side. On the other hand, the bird may have developed a preference for the opposite side of the key during the learning sessions. We have reported one experiment in which there was a significant positive correlation between the extent to which birds actually pecked on the opposite side of the key in training and testing and the extent to which they showed mirror-image reversal. More recent experiments indicate that the place where a bird pecks may be a rather unreliable indication of the part of the key it actually attends to. We still think it is likely that when behavior that appears to indicate mirror-image reversal occurs, it is actually governed by the tendency of some birds to attend to one side of the key during training and to the opposite side during testing.

We do not know whether a similar explanation holds for interocular mirror-image reversal in species other than the pigeon. It is at least clear that careful analysis of the cues governing mirror-image discrimination is necessary before an unequivocal interpretation is possible. As we shall see, response asymmetries or attentional asymmetries evidently play a rather general role in mirror-image discrimination. As a result it may not always be obvious precisely what an animal has learned in the course of its exposure to a mirror-image-stimulus discrimination task.

So far we have stressed the equivalence of mirror-image stimuli and the trouble animals have discriminating between them. Usually, however, animals *can* discriminate between them, albeit with difficulty. How do they manage to do so? One possibility is that the mirror-image duplication of memory traces is only partial, so that the original trace remains the dominant one. In this way asymmetry could be built up, although the buildup would be gradual. There is evidence that interhemispheric transfer is more or less complete in pigeons and that it is less so in cats and monkeys. In man it is now well known that there is considerable specialization of function within each hemisphere of the brain. In most people the left cerebral cortex seems to have the dominant role in speech, whereas the right cortex is apparently the more important for certain nonverbal perceptual tasks.

Mach thought the asymmetry that made possible the solution of mirror-image problems might reside in a motor function rather than in either a sensory or a perceptual one. He observed that mirror-image confusions occur less commonly for stimuli associated with writing than for stimuli that lack any motor association. This suggested to him that handedness might provide an important cue for mirror-image discrimination in man. The one-direction horizontal eye movements associated with reading probably also facilitate the discrimination of mirror-image letters and words.

Unlike handedness, which appears to be at least to some degree genetically determined, the direction of reading and writing seems to be merely a matter of convention. About A.D. 1500 there were as many scripts written and read from right to left as there were written and read from left to right. With the expansion of European culture in the centuries that followed, left-to-right scripts came to predominate. Even today, however, Hebrew and Arabic are written from right to left. In all cultures so far tested the majority of people are right-handed and right-eye dominant, so that there appears to be no causal relation between handedness and eye dominance on the one hand and direction of reading and writing on the other. Some early scripts, known as boustrophedon (literally an "ox-turning," or the plowing of alternate furrows in opposite directions), consisted of alternating left-to-right and right-to-left lines. In some instances the alternate lines were complete mirror images of each other, so that only the appropriate directional scan would provide each

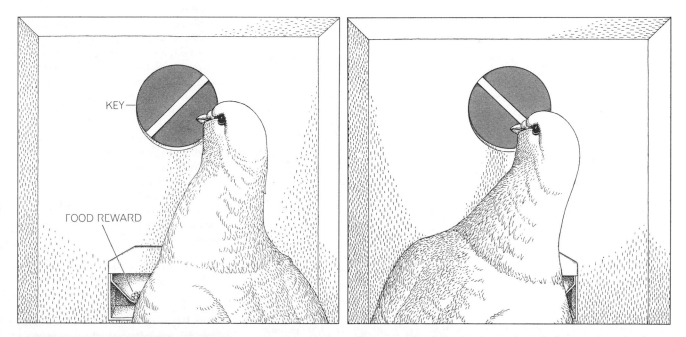

ASYMMETRICAL RESPONSES were noted in a pigeon presented with a pair of mirror-image stimuli in the authors' laboratory. On exposure to the positive stimulus, a 45-degree line, the pigeon (*left*) tilted its head to the right, making the line appear vertical. The same tilt of the head transformed the negative stimulus, a 135-degree line (*right*), into a horizontal line. The result was that the bird, rather than making a mirror-image discrimination, had simply learned to tell a vertical line from a horizontal one.

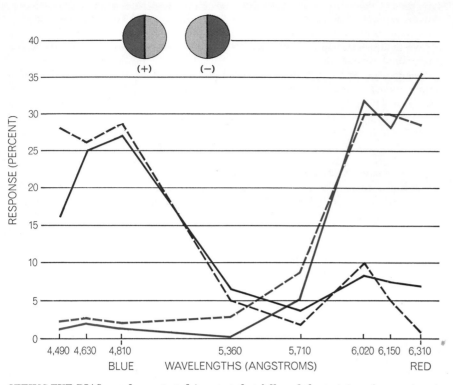

SEEING-EYE BIAS was demonstrated in a test that followed the training of two pairs of pigeons to peck a key for a reward when the left half of the key was red and the right blue, but not when the colors were reversed. Two birds were trained with only their right eye open (*black*) and two with only their left eye open (*color*). In the test the key was shown in various colors, including both blue and red. Pecking reached a maximum at the blue wavelength in the case of the right-eyed birds; in training they had attended to the right side of the key. In the case of the left-eyed birds, who had attended to the left side of the key, the maximum occurred at the red wavelength. J. Christopher Clarke conducted the color experiment in the authors' laboratory at the University of Auckland.

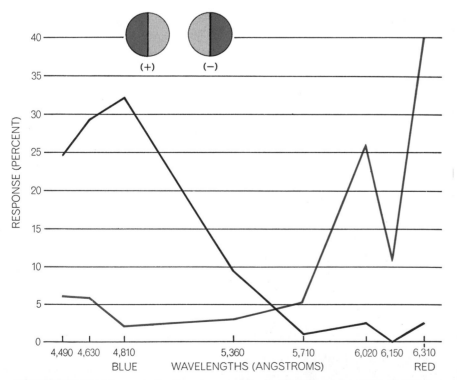

ATTENTION BIAS is not confined to pigeons trained with one eye closed. A second color experiment conducted by Clarke was identical with the one illustrated at top of page except that only two birds were trained, each with both eyes open. Even with unhindered vision one evidently attended only to the right side of the key (*black*) and the other to the left (*color*). The birds had learned not a mirror image but only a two-color discrimination.

symbol with its correct orientation and meaning.

We have observed that pigeons apparently develop spontaneous response asymmetries while learning mirror-image discriminations. In one of our experiments involving the ability to discriminate a 45-degree line from a 135-degree line two birds, each viewing the marked key with both eyes, tilted their heads consistently to the side. The task was thus transformed into one of discriminating a horizontal line from a vertical one [*see illustration on preceding page*]. In teaching red-blue (positive) v. blue-red (negative) discrimination to two other birds that were viewing the key with both eyes, we observed that one bird placed itself to the left side of the key and pecked on the left side whereas the other placed itself to the right side and pecked on the right side. For testing purposes the key was no longer divided in half but displayed a sequence of colors that included both blue and red. The test results showed that both birds had learned a color discrimination rather than a mirror-image discrimination. This result is similar to the one we described above for birds restricted to the use of one eye at a time, except that in the earlier instances attention to one side of the key during learning depended on which eye was covered, whereas the birds with both eyes uncovered apparently developed a spontaneous asymmetry.

In a sense, to say that the ability to discriminate between a real image and a mirror image is achieved through the development of response asymmetries is simply to push the question back a step; an animal with perfect bilateral symmetry could no more develop a response asymmetry than it could achieve mirror-image discrimination. If one accepts the premise that asymmetry must occur somewhere, however, the simplest form of it would be just such a unilateral asymmetrical response—the predominant use of one hand, a left-to-right eye scan or a tilt of the head to one side. This is indeed the simplest kind of left-right response differentiation. Moreover, it is all the asymmetry that is needed for even the most complex mirror-image discrimination.

Many aids to memory that assist left-right discrimination make use of existing or previously acquired asymmetries. Children probably first learn which is the left or the right side of their body or which is a left or a right turn by association with their "right" hand, that is, the hand they "write" with. The French solve the problem of what is left and right for a theater audience and what is left and right for an actor as follows. The left side of the stage is called the *jardin* (garden) and the right side the *cour* (court). For the audience the mnemonic device is *Jésus Christ:* the *J* stands for *jardin* (left) and the *C* for *cour* (right). For the actor *cour* is a reminder of *coeur* (heart), which of course beats most strongly on the left, a fact of which he may be particularly conscious before the curtain goes up on opening night.

Symmetries may be found in all forms of life. As Martin Gardner has written in *The Ambidextrous Universe,* it is not difficult to understand how various kinds of symmetry may have evolved. Primitive single-cell organisms, floating weightlessly in the sea without any fixed orientation relative to the earth, may have been naturally spherical, since there were no directional biases in the forces and stimuli that impinged on them. When organisms became anchored to the sea bottom or established themselves on land, the basis for a differentiated up-down axis came into being. For example, most plants have a rough radial symmetry, with an up-down axis but no obvious differentiation between front and back or left and right. It was probably the evolution of movement that gave rise to the distinction between front and back, but there would still be no basis for a distinction between left and right. Linear movement seems in fact to be most efficiently accomplished by a bilaterally symmetrical system, and where different forms of locomotion

have evolved independently of one another they are with very few exceptions bilaterally symmetrical. Given a bilaterally symmetrical motor apparatus, one might also expect sensory systems to evolve in a bilaterally symmetrical fashion. An organism moving around in the natural environment would encounter no asymmetries that favored either left or right in the long run, and it would therefore be maximally receptive to stimuli from the environment if it were equally sensitive to left and right.

There must also be some advantage to maintaining bilateral symmetry even in the face of asymmetrical experience. If an animal is attacked from the left and survives to learn from the experience, there would be an advantage to generalizing the learning in order to be able to cope with an attack from the right. Another advantage to maintaining symmetry is that things look the same from one side or the other; an animal can be recognized whether it is seen from the left profile or the right. In the natural environment there is more to be gained from mirror-image equivalence than from mirror-image discrimination.

Left-right asymmetry in man's nervous system may have evolved along with the use of tools. Many operations with tools require a greater contribution from one hand than from the other. It has been suggested that the origin of right-handedness lies in sword fighting. Since the heart is displaced slightly to the left of the body's midline, the odds in favor

of survival were improved, the reasoning goes, when the left hand performed the essentially passive function of supporting a shield and the right hand wielded the sword. The displacement of the heart is so slight, however, as to render the hypothesis rather implausible. In less sanguinary examples of tool use, such as hammering or chopping, one hand—usually the left—holds the material being worked and the other hand holds the tool. Jerome S. Bruner of Harvard University has proposed that there may be a similar relation between the two hemispheres of the brain with respect to speech, the right hemisphere being responsible for holding a context and the left working on the context to produce the actual speech. Bruner's proposal suggests a link between language and tool use.

In general, therefore, it appears that left-right asymmetries are particularly associated with the kinds of behavior that are no longer restricted to the natural environment. This conclusion reemphasizes our point that the large majority of left-right asymmetries exist only in the man-made environment. In tool use, in communication and in other kinds of symbolic behavior man is essentially freed from the symmetrical constraints imposed by the natural world. It is primarily with respect to these types of behavior that the human brain and nervous system have become lateralized. The results include increases in flexibility, in neural storage capacity and in the ability to make distinctions.

SPONTANEOUS MIRROR WRITING is the work of a five-year-old girl in a New Zealand school. The lighter, correctly oriented script is the teacher's; word order in the pupil's copy is consistent- ly right-to-left although some words and letters are in normal left-to-right form. Mirror writing is evidence in favor of the conclusion that interhemispheric memory transfers involve reversals.

9

LEARNING IN THE AUTONOMIC NERVOUS SYSTEM

LEO V. DICARA
January 1970

The heart beats and the stomach digests food without any obvious training, effort or even attention. That may be the basis of a curious prejudice against the visceral responses—the responses of glands, of cardiac muscle and of the smooth muscle of the alimentary canal and blood vessels—and against the autonomic nervous system, which controls them. Such responses are assumed to be quite different from, and somehow inferior to, the highly coordinated voluntary responses of skeletal muscles and the cerebrospinal nervous system that controls them. A corollary of this attitude has been the assumption that visceral responses can be "conditioned" but cannot be learned in the same way as skeletal responses. It turns out that these long-standing assumptions are not valid. There is apparently only one kind of learning; supposedly involuntary responses can be genuinely learned. These findings, which have profound significance for theories of learning and the biological basis of learning, should lead to better understanding of the cause and cure of psychosomatic disorders and of the mechanisms whereby the body maintains homeostasis, or a stable internal environment.

Learning theorists distinguish between two types of learning. One type, which is thought to be involuntary and therefore inferior, is classical, or Pavlovian, conditioning. In this process a conditioned stimulus (a signal of some kind) is presented along with an innate unconditioned stimulus (such as food) that normally elicits a certain innate unconditioned response (such as salivation); after a time the conditioned stimulus elicits the same response. The other type of learning—clearly subject to voluntary control and therefore considered superior—is instrumental, or trial-and-error, learning, also called operant conditioning. In this process a reinforcement, or reward, is given whenever the desired conditioned response is elicited by a conditioned stimulus (such as a certain signal). The possibilities of learning are limited in classical conditioning, because the stimulus and response must have a natural relationship to begin with. In instrumental learning, on the other hand, the reinforcement strengthens any immediately preceding response; a given response can be reinforced by a variety of rewards and a given reward can reinforce a variety of responses.

Differences in the conditions under which learning occurs through classical

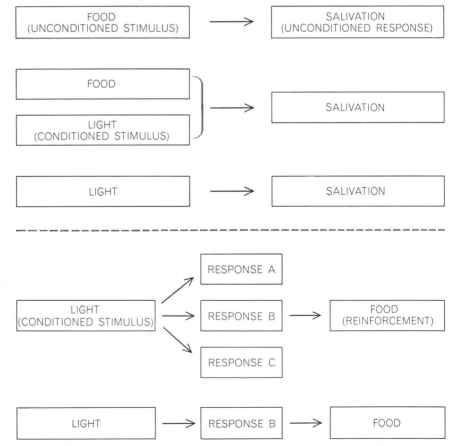

TWO TYPES OF LEARNING are classical conditioning and instrumental learning. Classical conditioning (*top*) begins with an unconditioned stimulus. The conditioned stimulus that is paired with it comes to substitute for it in producing the unconditioned response. In instrumental learning (*bottom*) a conditioned stimulus is presented along with an opportunity to respond in various ways. The correct response is reinforced, or rewarded. After several reinforcements the stimulus serves as a signal to perform the learned response.

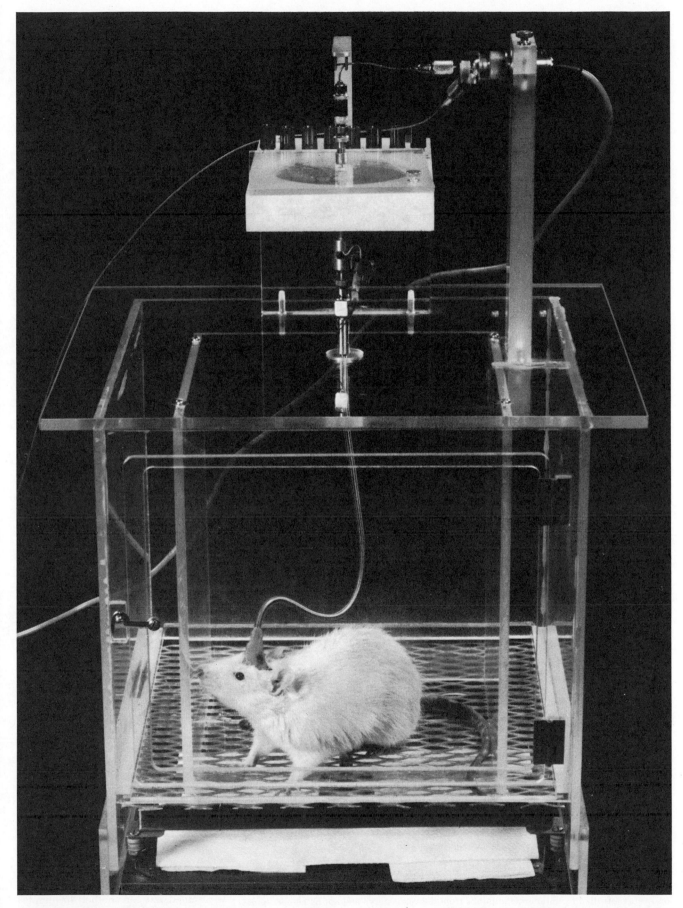

VISCERAL RESPONSES of active rats were measured with this experimental setup. The necessary tubes and wires (in this case including a plastic catheter to sense blood pressure in an abdominal artery) are led from the rat's skull through a protective steel spring to a mercury connector, a fluid swivel that permits free movement. The platform is wired to record the rat's activity.

conditioning and through instrumental learning have been cited to show that the two processes are two distinct phenomena that operate through different neurophysiological mechanisms. The traditional belief has been that the involuntary and inferior visceral responses can be modified only by the correspondingly inferior type of learning—classical conditioning—and not by the superior and voluntary instrumental learning, which has been thought to modify only voluntary, skeletal responses.

Not all learning theorists accepted this distinction. For many years Neal E. Miller of Rockefeller University has held that classical conditioning and instrumental learning are not two basically different phenomena but rather two manifestations of the same phenomenon under different conditions—that there is, in fact, only one kind of learning. To support such a position he had to show that instrumental training procedures can produce learning of any visceral responses that can be acquired through classical conditioning, and the demonstration had to be very clear and convincing in the face of the ingrained belief that such learning is simply not possible.

Research on the instrumental modification of visceral responses comes up against a basic problem: most such responses can be affected by voluntary activities such as the tensing of muscles or changes in the rate or pattern of breathing. It is therefore hard to rule out completely the possibility that the experimental subject has not directly learned to control a visceral response through the autonomic system but rather has learned to execute some subtle and undetectable skeletal response that in turn modifies the visceral behavior. (A skilled disciple of yoga, for example, can stop his heart sounds by controlling his rib cage and diaphragm muscles so that pressure within the chest is increased to the point where the venous return of blood to the heart is considerably retarded.)

To guard against the contamination of experimental results by such "cheating," careful controls and detailed statistical analysis of data are required. The primary control Miller and I apply in our animal experiments is paralysis of the subject's skeletal muscles. This is accomplished by administering a drug of the curare family (such as *d*-tubocurarine) that blocks acetylcholine, the chemical transmitter by which cerebrospinal nerve impulses are delivered to skeletal muscles, but does not interfere with consciousness or with the transmitters that mediate autonomic responses. A curarized animal cannot breathe and must therefore be maintained on a mechanical respirator. Moreover, it cannot eat or drink, and so the possibilities of rewarding it are limited. We rely on two methods of reinforcement. One is electrical stimulation of a "pleasure center" in the brain, the medial forebrain bundle in the hypothalamus, and the other is the avoidance of or escape from a mildly unpleasant electric shock.

Utilizing these techniques, we have shown that animals can learn visceral responses in the same way that they learn skeletal responses. Specifically, we have produced, through instrumental training, increases and decreases in heart rate, blood pressure, intestinal contractions, control of blood-vessel diameter and rate of formation of urine. Other investigators have demonstrated significant instrumental learning of heart-rate and blood-pressure control by human beings and have begun to apply the powerful techniques developed in animal experiments to the actual treatment of human cardiovascular disorders.

After Miller and his colleagues Jay Trowill and Alfredo Carmona had achieved promising preliminary results (including the instrumental learning of salivation in dogs, the classical response of classical conditioning), he and I undertook in 1965 to show that there are no real differences between the two kinds of learning: that the laws of learning observed in the instrumental training of skeletal responses all apply also to the instrumental training of visceral responses. We worked with curarized rats, which we trained to increase or to decrease their heart rate in order to obtain pleasurable brain stimulation. First we rewarded small changes in the desired direction that occurred during "time in" periods, that is, during the presentation of light and tone signals that indicated when the reward was available. Then we set the criterion (the level required to obtain a reward) at progressively higher levels and thus "shaped" the rats to learn increases or decrease in heart rate of about 20 percent in the course of a 90-minute training period [*see illustration on page 78*].

These changes were largely overall increases or decreases in the "base line" heart rate. We were anxious to demonstrate something more: that heart rate, like skeletal responses, could be brought under the control of a discriminative stimulus, which is to say that the rats could learn to respond specifically to the light and tone stimuli that indicated when a reward was available and not to respond during "time out" periods when they would not be rewarded. To this end we trained rats for another 45 minutes at the highest criterion level. When we began discrimination training, it took the

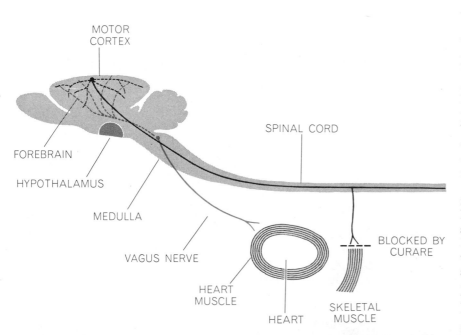

CURARE paralyzes skeletal muscles. It ensures, for example, that a change in heart rate has been controlled by autonomic impulses from the vagus nerve and not by cerebrospinal impulses to skeletal muscles. The two nervous systems are not completely separate: visceral responses have representation at higher brain centers in the cortex (**broken lines**).

rats some time after the beginning of each stimulus period to meet the criterion and get the reward; by the end of the training they were changing their heart rate in the rewarded direction almost immediately after the time-in period began [*see illustration on page* 79].

In skeletal instrumental training discrimination is also learned between a positive stimulus, response to which is rewarded, and a negative stimulus, response to which is not rewarded. Our animals learned to respond with the proper visceral behavior to one stimulus (such as a light) and not to respond to another (such as a tone). Moreover, once an animal has learned to discriminate between positive and negative cues for a given skeletal response, it is easier for it to respond similarly with a different response for the same reward. We found that this phenomenon of transfer also appeared in visceral training: rats that showed the best discrimination between a positive and a negative stimulus for a skeletal response (pressing a bar) also showed the best discrimination when the same stimuli were used for increased or decreased heart rate.

Two other properties of instrumental training are retention and extinction. To test for retention we gave rats a single training session and then returned them to their home cages for three months. When they were again curarized and tested, without being reinforced, rats in both the increase group and the decrease group showed good retention by exhibiting reliable changes in the direction for which they had been rewarded three months earlier. Although learned skeletal responses are remembered well, they can be progressively weakened, or experimentally extinguished, by prolonged trials without reward. We have observed this phenomenon of extinction in visceral learning also. To sum up, all the phenomena of instrumental training that we have tested to date have turned out to be characteristic of visceral as well as skeletal responses.

The experiments I have described relied on electrical stimulation of the brain as a reinforcement. In order to be sure that there was nothing unique about brain stimulation as a reward for visceral learning, Miller and I did an experiment with electric-shock avoidance, the other of the two commonly used rewards that can conveniently be administered to paralyzed rats. A shock signal was presented to the curarized rats. After it had been on for five seconds it was accompanied by brief pulses of mild

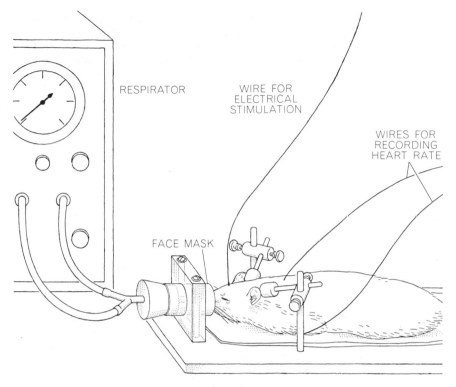

CURARIZED RATS cannot breathe and must be fitted with a face mask connected to a respirator. Such usual instrumental-learning rewards as food and water cannot be used.

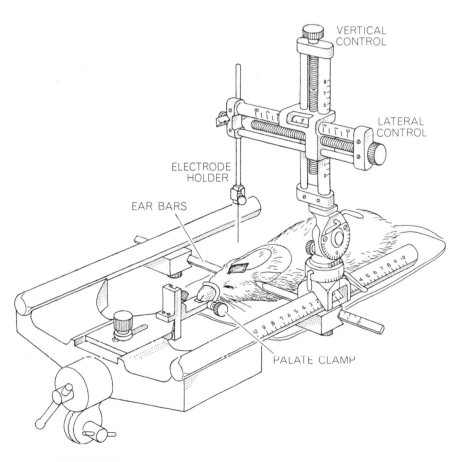

REWARD for visceral learning is either electrical stimulation of the brain or avoidance of electric shock. For brain stimulation an electrode implanted in the brain of an anesthetized rat is guided to a "pleasure center" in the hypothalamus with the aid of a stereotactic device.

shock delivered to the rat's tail. During the first five seconds the animal could turn off the shock signal and avoid the shock by making the correct heart-rate response; failing that, it could escape the shock by making the correct response and thus turning off both the signal and the shock.

In the course of a training session we mixed shock trials with "safe" trials and "blank" trials at random. During a safe trial we presented a different signal and did not administer a shock; during a blank trial there was no signal or shock. For half of the rats the shock signal was a tone and the safe signal a flashing light; for the other half the stimuli were reversed. The rats that were rewarded for increasing their heart rate learned to increase it and those that were rewarded for decreasing the rate learned to decrease it. In part the learning represented a general change in base line, as indicated by the trend of the heart rate during blank trials. Beyond this, however, the rats clearly learned to discriminate. As their training progressed, the shock signal began to elicit a greater change in the rewarded direction than the blank trials did. Conversely, the safe signal elicited a trend in the opposite direction—toward the base line represented by the data for the blank trials [*see illustration on page 80*].

At this point we had shown that instrumental learning of visceral responses follows the laws of skeletal instrumental training and that it is not limited to a particular kind of reward. We also showed that the response itself is not limited: we trained rats to raise and lower their systolic blood pressure in much the same way. These results were all obtained, however, with animals that were paralyzed. Would normal, active animals also learn a visceral response? If so, could that response be shown to be independent of skeletal activity? We designed a special experimental cage and the necessary equipment to make possible the recording of various responses of active rats [*see illustration on page 75*], and we established that heart-rate and blood-pressure changes could be learned by noncurarized animals. The heart-rate learning persisted in subsequent tests during which the same animals were paralyzed by curare, indicating that it had not been due to the indirect effects of overt skeletal responses. This conclusion was strengthened when, on being retrained without curare, the two groups of animals displayed increasing differences in heart rate, whereas any differences in respiration and general level of activity continued to decrease.

We noted with interest that initial learning in the noncurarized state was slower and less effective than it had been in the previous experiments under curare. Moreover, a single training session under curare facilitated later learning in the noncurarized state. It seems likely that paralysis eliminated "noise" (the confusing effects of changes in heart action and blood-vessel tone caused by skeletal activity) and perhaps also made it possible for the animal to concentrate on and sense the small changes accomplished directly by the autonomic system.

In all these studies the fact that the same reward could produce changes in opposite directions ruled out the possibility that the visceral learning was caused by some innate, unconditioned effect of the reward. Furthermore, the fact that the curarized rats were completely paralyzed, which was confirmed by electromyographic traces that would have recorded any activity of the skeletal muscles, ruled out any obvious effect of the voluntary responses. It was still possible, however, that we were somehow inducing a general pattern of arousal or were training the animals to initiate impulses from the higher brain centers that would have produced skeletal movements were it not for the curare, and that it was the innate effect of these central commands to struggle and relax that were in turn changing the heart rate. Such possibilities made it desirable to discover whether or not changes in heart rate could be learned independently of changes in other autonomic responses that would occur as natural concomitants of arousal.

To this end Miller and Ali Banuazizi compared the instrumental learning of heart rate with that of intestinal contraction in curarized rats. They chose these two responses because the vagus nerve innervates both the heart and the gut, and the effect of vagal activation on both organs is well established. In order to record intestinal motility they inserted a water-filled balloon in the large intestine. Movement of the intestine wall caused fluctuations in the water pressure that were changed into electric voltages by a pressure transducer attached to the balloon.

The results were clear-cut. The rats rewarded (by brain stimulation) for increases in intestinal contraction learned an increase and those rewarded for decreases learned a decrease, but neither

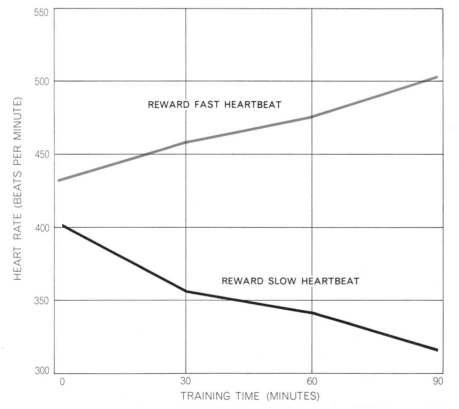

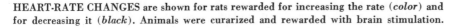

HEART-RATE CHANGES are shown for rats rewarded for increasing the rate (*color*) and for decreasing it (*black*). Animals were curarized and rewarded with brain stimulation.

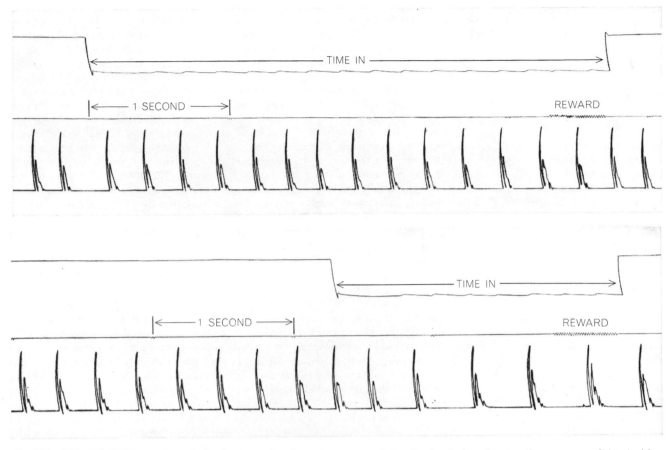

ELECTROCARDIOGRAMS made at the beginning and at the end of an extra period of training demonstrate discrimination. At first the rat takes some time after the onset of stimulus ("time in") to respond (by slowing its heartbeat) and earn a reward (top). After 45 minutes of discrimination training the rat responds more directly: it slows its heartbeat soon after time-in period begins (bottom).

group showed an appreciable change in heart rate. The group that was rewarded for increases in heart rate learned an increase and the group rewarded for decreases learned a decrease, but neither heart-rate group showed an increase in intestinal contraction [see illustrations on page 82]. Moreover, the heart-rate and intestinal learning were negatively correlated: the better the response being rewarded was learned, the less change there was in the unrewarded response. These results showed that the instrumental learning of two visceral responses can occur independently of each other and that what is learned is specifically the rewarded response. They ruled out the possibility that the learning was mediated by a general reaction such as arousal.

There was still a remote possibility to be eliminated: The central impulses I mentioned might be initiated selectively toward muscles that affect the intestines when intestinal changes are rewarded and toward muscles that affect heart rate when heart-rate changes are rewarded. Miller and I therefore trained curarized rats to increase or decrease their heart

rate and then tested them in the non-curarized state for transfer of learning. We reasoned that if heart-rate changes were not directly learned under curare but rather were mediated by the learning of central impulses to skeletal muscles, movement of such muscles would betray the fact if the learning was transferred to the noncurarized state. We found that learned increases and decreases of about 10 percent did transfer independently of muscle movement: the differences between the two groups in heart rate were too large to be accounted for by the differences between them in respiration or general level of activity.

The strongest argument against attempts to explain visceral learning as a response to skeletal movement or central motor impulses is this kind of specificity. As more and more different visceral responses are recorded and the learning of them is shown to be specific, it becomes harder to think of enough different voluntary responses to account for them all. We have shown, for example, that curarized rats can learn to make changes in the dilation and constriction of blood vessels in the skin and to make these

vasomotor changes independently of changes in heart rate and blood pressure. Indeed, the rats can be trained to make these changes specific to a single structure: they can dilate the blood vessels in one ear more than those in the other ear! This could not be the result of heart-rate or blood-pressure changes, which would affect both ears equally. We also obtained instrumental learning in the rate of urine formation by the kidneys, independent of blood pressure or heart rate. The increases and decreases in the amount of urine produced were achieved by specific changes in the arteries of the kidneys that resulted in an increase or decrease in the blood flow through the kidneys.

In addition to buttressing the case for instrumental learning of visceral responses, these striking results suggest that vasomotor responses, which are mediated by the sympathetic division of the autonomic nervous system, are capable of much greater specificity than was believed possible. This specificity is compatible with an increasing body of evidence that various visceral responses have specific representation at the cerebral cortex, that is, that they have neural connections of some kind to higher brain centers.

Some recent experiments indicate that not only visceral behavior but also the electrical activity of these higher brain centers themselves can be modified by direct reinforcement of changes in brain activity. Miller and Carmona trained noncurarized cats and curarized rats to change the character of their electroencephalogram, raising or lowering the voltage of the brain waves. A. H. Black of McMaster University in Canada trained dogs to alter the activity of one kind of brain wave, the theta wave. More recently Stephen S. Fox of the University of Iowa used instrumental techniques to modify, both in animals and in human subjects, the amplitude of an electrical event in the cortex that is ordinarily evoked as a visual response.

We are now trying to apply similar techniques to modify the electrical activity of the vagus nerve at its nucleus in the lowermost portion of the brain. Preliminary results suggest that this is possible. The next step will be to investigate the visceral consequences of such modification. This kind of work may open up possibilities for modifying the activity of specific parts of the brain and the functions they control and thereby learning more about the functions of different parts of the brain.

Controlled manipulation of visceral responses by instrumental training also makes it possible to investigate the mechanisms that underlie visceral learning. We have made a beginning in this direction by considering the biochemical consequences of heart-rate training and specifically the role of the catecholamines, substances such as epinephrine and norepinephrine that are synthesized in the brain and in sympathetic-nerve tissues. Norepinephrine serves as a nerve-impulse transmitter in the central nervous system. Both substances play roles in the coordination of neural and glandular activity, influencing the blood vessels, the heart and several other organs. Alterations in heart rate produced by increased sympathetic-nerve activity in the heart, for example, are accompanied by changes in the synthesis, uptake and utilization of catecholamines in the heart, suggesting that it may be possible to influence cardiac catecholamine metabolism through instrumental learning of heart-rate responses. This would be important in view of the possible role of norepinephrine in essential hypertension (high blood pressure) and congestive heart failure; it might also help to establish the role of learning and experience in the development of certain psychosomatic disorders.

Eric Stone and I found that the level of catecholamines in the heart varies with heart-rate training. After three hours of training under curare, rats trained to increase their heart rate have a significantly higher concentration of cardiac catecholamines than rats trained to decrease their heart rate. Experiments are now under way to determine how long such biochemical differences between the two groups persist after training and whether the heart-rate conditioning has long-range effects on the heart and on the excitability of the sympathetic nerves. When we examined the brains of rats in the two groups we found a similar biochemical difference: the animals trained to increase their heart rate had a significantly higher level of norepinephrine in the brain stem than rats trained to decrease heart rate. Brain norepinephrine helps to determine the excitability of the central nervous system and is involved in emotional behavior. We have therefore started experiments to see whether or not changes in sympathetic excitability obtained by cardiovascular instrumental training are related to changes in the metabolism of norepinephrine and, if so, in which areas of the brain these metabolic changes are most apparent.

Is the capacity for instrumental learning of autonomic responses just a useless by-product of the capacity for cerebrospinal, skeletal-muscle learning? Or does it have a significant adaptive function in helping to maintain homeostasis, a stable internal environment? Skeletal responses operate on the external environment; there is obvious survival value in the ability to learn a response that brings a reward such as food, water or escape from pain. The responses mediated by the autonomic system, on the other hand, do not have such direct effects on the external environment. That was one of the reasons for the persistent belief that they are not subject to instrumental learning. Yet the experiments I have described demonstrate that visceral responses are indeed subject to instrumental training. This forces us to think of the internal behavior of the visceral organs in the same way we think of the external,

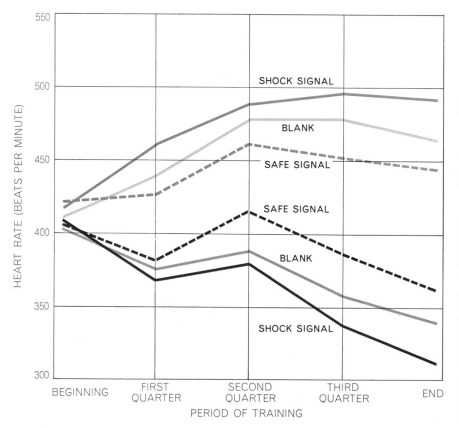

DISCRIMINATION is demonstrated by these curves for rats that were trained to increase (*color*) and decrease (*black*) heart rate and were rewarded by avoidance of shock. The results for blank trials (no signal or shock) show "base line" learning. The results for shock-signal and safe-signal trials show discriminating responses to more specific stimuli.

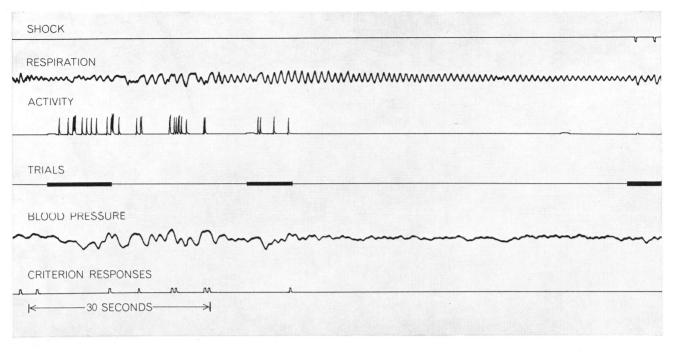

SHOCK

RESPIRATION

ACTIVITY

TRIALS

BLOOD PRESSURE

CRITERION RESPONSES

|←——— 30 SECONDS ———→|

POLYGRAPH RECORD, a small portion of which is reproduced, records a free-moving rat's respiration, activity and systolic blood pressure. It also shows when trials took place, whether the blood-pressure increase met the criterion and whether, not having met criterion, the animal received an electric shock. This record was made by an animal being tested as in the illustration on page 75.

observable behavior of the skeletal muscles, and therefore to consider its adaptive value to homeostasis.

In a recent experiment George Wolf, Miller and I found that the correction of a deviation from homeostasis by an internal, glandular response (rather than by an external response such as eating or drinking) can serve as a reward to reinforce learning. We injected albino rats with an antidiuretic hormone (ADH) if they chose one arm of a *T*-shaped maze and with a control solution (a minute amount of isotonic saline solution) if they chose the other arm. Before running the maze each rat had been given an excess of water through a tube placed in the stomach, so that the antidiuretic hormone was maladaptive: it interfered with the kidney response that was necessary to get rid of the excess water and restore homeostasis, whereas the control solution did not interfere. The rats learned to select the side of the maze that ensured an injection of saline solution, so that their own glandular response to the excess water could restore homeostasis. Then we did the same experiment with rats that suffered from diabetes insipidus, a disorder in which too much urine is passed and it is insufficiently concentrated. These rats had been tube-fed an excess of a highly concentrated salt solution. Now the homeostatic effects of the two injections were reversed: the ADH was adaptive, tend-

ing to concentrate the urine and thereby get rid of the excess salt, whereas the control solution had no such effect. This time the rats selected the ADH side of the maze. As a control we tested normal rats that were given neither water nor concentrated saline solution, and we found they did not learn to choose either side of the maze in order to obtain or avoid the antidiuretic hormone.

In many experiments a deficit in water or in salt has been shown to serve as a drive to motivate learning; the external response of drinking water or saline solution—thus correcting the deficit—functions as a reward to reinforce learning. What our experiment showed was that the return to a normal balance can be effected by action that achieves an internal, glandular response rather than by the external response of drinking.

Consider this result along with those demonstrating that glandular and visceral responses can be instrumentally learned. Taken together, they suggest that an animal can learn glandular and visceral responses that promptly restore a deviation from homeostasis to the proper level. Whether such theoretically possible learning actually takes place depends on whether innate homeostatic mechanisms control the internal environment so closely and effectively that deviations large enough to serve as a drive are not allowed. It may be that innate controls are ordinarily accurate

enough to do just that, but that if abnormal circumstances such as disease interfere with innate control, visceral learning reinforced by a return to homeostasis may be available as an emergency replacement.

Are human beings capable of instrumental learning of visceral responses? One would think so. People are smarter than rats, and so anything rats can do people should be able to do better. Whether they can, however, is still not completely clear. The reason is largely that it is difficult to subject human beings to the rigorous controls that can be applied to animals (including deep paralysis by means of curare) and thus to be sure that changes in visceral responses represent true instrumental learning of such responses.

One recent experiment conducted by David Shapiro and his colleagues at the Harvard Medical School indicated that human subjects can be trained through feedback and reinforcement to modify their blood pressure. Each success (a rise in pressure for some volunteers and a decrease for others) was indicated by a flashing light. The reward, after 20 flashes, was a glimpse of a nude pinup picture. (The volunteers were of course male.) Most subjects said later they were not aware of having any control over the flashing light and did not in fact know what physiological function was being

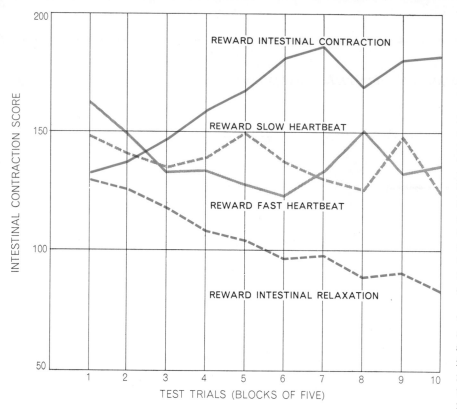

INTESTINAL CONTRACTION is learned independently of heart-rate changes. Contractions are increased by rats rewarded for increases (*colored line*) and decreased by rats rewarded for decreases (*broken colored line*). The intestinal-contraction score does not change appreciably, however, in rats rewarded for increasing or decreasing heart rate (*gray*).

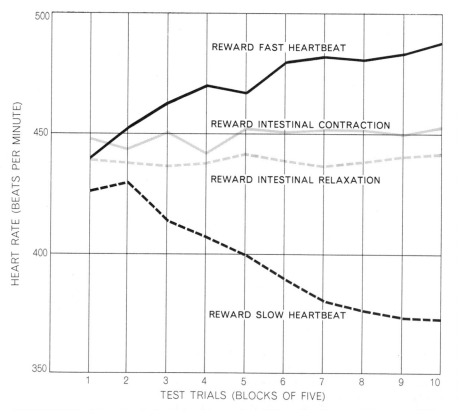

SPECIFICITY of learning is shown by this graph and the one at the top of the page. Here the results for heart rate rather than intestinal contraction are shown for the same animals. Rats rewarded for changing their heart rate change it in the appropriate direction (*black lines*). Rats rewarded for intestinal changes do not change heart rate (*light colored lines*).

measured, and so they presumably had not exerted any voluntary effort (at least not consciously and deliberately) to modify the response.

Whatever is actually being learned by such subjects, the extent of learning is clearly less than can be achieved in animals. In one of our experiments the average difference in blood pressure between the two groups of curarized rats was 58 millimeters of mercury. Shapiro's two human groups, in contrast, yielded a comparable difference of about four millimeters. Clearly curarized rats do better than noncurarized people, but that is not really surprising. The difference between the noncurarized rats and the noncurarized human subjects is much smaller [*see bottom illustration on opposite page*].

The curare effect here is in line with what is seen in experiments with a single species. What does it mean? I mentioned above that initial training under curare facilitated further training in the noncurarized state. Perhaps the curare keeps the animal from being confused (as it may be in the noncurarized state) when a small change in the correct direction that is produced by direct control of the visceral response is obscured by a larger change in the opposite direction that is accomplished through skeletal activity and is therefore not rewarded. It is also possible that the curare helps to eliminate variability in the stimulus and to shift the animal's attention from distracting skeletal activity to the relevant visceral activity. It may be possible to facilitate visceral learning in humans by training people (perhaps through hypnosis) to breathe regularly, to relax and to concentrate in an attempt to mimic the conditions produced by curarization.

The evidence for instrumental learning of visceral responses suggests that psychosomatic symptoms may be learned. John I. Lacey of the Fels Research Institute has shown that there is a tendency for each individual to respond to stress with his own rather consistent sequence of such visceral responses as headache, queasy stomach, palpitation or faintness. Instrumental learning might produce such a hierarchy. It is theoretically possible that such learning could be carried far enough to create an actual psychosomatic symptom. Presumably genetic and constitutional differences among individuals would affect the susceptibility of the various organ systems. So would the extent to which reinforcement is available. (Does a child's mother keep him home from school when he complains of headache? When he looks pale?) So also would the extent to which visceral learning is effective in the various organ systems.

We are now trying to see just how far we can push the learning of visceral responses—whether it can be carried far enough in noncurarized animals to produce physical damage. We also want to see if there is a critical period in the animal's infancy during which visceral learning has particularly intense and long-lasting effects. Some earlier experiments bear on such questions. For example, during training under curare seven rats in a group of 43 being rewarded for slowing their heart rate died, whereas none of 41 being rewarded for an increase in heart rate died. This statistically reliable difference might mean one of two things. Either training to speed the heart rate helps a rat to resist the stress of curare or the reward for slowing the heart rate is strong enough to overcome innate regulatory mechanisms and induce cardiac arrest.

If visceral responses can be modified by instrumental learning, it may be possible in effect to "train" people with certain disorders to get well. Such therapeutic learning should be worth trying on any symptom that is under neural control, that can be continuously monitored and for which a certain direction of change is clearly advisable from a medical point of view. For several years Bernard Engel and his colleagues at the Gerontology Research Center in Baltimore have been treating cardiac arrhythmias (disorders of heartbeat rhythm) through instrumental training. Heart function has been significantly improved in several of their patients. Miller and his colleagues at the Cornell University Medical College treated a patient with long-standing tachycardia (rapid heartbeat). For two weeks the patient made almost no progress, but in the third week his learning improved; since then he has been able to practice on his own and maintain his slower heart rate for several months. Clark T. Randt and his colleagues at the New York University School of Medicine have had some success in training epileptic patients to suppress paroxysmal spikes, an abnormal brain wave.

It is far too early to promise any cures. There is no doubt, however, that the exciting possibility of applying these powerful new techniques to therapeutic education should be investigated vigorously at the clinical as well as the experimental level.

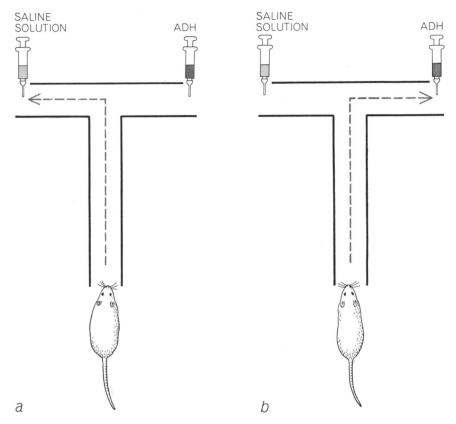

VISCERAL RESPONSE that adjusts the internal environment can serve as a reward to reinforce learning. Rats "loaded" with water (a) learned to choose the side of a *T*-maze that resulted in an injection of a control solution rather than one of antidiuretic hormone (ADH), which would interfere with water excretion. (The arms associated with each reward were changed at random.) Rats loaded with salt (b), on the other hand, for whom the hormone would induce the proper kidney response, learned to pick the ADH-associated arm.

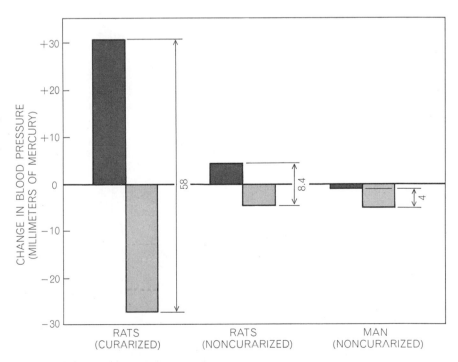

COMPARISON of blood-pressure learning in rats and humans rewarded for increasing (*dark gray bars*) and for decreasing (*light gray*) blood pressure shows that the difference between curarized and noncurarized subjects is greater than the difference between species.

III

ALTERED STATES OF AWARENESS: EXTERNAL CONTROL

III

ALTERED STATES OF AWARENESS: EXTERNAL CONTROL

INTRODUCTION

Today, the most popular external agents for altering awareness are drugs of various kinds. In America, alcohol has been a perennial favorite. A rapidly growing contender for first place, at least among the young, is marihuana, one of the drugs derived from the hemp plant, *Cannabis sativa*. In some cultures, various forms of the plant have been used extensively for centuries.

Such naturally occurring hallucinogens as mescaline and psilocybin are similarly time-honored, and antedate such synthetic hallucinogens as LSD by centuries. These drugs have, to varying degrees, the capacity to alter awareness. There has been—and there no doubt will continue to be—a heated debate over the use of these awareness-altering drugs.

When we consider the current controversy over the use of marihuana, it seems inconceivable that Western physicians could ever have prescribed the drug for complaints ranging from cramps to coughing—yet such prescriptions were once common. Lester Grinspoon, in "Marihuana," carefully considers what science has learned about the use of this from the psychological, physiological, and social points of view. The conclusions reached by Grinspoon may well outrage some people, may surprise certain others, and may please yet others; yet these conclusions represent a conservative synthesis of the scientific research on the effects of this drug up until the time the article was published.

The alkaloids that make up the group of drugs known as hallucinogens (also as psychotommetic or psychedelic drugs) are powerful agents for the external alteration of awareness. Normal perceptions often undergo startling transformations under the influence of these drugs. The neuroscientist is interested in another facet of these drugs—their similarity to several brain chemicals intimately involved in the transmission of neural activity. Frank Barron, Murray E. Jarvik, and Sterling Bunnell, Jr., in their article "The Hallucinogenic Drugs," examine the behavioral and physiological effects of these chemicals. Their conclusion: "The hallucinogens, like so many other discoveries of man, are analogous to fire which can burn down the house or spread through the house life-sustaining warmth."

Chemicals are not the only agents for the external alteration of awareness. We can, for example, effectively alter awareness by distorting the visual input to the brain. This distortion may be produced by special prism goggles, which require the brain to make adjustments in order to cope with the visual world. Thus, an experimental subject's awareness of the visual world, when he first puts on a pair of prism goggles, is one of confusion and chaos. In time, however, order arises from the disorder—which implies that the brain itself has adjusted to the distortion so that it is able to extract meaning from the distorted signal. Ivo Kohler, in his article "Experiments with Goggles," proposes that the mechanism of the brain's adjustment to the distorted visual world is the same as that of the brain's operation under normal conditions. Thus, we are investigating a normal phenomenon, not an abnormal one.

The brain of man consists of two matched hemispheres. When, for medical reasons, the two hemispheres are surgically separated, it is possible to observe separately the functions of each of them. Michael S. Gazzaniga, in his article "The Split Brain in Man," points out that the levels of awareness and cognition are unequally represented in the two hemispheres: people who have undergone such surgery quite literally possess two brains, perhaps even two separate "consciousnesses," each separately capable of highly complex mental operations. These people, although few in number, provide us with dramatic evidence of a basic principle of brain function in man in relation to states of awareness.

Also included in this section is "The Physiology of Meditation" by Robert Keith Wallace and Herbert Benson. (Ideally, this article belongs in Section II, but because it did not appear in SCIENTIFIC AMERICAN until the production of this book was nearly complete, the choice was either to leave it out or to splice it onto the end.) Wallace and Benson discuss the physiological changes that take place in a person practicing "transcendental meditation." This state of awareness is similar to the meditative state achieved by yogis and other Eastern mystics. The authors show that the meditative state is indeed a unique one — it is distinct from relaxed wakefulness, sleep, and hypnosis. The suggestion is offered that the use of these meditative techniques might be an adaptive response to the increasing pressures of a highly complex environment.

10

MARIHUANA

LESTER GRINSPOON
December 1969

The earliest record of man's use of marihuana is a description of the drug in a Chinese compendium of medicines, the herbal of Emperor Shen Nung, dated 2737 B.C. Marihuana was a subject of extravagant social controversy even in ancient times: there were those who warned that the hemp plant lined the road to Hades, and those who thought it led to paradise. Its use as an intoxicant spread from China to India, then to North Africa and from there, about A.D. 1800, to Europe, perhaps primarily through troops of Napoleon's army returning from the Egyptian campaign. In the Western Hemisphere marihuana has been known for centuries in South and Central America, but it did not begin to be used in the U.S. to any significant extent until about 1920. Since the hemp plant *Cannabis sativa*, the source of the drug in its various forms, is a common weed growing freely in many climates, there is no way of knowing precisely how extensive the world usage of the drug may be today. A United Nations survey in 1950 estimated that its users then numbered some 200 million people, principally in Asia and Africa.

Cannabis sativa has a long history of use as a source of fiber, as a drug in tribal religious ceremonies and as medicine, particularly in India. In the 19th century the drug was widely prescribed in the Western world for various ailments and discomforts, such as cough-

ing, fatigue, rheumatism, asthma, delirium tremens, migraine headache and painful menstruation. Although its use was already declining somewhat because of the introduction of synthetic hypnotics and analgesics, it remained in the U.S. *Pharmacopoeia* until 1937. The difficulties imposed on its use by the Tax Act of 1937 completed its medical demise.

In any case, throughout history the principal interest in the hemp plant has been in its properties as an agent for achieving euphoria. The name marihuana is said to be a corruption of the Portuguese word *mariguango*, meaning intoxicant. The drug's ubiquity is evidenced in the multitude of vernacular terms by which it is known; in the U.S. it is variously called the weed, stuff, Indian hay, grass, pot, tea, maryjane and other names. In this country it is almost invariably smoked (usually as a cigarette called a reefer or a joint), but elsewhere the drug is often taken in the form of a drink or in foods such as sweetmeats.

Drug preparations from the hemp plant vary widely in quality and potency, depending on the climate, soil, cultivation and method of preparation. The drug is obtained almost exclusively from the female plant. When the cultivated plant is fully ripe, a sticky, golden yellow resin with a minty fragrance covers its flower clusters and top leaves. The plant's resin contains the active substances. Preparations of the drug come

in three grades, identified by Indian names. The cheapest and least potent, called bhang, is derived from the cut tops of uncultivated plants and has a low resin content. Most of the marihuana smoked in the U.S. is of this grade. To the discriminating Hindu bhang is a crude substitute for ganja, a little like the difference between beer and fino Scotch, and it is scorned by all but the very poorest in India. Ganja is obtained from the flowering tops and leaves of carefully selected, cultivated plants, and it has a higher quality and quantity of resin. The third and highest grade of the drug, called charas in India, is made from the resin itself, carefully scraped from the tops of mature plants. Only this version of the drug is properly called hashish; the common supposition that hashish refers to all varieties of cannabis drugs is incorrect. Charas, or hashish, is five to eight times stronger in effect than the most potent marihuana regularly available in the U.S.

The chemistry of the cannabis drugs is extremely complex and not completely understood. In the 1940's it was determined that the active constituents are various isomers of tetrahydrocannabinol. Recently one of these isomers, called the delta-1 form, has been synthesized and is believed to be the primary active component of marihuana. The drug's effects, however, probably also involve other components and the

SEPALS

MALE

STAMENS

PISTILS

BRACT

FEMALE

HEMP PLANT (*CANNABIS SATIVA*) is a common weed growing freely in many parts of the world, where it is used as a medicine, an intoxicant and a source of fiber. It is classified as a dioecious plant, that is, the male reproductive parts are on one individual (*left*) and the female parts are on another (*right*). Details of the two types of flower are shown at bottom. The active substances in the drug are contained in a sticky yellow resin that covers the flower clusters and top leaves of the female plant when it is ripe.

form in which it is taken. About 80 derivatives of cannabinol have been prepared, and some of these have been tested for effects in animals or in human volunteers.

The effects of cannabis (used here as a general term for the various forms of the psychoactive products of the plant) in animals are confined to the central nervous system. The drug does not noticeably affect the gross behavior of rats or mice or simple learning in rats; it does, however, calm mice that have been made aggressive by isolation, and in dogs it induces a dreamy, somnolent state reminiscent of the last stage of a human "high." In large doses cannabis produces in animals symptoms such as vomiting, diarrhea, fibrillary tremors and failure of muscular coordination. Lethal doses have been established for a few animals; given by mouth, the lethal dose for cats, for example, is three grams of charas, eight grams of ganja or 10 grams of bhang per kilogram of body weight. Huge doses have been given to dogs without causing death, and there has been no reported case of a fatality from the drug in man.

The psychic effects of the drug have been described in a very extensive literature. Hashish long ago acquired a lurid reputation through the writings of literary figures, notably the group of French writers (Baudelaire, Gautier, Dumas *père* and others) who formed Le Club des Hachichins (hashish smokers) in Paris in the 1850's. Their reports, written under the influence of large amounts of hashish, must be discounted as exaggerations that do not apply to moderate use of the drug. Hashish is supposed to have been responsible for Baudelaire's psychosis and death, but the story overlooks the fact that he had been an alcoholic and suffered from tertiary syphilis.

Bayard Taylor, the American writer, lecturer and traveler best known for his translation of Goethe's *Faust,* wrote one of the first accounts of a cannabis experience in terms that began to approach a clinical description. He tried the drug in a spirit of inquiry during a visit to Egypt in 1854 and related the effects as follows: "The sensations it then produced were...physically of exquisite lightness and airiness—mentally of a wonderfully keen perception of the ludicrous in the most simple and familiar objects. During the half hour in which it lasted, I was at no time so far under its control that I could not, with the clearest perception, study the changes through which I passed. I noted with careful attention the fine sensations which spread through-

out the whole tissue of my nervous fibers, each thrill helping to divest my frame of its earthly and material nature, till my substance appeared to me no grosser than the vapours of the atmosphere, and while sitting in the calm of the Egyptian twilight I expected to be lifted up and carried away by the first breeze that should ruffle the Nile. While this process was going on, the objects by which I was surrounded assumed a strange and whimsical expression.... I was provoked into a long fit of laughter. The Hallucination died away as gradually as it came, leaving me overcome with a soft and pleasant drowsiness, from which I sank into a deep, refreshing sleep."

Perhaps the most detailed clinical account is that of the noted New York psychiatrist Walter Bromberg, who in 1934 described the psychic effects on the basis of many observations and talks with people while they were under the influence of marihuana and of his own experience with the drug. "The intoxication," he wrote, "is initiated by a period of anxiety within 10 to 30 minutes after smoking, in which the user sometimes... develops fears of death and anxieties of vague nature associated with restlessness and hyper-activity. Within a few minutes he begins to feel more calm and soon develops definite euphoria; he becomes talkative...is elated, exhilarated ...begins to have...an astounding feeling of lightness of the limbs and body... laughs uncontrollably and explosively... without at times the slightest provocation...has the impression that his conversation is witty, brilliant.... The rapid flow of ideas gives the impression of brilliance of thought and observation [but] confusion appears on trying to remember what was thought...he may begin to see visual hallucinations...flashes of light or amorphous forms of vivid color which evolve and develop into geometric figures, shapes, human faces and pictures of great complexity.... After a longer or shorter time, lasting up to two hours, the smoker becomes drowsy, falls into a dreamless sleep and awakens with no physiologic after-effects and with a clear memory of what had happened during the intoxication."

Most observers confirm Bromberg's account as a composite description of marihuana highs. They find that the effects from smoking marihuana last for two to four hours, and from ingestion of the drug, for five to 12 hours. For a new user the initial anxiety that sometimes occurs is alleviated if supportive friends are present; experienced users

occasionally describe it as "happy anxiety." It is contended that the intoxication heightens sensitivity to external stimuli, reveals details that would ordinarily be overlooked, makes colors seem brighter and richer, brings out values in works of art that previously had little or no meaning to the viewer and enhances the appreciation of music. Many jazz musicians have said they perform better under the influence of marihuana, but this has not been objectively confirmed.

The sense of time is distorted: 10 minutes may seem like an hour. Curiously, there is often a splitting of consciousness, so that the smoker, while experiencing the high, is at the same time an objective observer of his own intoxication. He may, for example, be afflicted with paranoid thoughts yet at the same time be reasonably objective about them and even laugh or scoff at them and in a sense enjoy them. The ability to retain a degree of objectivity may explain the fact that many experienced users of marihuana manage to behave in a perfectly sober fashion in public even when they are highly intoxicated.

Marihuana is definitely distinguishable from other hallucinogenic drugs such as LSD, DMT, mescaline, peyote and psilocybin. Although it produces some of the same effects, it is far less potent than these other drugs. It does not alter consciousness to nearly so great an extent as they do nor does it lead to increasing tolerance to the drug dosage. Moreover, marihuana smokers can usually gauge the effects accurately and thus control the intake of the drug to the amount required to produce the desired degree of euphoria.

Let us consider now what has been learned from attempts to obtain objective measurements of the effects of the use of marihuana: psychological, physiological, psychic and social. There is a large literature on these studies, extending over a century or more and particularly voluminous in the 1960's. Although most of the studies leave much to be desired methodologically, many nonetheless add to the total of our knowledge about the drug.

An intensive investigation exploring various aspects of the marihuana problem was conducted in the 1930's by a committee appointed by Mayor Fiorello La Guardia of New York. In this inquiry Robert S. Morrow examined the effects of the drug on psychomotor functions and certain sensory abilities. He found that even in large doses marihuana did

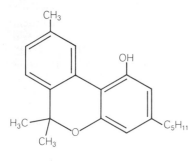

CANNABINOL

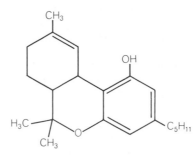

Δ¹-TRANS-TETRAHYDROCANNABINOL

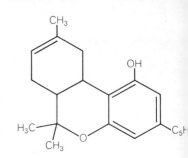

Δ⁶-TRANS-TETRAHYDROCANNABIN

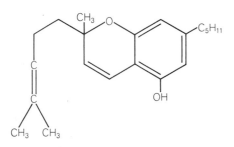

CANNABICHROMENE

CANNABIDIOL

CANNABIDIOLIC ACID

ACTIVE CONSTITUENTS of the cannabis drugs include various derivatives of cannabinol, only a few of which are represented by the molecular diagrams on these two pages. One of the isomers of tetrahydrocannabinol, called the delta-1 form (*second from left in*

not affect performance on tests of the speed of tapping or the quickness of response to simple stimuli. Nor did it impair hearing acuity, musical ability or the ability to judge short time periods or short distances accurately. The drug did affect steadiness of the hand and body and the reaction time for complex stimuli.

More recently Lincoln D. Clark and Edwin N. Nakashima of the University of Utah College of Medicine used eight tests of perception, coordination and learning to examine subjects who received doses of marihuana by mouth. They found that performance on six of the eight tests was not impaired even by high doses of the drug. The two tasks on which performance was affected were reaction time and learning of a digit code; however, in the case of the former this conclusion was based on data from only two subjects and in the latter test it was based on data from five subjects, one of whom actually showed improvement while receiving the drug.

Andrew T. Weil, Norman E. Zinberg and Judith M. Nelsen of the Boston University School of Medicine recently applied other tests to two different groups of subjects, one group consisting of chronic users of marihuana, the other of

persons experiencing the drug for the first time. In ability to maintain sustained attention (the "Continuous Performance Test") the performance of both groups was unaffected either by a low dose or by a high dose of the drug. In cognitive functioning (the "Digit Symbol Substitution Test") the drug-naïve group showed some impairment during the high, but the performance of experienced users of marihuana showed no significant impairment and in fact on the higher doses revealed a trend toward improvement. In muscular coordination and attention (the "Pursuit Rotor Test") the results were the same as in the DSST, but in this case the improvement in the chronic users' performance may have been due simply to practice at the task. Nine subjects receiving the drug for the first time were also tested for the effect on their time sense. Before taking the drug the subjects had shown that in the undrugged state they could come within two minutes of estimating a five-minute interval correctly. After receiving a placebo no subject changed his guess of a five-minute time span. While intoxicated on a low dose three subjects roughly doubled their estimate of a five-minute time span, and while on a high dose four increased their estimates.

In the La Guardia study Florence Halpern investigated marihuana's effects on intellectual functioning. She found that the subjects' scores on intelligence tests, particularly where number concepts were involved, tended to decline during the mature stages of a high. Their performance returned to normal afterward. In some tests of memory and of verbal facility the performances either were not impaired or actually were improved under the influence of low doses of the drug. She concluded that where intellectual performance was reduced the lowered scores were due to a loss of speed and accuracy during the intoxication.

A number of investigators, including members of the La Guardia study, Weil's group and others, have examined the physical and physiological effects of marihuana intoxication. Occasionally there may be nausea, vomiting and diarrhea, particularly if the drug is taken by mouth. Usually, however, the bodily symptoms accompanying the high are slight. There is only very slight, if any, dilatation of the pupils accompanied by a sluggish pupillary response to light, slight tremors and a mild lack of coordination. A consistently observed physiological effect is increase in the pulse rate

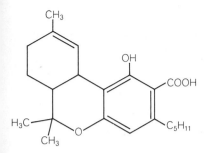

TRANS-TETRAHYDROCANNABINOLIC ACID

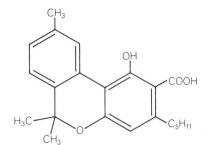

CANNABINOLIC ACID

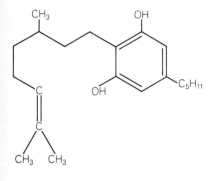

CANNABIGEROL

CANNABIGEROLIC ACID

top row), has been synthesized and is believed to be the primary active component of mari-huana. The drug's intoxicating effects, however, probably involve other components as well.

[*see illustration on page 95*]; in addition there may be a slight rise in the blood pressure. Urination tends to increase in frequency and perhaps in amount. Often the mouth and throat feel dry, causing thirst. One of the most striking results of the intoxication is a sense of hunger. It generates a high appreciation of food, so that a person under the influence may approach an ordinary dish with the anticipation of a gourmet confronting a special treat. This effect suggests that the drug might be useful in the treatment of the pathological loss of appetite known as anorexia nervosa.

There is now an abundance of evidence that marihuana is not an addictive drug. Cessation of its use produces no withdrawal symptoms, nor does a user feel any need to increase the dosage as he becomes accustomed to the drug. Investigators have found that habituation to marihuana is not as strong as to tobacco or to alcohol. Bromberg concluded that marihuana is not habit-forming, and that it is used to serve "the hedonistic elements of the personality." It is certainly possible that in some people this desire may develop into a dependency on the drug for the experience of pleasure or respite from psychic pain.

Can such a use be called abuse of the drug? The term "abuse" is difficult to define; its interpretation varies from culture to culture and from custom to custom. If abuse is measured in terms of the danger to the individual and society, then it must be pointed out that although the dangers of alcoholism and even of social drinking are well established, social drinking is not considered abuse in the U.S. The dangers of the use of marihuana, on the other hand, have not yet been clearly determined.

The prevailing public attitude toward marihuana in the U.S. is charged with a hyperemotional bias. In part this is the product of an "educational campaign" initiated in the 1930's by the Federal Bureau of Narcotics (since renamed the Bureau of Narcotics and Dangerous Drugs), a campaign that has disseminated much distortion and misinformation about the drug [*see illustration on next page*]. There are also cultural and social factors that contribute to the public apprehension about marihuana. The still powerful vestige of the Protestant ethic in this country condemns marihuana as an opiate used solely for the pursuit of pleasure (whereas alcohol is accepted because it lubricates the wheels of commerce and catalyzes social

intercourse). Marihuana's effect in producing a state of introspection and bodily passivity is repellent to a cultural tradition that prizes activity, aggressiveness and achievement. And it may well be that social prejudices enter into the public alarm concerning the drug: prejudice on the part of the older generation, which sees marihuana as a symbol of the alienation of the young, and on the part of the white population, which, perhaps largely unconsciously, regards marihuana as a nonwhite drug that is rapidly invading the white community, because until fairly recently the smoking of marihuana took place mainly in the ghettos of Negroes, Puerto Ricans and people of Mexican origin. It is perhaps no accident that some of the Southern states have most severe laws against the distribution of marihuana, carrying penalties of life imprisonment or even death in some cases.

If we are to find a rational and effective approach to the problem of the increasing use of marihuana in the U.S., we obviously need to reduce the emotionalism surrounding the subject and replace myths with facts as far as they can be determined. Let us examine the current suppositions about the drug.

Does marihuana lead its users to the use of narcotics? The 1937 Federal law that made the cannabis drugs illegal led to a rise in price that provided an incentive to pushers of narcotics to also handle marihuana without any additional legal risk. The resulting potential for the exposure of users to both types of drugs might have been expected to lead to an increase in the use of narcotics that was significantly related to the increasing use of marihuana. No such relation has been found in several studies that have looked into this question, including the La Guardia study and a U.S. Presidential task force investigation of narcotics and drug abuse. It is true that the Federal study showed that among heroin users about 50 percent had had experience with marihuana; the study also found, however, that most of the heroin addicts had been users of alcohol and tobacco. There is no evidence that marihuana is more likely than alcohol or tobacco to lead to the use of narcotics.

Does marihuana incite people to aggression and violent criminal behavior, as some investigators have maintained? In an intensive study of the marihuana problem in Manhattan, Bromberg found no indication of such a relation. "No cases of murder or sexual crime due to marihuana were established." Reviewing a case that had been cited by the Federal Bureau of Narcotics, of a man who was alleged to have confessed to murdering a friend while under the influence of marihuana, Bromberg found on examination of the individual that he was a psychopathic liar and that there was "no indication in the examination or history" that he had ever used marihuana or any other drug. A psychiatric investigator in Nigeria, T. Asuni, noted that an underprivileged community had a high incidence both of crime and of the use of hashish, but he concluded that these statistics were attributable to the frustrations of the people's lives rather than to a relation between the drug and crime. Indeed, two investigators of the use of the drug in India, R. N. Chopra and G. S. Chopra, have contended that instead of inciting criminal behavior cannabis tends to suppress it; the intoxication induces a lethargy that is not conducive to any physical activity, let alone

the committing of crimes. The release of inhibitions results in verbal rather than behavioral expression. During the high the marihuana user may say things he would not ordinarily say, but he generally will not do things that are foreign to his nature. If he is not normally a criminal, he will not commit a crime under the influence of the drug.

Does marihuana induce sexual debauchery? This popular impression may owe its origin partly to the fantasies of dissolute writers and partly to the fact that in times past users in the Middle East laced the drug with aphrodisiacs. There is no evidence that cannabis stimulates sexual desire or power; this is conceded even by Ahmed Benabud, a Moroccan psychiatrist and investigator of the drug who condemns it severely on psychological grounds. There are those, on the other hand, who contend that marihuana weakens sexual desire—with equally little substantiation. Some marihuana users report that the high en-

hances the enjoyment of sexual intercourse. This may be true in the same sense that the enjoyment of art and music is apparently enhanced. It is questionable, however, that the intoxication breaks down moral barriers that are not already broken.

Does marihuana lead to physical and mental degeneracy? Reports from many investigators, particularly in Egypt and in parts of the Orient, indicate that long-term users of the potent versions of cannabis are indeed typically passive, nonproductive, slothful and totally lacking in ambition. It is possible that chronic use of the drug in its stronger forms may in fact have debilitating effects, as prolonged heavy drinking does. There is another possible explanation, however. Many of those who take up cannabis are people who are hungry, sick, hopeless or defeated, seeking through this inexpensive drug to soften the impact of an otherwise unbearable reality. In most situations one cannot be certain which came

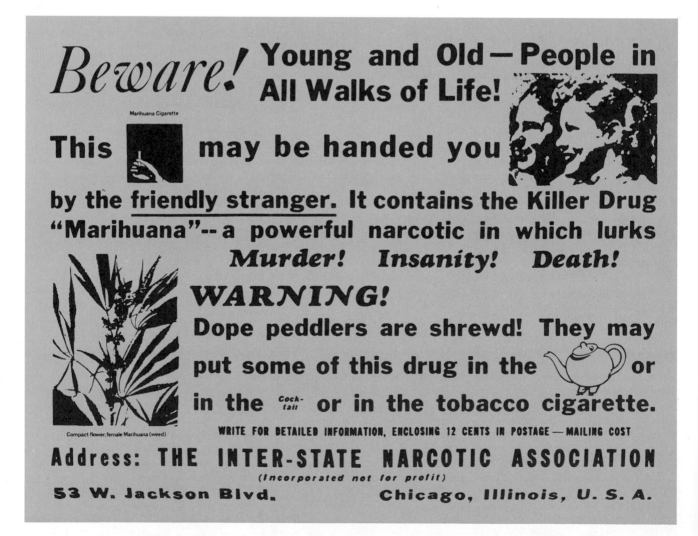

ANTIMARIHUANA POSTER is part of the "educational campaign describing the drug, its identification and evil effects" supported in the U.S. since the 1930's by the Federal Bureau of Narcotics (since renamed the Bureau of Narcotics and Dangerous Drugs).

first: the drug on the one hand or the depression or personality disorder on the other. This question applies to many of the "potheads" in the U.S. An intensive study of college students who had taken to marihuana showed that many of them had suffered serious conflicts or depression long before they began to use the drug.

There is a substantial body of evidence that moderate use of marihuana does not produce physical or mental deterioration. One of the earliest and most extensive studies of this question was an investigation conducted by the British Government in India in the 1890's. The real motive for the inquiry is suspected to have been to establish that cannabis was more dangerous than Scotch whisky, from whose sale the government could obtain a great deal more tax revenue. Nevertheless, the investigation was carried out with typical British impartiality and thoroughness. The investigating agency, called the Indian Hemp Drug Commission, interviewed some 800 persons, including cannabis users and dealers, physicians, superintendents of insane asylums, religious leaders and a variety of other authorities, and in 1894 published a report running to more than 3,000 pages. It concluded that there was no evidence that moderate use of the cannabis drugs produced any disease or mental or moral damage or that it had any more tendency to lead to excess than the moderate use of whisky did.

In the La Guardia study in New York City an examination of chronic users who had averaged about seven marihuana cigarettes a day (a comparatively high dosage) over a long period (the mean was eight years) showed that they had suffered no mental or physical decline as a result of their use of the drug. A similar study by H. L. Freedman and M. J. Rockmore, examining 310 Army men who had used marihuana for an average of seven years, produced the same finding.

In the effort to obtain a rational perspective on the marihuana problem one is inevitably drawn repeatedly to comparisons between this drug and alcohol and to the public attitudes toward the two drugs. The habit called social drinking is considered as American as apple pie, and it receives about as much public acceptance. Yet even this kind of drinking carries clearly demonstrated hazards and consequences of a most serious nature. Life insurance statistics show that social drinkers have considerably higher than average mortality rates from all the leading causes of

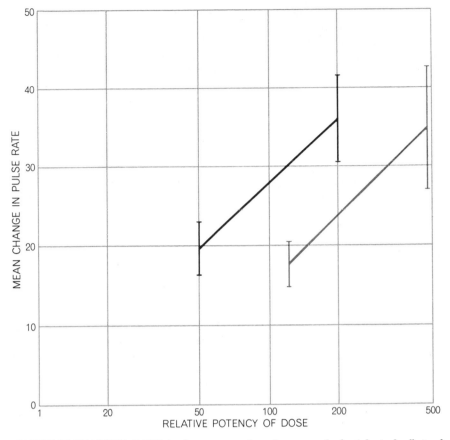

INCREASE IN PULSE RATE is the most consistently reported physiological effect of marihuana intoxication. In this graph, based on the work of Harris Isbell and his colleagues at the University of Kentucky, the two lines show the pulse responses to varying doses of pure synthetic delta-1-tetrahydrocannabinol, taken both by smoking (*left*) and orally (*right*). In most cases the physiological effects of a marihuana "high" are slight.

death: diseases of the heart and circulatory system, cancer, diseases of the digestive system, homicides, suicides and motor-vehicle and other accidents. A majority of drivers killed in vehicle accidents are found to have been drinking. In contrast, there has been no evidence so far that marihuana contributes to the development of any organic disease, and in the only investigation to date of the effect on driving, a controlled study conducted recently by the Bureau of Motor Vehicles of the state of Washington, it was found that marihuana causes significantly less impairment of driving ability than alcohol does [*see illustration on page 97*].

Perhaps the weightiest charge made against cannabis is that it may lead to psychosis or at least to personality disorders. There is a vast literature on this subject, and it divides into all shades of opinion. Many psychiatrists in India, Egypt, Morocco and Nigeria have declared emphatically that the drug can produce insanity; others insist that it does not. One of the authorities most

often quoted in support of the indictment is Benabud of Morocco. He believes that the drug produces a specific syndrome, called "cannabis psychosis." His description of the identifying symptoms is far from clear, however, and other investigators dispute the existence of such a psychosis. The symptoms said to be characteristic of this syndrome are also common to other acute toxic states including, particularly in Morocco, those associated with malnutrition and endemic infections. Benabud estimates that the number of kif (marihuana) smokers suffering from all types of psychosis is not more than five per 1,000; this rate, however, is lower than the estimated total incidence of all psychoses in populations of other countries. Thus one would have to assume either that there is a much lower prevalence of psychoses other than "cannabis psychosis" among kif smokers in Morocco or that there is no such thing as a "cannabis psychosis," and that the drug is contributing little or nothing to the prevalence rate for psychoses.

The American psychiatrist Bromberg,

in a report of one of his studies, listed 31 patients whose psychoses he attributed to the toxic effects of marihuana. Of these 31, however, seven patients were already predisposed to functional psychoses that were only precipitated by the drug, seven others were later found to be schizophrenics, one was later diagnosed as a manic-depressive and a number of others may have had an acute and temporary attack of psychosis (the "five-day schizophrenia") that could have been mistaken for a drug reaction.

Bromberg found no psychotics among 67 imprisoned criminals who had been users of marihuana. Freedman and Rockmore found none among the 310 marihuana-smoking soldiers they studied, and similar findings have been reported in several other studies of sizable samples. The Chopras in India, in examinations of a total of 1,238 cannabis users, found only 13 to be psychotic, which is about the usual rate of incidence of psychosis in the total population in Western countries. In the La Guardia study nine out of 77 subjects who were studied intensively had a history of psychosis; this high rate could be attributed, however,

to the fact that all the subjects were patients in hospitals or institutions. Samuel Allentuck and K. H. Bowman, the psychiatrists who examined this group, concluded that "marihuana will not produce psychosis de novo in a well-integrated, stable person."

This is not to say that the drug may not precipitate an acute anxiety state with paranoid thoughts or even a temporary psychosis in a susceptible person. A drug that alters the state of consciousness and distorts perception and the body image may well tip a delicately balanced ego, already overburdened with anxiety, into a schizophrenic reaction. In our clinical research program at the Massachusetts Mental Health Center in Boston we surveyed the cases of 41 patients who had been admitted in an acute state of schizophrenia. Six of the patients had used marihuana at one time or another, but in four cases the drug experience had occurred long before the schizophrenic breakdown. In the other two cases a careful study of the entire history failed to indicate definitely whether the drug had or had not precipitated the psychosis.

Very little research attention has been given to the possibility that marihuana might *protect* some people from psychosis. Among users of the drug the proportion of people with neuroses or personality disorders is usually higher than in the general population; one might therefore expect the incidence of psychoses also to be higher in this group. The fact that it is not suggests that for some mentally disturbed people the escape provided by the drug may serve to prevent a psychotic breakdown.

A century ago a French physician, Jacques Joseph Moreau de Tours, reported that he had successfully treated melancholia and other chronic mental illnesses with an extract of cannabis. Several other physicians in France, Germany and England tried the drug, with conflicting results. In the 1940's some interest developed in synhexyl, a synthetic tetrahydrocannabinol, as an apparently promising treatment for depressive psychoses; in the only controlled study, however, this particular drug was found to be no more effective than a placebo.

Tests of the use of cannabis to help

	15 MINUTES			90 MINUTES		
NAÏVE SUBJECTS	PLACEBO	LOW DOSE	HIGH DOSE	PLACEBO	LOW DOSE	HIGH DOSE
1	−3	—	+5	−7	+4	+8
2	+10	−8	−17	−1	−15	−5
3	−3	+6	−7	−10	+2	−1
4	+3	−4	−3			−7
5	+4	+1	−7	+6		−8
6	−3	−1	−9	+3	−5	−12
7	+2	−4	−6	+3	−5	−4
8	−1	+3	+1	+4	+4	−3
9	−1		−4	+6	−1	−10
MEAN	+0.9	−1.2	−5.1	+0.4	−2.6	−3.9
STANDARD ERROR	1.4	1.4	2.1	1.9	2.0	2.0
CHRONIC USERS			HIGH DOSE			HIGH DOSE
10			−4			−16
11			+1			+6
12			+11			+18
13			+3			+4
14			−2			−3
15			−6			+8
16			−4			
17			+3			
MEAN			+0.25			+2.8
STANDARD ERROR			1.9			4.7

TEST OF COGNITIVE FUNCTIONING (called "Digit Symbol Substitution Test") was administered recently by Andrew T. Weil, Norman E. Zinberg and Judith M. Nelsen of the Boston University School of Medicine to two different groups of subjects, one group consisting of chronic users of marihuana, the other of persons experiencing the drug for the first time. A sample of the test is shown at left; the results of the study are summarized at right. On a signal from the examiner the subject was required to fill as many of the empty spaces as possible with the appropriate symbols. The code was always available to the subject during the 90-second administration of the test. The results were tabulated in terms of the change in scores from a base-line score (number correct before smoking marihuana) both 15 minutes and 90 minutes after the smoking session. On the average Weil and his colleagues found that the drug-naïve group showed some impairment during the high (*top right*), but the performance of experienced users of marihuana showed no significant impairment and in fact on the higher doses revealed a slight trend toward improvement (*bottom right*).

drug addicts withdraw from the use of narcotics have yielded more promising results. The first medical use for this purpose was reported in 1889 by an English physician, Edward Birch, who treated a chloral hydrate addict and an opium addict by replacing their drugs with cannabis and found they were then able to discontinue the cannabis without withdrawal symptoms. Similar successes were obtained more recently in two notable trials: one reported in 1942 by Allentuck and Bowman, who tapered off opiate addicts with a marihuana derivative, and another in 1953 by two North Carolina physicians, L. S. Thompson and R. C. Proctor, who withdrew patients from addiction to narcotics, barbiturates and alcohol by the use of pyrahexyl, a tetrahydrocannabinol.

Curiously, these encouraging results have not been followed up by large-scale clinical trials or basic research. It seems that research on the possible medical uses of marihuana is discouraged by the lingering common impression that it is addictive and by the fact that the drug is outlawed and difficult to obtain legally even for research purposes.

Indispensable to an understanding of marihuana's effects and of the present burgeoning spread of its use is the study in depth of people's motivations for using it. In India, where the use is not illegal and therefore not complicated by anxieties arising from that cause, cannabis serves the clear-cut purpose of simple relief from the dreariness and hardships of poverty. The Chopras note that during the harvest season the consumption of the drug increases by 50 percent among farmers in some areas. These authors observe: "A common practice amongst laborers engaged in building or excavation work is to have a few pulls at a ganja pipe or to drink a glass of bhang toward the evening. This produces a sense of well-being, relieves fatigue, stimulates the appetite and induces a feeling of mild stimulation which enables the worker to bear more cheerfully the strain of the daily routine of life."

This simple motivation goes far to explain the fact that in the U.S. marihuana first came into wide use in the ghettos. Several studies of population samples in the Army have shown that 87 percent or more of the marihuana users there were Negroes. Inquiring into the motivations of the 310 marihuana smokers they studied, Freedman and Rockmore found that the responses generally ran in this vein: the drug gave its users "a good feeling"; it was a substitute for whisky; "I feel bad all the time—weeds make me feel better"; "It makes me sleep and eases my pain"; "It makes me feel like I'm a man." For many the drug was evidently an escape from feelings of inadequacy, personal frustrations, anxiety and/or depression.

One must look beyond personal factors, however, to account for the current vogue of marihuana among large portions of the U.S. population. A study of 54 psychiatric patients who were white, middle-class college graduates, for example, elicited the responses that they took up marihuana out of curiosity, to go along with friends, for stimulation or for an unusual experience. Among the youth of this country marihuana has a powerful attraction for those who have a tendency to introspection and meditation or an urge to retire from involvement in society. For many the use of the illegal drug is an act of defiance of the "establishment."

As C. P. Snow has observed: "Uneasiness seems to be becoming part of the climate of our time." It is difficult to avoid the conclusion that the increasing use of marihuana is in part related to the fearful threats of overpopulation, racial conflict and nuclear war. Conversely, the same threats may indirectly be contributing to the emotional campaign against this drug. It is conceivable that some of the affect generated in the population by the violence and martial spirit of our time is being displaced onto issues such as marihuana. Regarded as essentially evil and dangerous, adopted by hippies, yippies and others who demonstrate and call attention to the aspects of reality and the threats of doom that most of us find too distressing to confront, marihuana is a natural target as a scapegoat.

In short, the anxiety and sense of helplessness generated by the dangers of our time may be focused in some degree on marihuana, driving some people to protective immersion in the drug and arousing others to a crusade against it. Although either of these responses may have some adaptive value for the individual psyche, neither contributes toward the development of a more secure world.

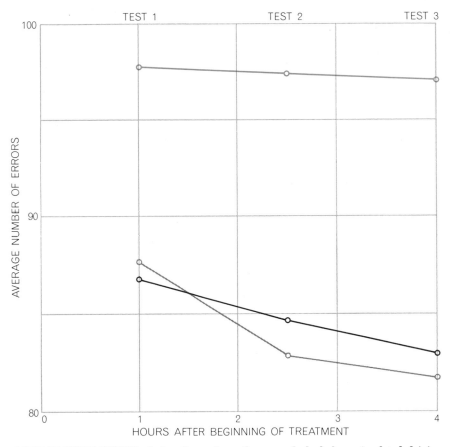

COMPARATIVE STUDY of the effects of marihuana and alcohol on simulated driving performance was conducted by the Bureau of Motor Vehicles of the state of Washington. The graph shows average number of errors on tests administered at three stages after treatment with alcohol (*color*), marihuana (*black*) and a placebo (*gray*). In general it was found that marihuana causes significantly less impairment of driving ability than alcohol does.

11

THE HALLUCINOGENIC DRUGS

FRANK BARRON, MURRAY JARVIK AND STERLING BUNNELL, JR.

April 1964

Human beings have two powerful needs that are at odds with each other: to keep things the same, and to have something new happen. We like to feel secure, yet at times we like to be surprised. Too much predictability leads to monotony, but too little may lead to anxiety. To establish a balance between continuity and change is a task facing all organisms, individual and social, human and non-human.

Keeping things predictable is generally considered one of the functions of the ego. When a person perceives accurately, thinks clearly, plans wisely and acts appropriately—and represses maladaptive thoughts and emotions—we say that his ego is strong. But the strong ego is also inventive, open to many perceptions that at first may be disorganizing. Research on the personality traits of highly creative individuals has shown that they are particularly alert to the challenge of the contradictory and the unpredictable, and that they may even court the irrational in their own make up as a source of new and unexpected insight. Indeed, through all recorded history and everywhere in the world men have gone to considerable lengths to seek unpredictability by disrupting the functioning of the ego. A change of scene, a change of heart, a change of mind: these are the popular prescriptions for getting out of a rut.

Among the common ways of chang-ing "mind" must be reckoned the use of intoxicating substances. Alcohol has quite won the day for this purpose in the U.S. and much of the rest of the world. Consumed at a moderate rate and in sensible quantities, it can serve simultaneously as a euphoriant and tranquilizing agent before it finally dulls the faculties and puts one to sleep. In properly disposed individuals it may dissolve sexual inhibitions, relieve fear and anxiety, or stimulate meditation on the meaning of life. In spite of its costliness to individual and social health when it is used immoderately, alcohol retains its rank as first among the substances used by mankind to change mental experience. Its closest rivals in popularity are opium and its derivatives and various preparations of cannabis, such as hashish and marijuana.

This article deals with another group of such consciousness-altering substances: the "hallucinogens." The most important of these are mescaline, which comes from the peyote cactus *Lophophora williamsii;* psilocybin and psilocin, from such mushrooms as *Psilocybe mexicana* and *Stropharia cubensis;* and d-lysergic acid diethylamide (LSD), which is derived from ergot (*Claviceps purpurea*), a fungus that grows on rye and wheat. All are alkaloids more or less related to one another in chemical structure.

Various names have been applied to this class of substances. They produce distinctive changes in perception that are sometimes referred to as hallucinations, although usually the person under the influence of the drug can distinguish his visions from reality, and even when they seem quite compelling he is able to attribute them to the action of the drug. If, therefore, the term "hallucination" is reserved for perceptions that the perceiver himself firmly believes indicate the existence of a corresponding object or event, but for which other observers can find no objective basis, then the "hallucinogens" only rarely produce hallucinations. There are several other names for this class of drugs. They have been called "psychotomimetic" because in some cases the effects seem to mimic psychosis [see "Experimental Psychoses," by six staff members of the Boston Psychopathic Hospital; SCIENTIFIC AMERICAN, June, 1955]. Some observers prefer to use the term "psychedelic" to suggest that unsuspected capacities of the imagination are sometimes revealed in the perceptual changes.

The hallucinogens are currently a subject of intense debate and concern in medical and psychological circles. At issue is the degree of danger they present to the psychological health of the person who uses them. This has become an important question because of a rapidly increasing interest in the drugs among laymen. The recent controversy at Harvard University, stemming at first from methodological disagreements

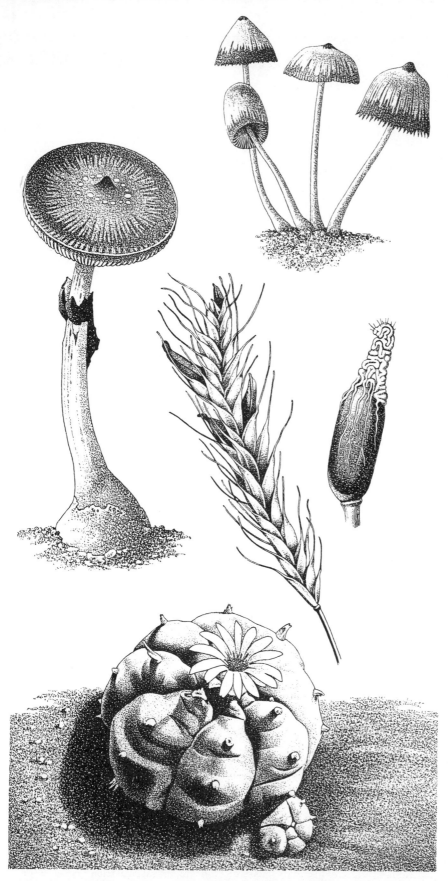

NATURAL SOURCES of the main hallucinogens are depicted. Psilocybin comes from the mushrooms *Stropharia cubensis* (*top left*) and *Psilocybe mexicana* (*top right*). LSD is synthesized from an alkaloid in ergot (*Claviceps purpurea*), a fungus that grows on cereal grains; an ergot-infested rye seed head is shown (*center*) together with a larger-scale drawing of the ergot fungus. Mescaline is from the peyote cactus *Lophophora williamsii* (*bottom*).

among investigators but subsequently involving the issue of protection of the mental health of the student body, indicated the scope of popular interest in taking the drugs and the consequent public concern over their possible misuse.

There are, on the other hand, constructive uses of the drugs. In spite of obvious differences between the "model psychoses" produced by these drugs and naturally occurring psychoses, there are enough similarities to warrant intensive investigation along these lines. The drugs also provide the only link, however tenuous, between human psychoses and aberrant behavior in animals, in which physiological mechanisms can be studied more readily than in man. Beyond this many therapists feel that there is a specialized role for the hallucinogens in the treatment of psychoneuroses. Other investigators are struck by the possibility of using the drugs to facilitate meditation and aesthetic discrimination and to stimulate the imagination. These possibilities, taken in conjunction with the known hazards, are the bases for the current professional concern and controversy.

In evaluating potential uses and misuses of the hallucinogens, one can draw on a considerable body of knowledge from such disciplines as anthropology, pharmacology, biochemistry, psychology and psychiatry.

In some primitive societies the plants from which the major hallucinogens are derived have been known for millenniums and have been utilized for divination, curing, communion with supernatural powers and meditation to improve self-understanding or social unity; they have also served such mundane purposes as allaying hunger and relieving discomfort or boredom. In the Western Hemisphere the ingestion of hallucinogenic plants in pre-Columbian times was limited to a zone extending from what is now the southwestern U.S. to the northwestern basin of the Amazon. Among the Aztecs there were professional diviners who achieved inspiration by eating either peyote, hallucinogenic mushrooms (which the Aztecs called *teo-nanacatyl*, or "god's flesh") or other hallucinogenic plants. *Teo-nanacatyl* was said to have been distributed at the coronation of Montezuma to make the ceremony seem more spectacular. In the years following the conquest of Mexico there were reports of communal mushroom rites among the Aztecs and other Indians of southern Mexico. The communal use has almost died out today, but in several

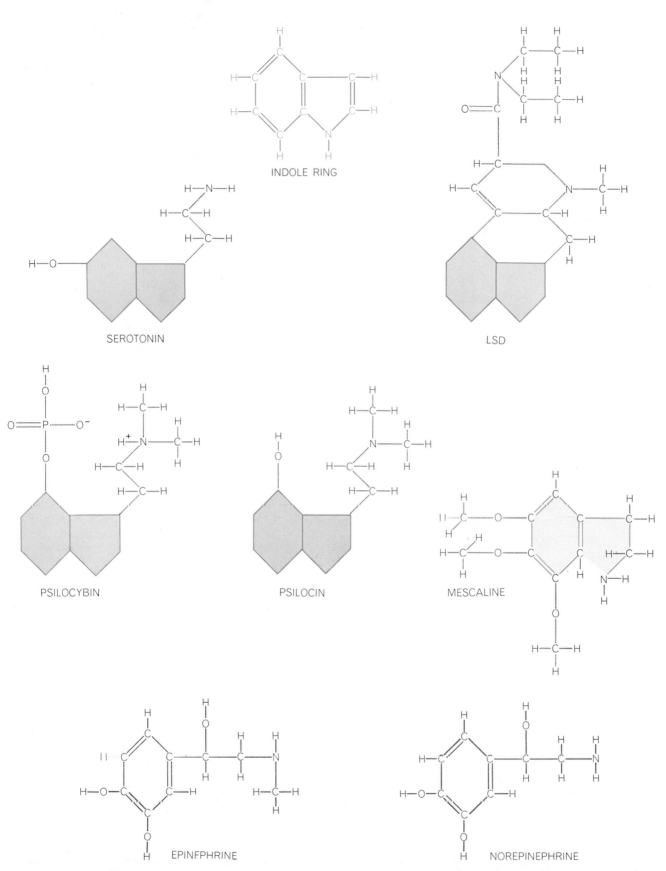

CHEMICAL RELATIONS among several of the hallucinogens and neurohumors are indicated by these structural diagrams. The indole ring (*in color at top*) is a basic structural unit; it appears, as indicated by the colored shapes, in serotonin, LSD, psilocybin and psilocin. Mescaline does not have an indole ring but, as shown by the light color, can be represented so as to suggest its relation to the ring. The close relation between mescaline and the two catechol amines epinephrine and norepinephrine is also apparent here.

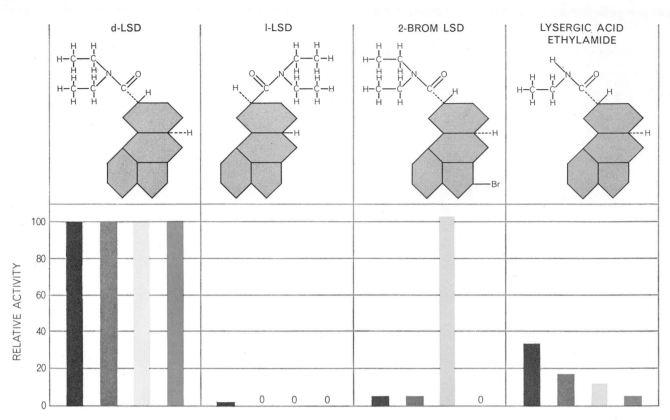

SLIGHT CHANGES in LSD molecule produce large changes in its properties. Here LSD (*left*) is used as a standard, with a "relative activity" of 100 in toxicity (*dark gray bar*), fever-producing effect (*light gray*), ability to antagonize serotonin (*light color*) and typical psychotomimetic effects (*dark color*). The stereoisomer of LSD (*second from left*) in which the positions of the side chains are reversed, shows almost no activity; the substitution of a bromine atom (*third from left*) reduces the psychotomimetic effect but not the serotonin antagonism; the removal of one of the two ethyl groups (*right*) sharply reduces activity in each of the areas.

tribes the medicine men or women (*curanderos*) still partake of *Psilocybe* and *Stropharia* in their rituals.

In the arid region between the Rio Grande and central Mexico, where the peyote cactus grows, the dried tops of the plants ("peyote buttons") were eaten by Indian shamans, or medicine men, and figured in tribal rituals. During the 19th century the Mescalero Apaches acquired the plant and developed a peyote rite. The peyotism of the Mescaleros (whence the name mescaline) spread to the Comanches and Kiowas, who transformed it into a religion with a doctrine and ethic as well as ritual. Peyotism, which spread rapidly through the Plains tribes, became fused with Christianity. Today its adherents worship God as the great spirit who controls the universe and put some of his power into peyote, and Jesus as the man who gave the plant to the Indians in a time of need. Saturday-night meetings, usually held in a traditional tepee, begin with the eating of the sacramental peyote; then the night is spent in prayer, ritual singing and introspective contemplation, and in the morning there is a communion breakfast of corn, game and fruit.

Recognizing the need for an effective organization to protect their form of worship, several peyote churches joined in 1918 to form the Native American Church, which now has about 225,000 members in tribes from Nevada to the East Coast and from the Mexican border to Saskatchewan. It preaches brotherly love, care of the family, self-reliance and abstinence from alcohol. The church has been able to defeat attempts, chiefly by the missionaries of other churches, to outlaw peyote by Federal legislation, and it has recently brought about the repeal of antipeyote legislation in several states.

The hallucinogens began to attract scholarly interest in the last decade of the 19th century, when the investigations and conceptions of such men as Francis Galton, J. M. Charcot, Sigmund Freud and William James introduced a new spirit of serious inquiry into such subjects as hallucination, mystical experience and other "paranormal" psychic phenomena. Havelock Ellis and the psychiatrist Silas Weir Mitchell wrote accounts of the subjective effects of peyote, or Anhalonium, as it was then called. Such essays in turn stimulated

the interest of pharmacologists. The active principle of peyote, the alkaloid called mescaline, was isolated in 1896; in 1919 it was recognized that the molecular structure of mescaline was related to the structure of the adrenal hormone epinephrine.

This was an important turning point, because the interest in the hallucinogens as a possible key to naturally occurring psychoses is based on the chemical relations between the drugs and the neurohumors: substances that chemically transmit impulses across synapses between two neurons, or nerve cells, or between a neuron and an effector such as a muscle cell. Acetylcholine and the catechol amines epinephrine and norepinephrine have been shown to act in this manner in the peripheral nervous system of vertebrates; serotonin has the same effect in some invertebrates. It is frequently assumed that these substances also act as neurohumors in the central nervous system; at least they are present there, and injecting them into various parts of the brain seems to affect nervous activity.

The structural resemblance of mescaline and epinephrine suggested a possible link between the drug and mental illness: Might the early, excited stage of schizophrenia be produced or at least triggered by an error in metabolism that produced a mescaline-like substance? Techniques for gathering evidence on this question were not available, however, and the speculation on an "M-substance" did not lead to serious experimental work.

When LSD was discovered in 1943, its extraordinary potency again aroused interest in the possibility of finding a natural chemical activator of the schizophrenic process. The M-substance hypothesis was revived on the basis of reports that hallucinogenic effects were produced by adrenochrome and other breakdown products of epinephrine, and the hypothesis appeared to be strengthened by the isolation from human urine of some close analogues of hallucinogens. Adrenochrome has not, however, been detected in significant amounts in the human body, and it seems unlikely that the analogues could be produced in sufficient quantity to effect mental changes.

The relation between LSD and serotonin has given rise to the hypothesis that schizophrenia is caused by an imbalance in the metabolism of serotonin, with excitement and hallucinations resulting from an excess of serotonin in certain regions of the brain, and depressive and catatonic states resulting from a deficiency of serotonin. The idea arose in part from the observation that in some laboratory physiological preparations LSD acts rather like serotonin but in other preparations it is a powerful antagonist of serotonin; thus LSD might facilitate or block some neurohumoral action of serotonin in the brain.

The broad objection to the serotonin theory of schizophrenia is that it requires an oversimplified view of the disease's pattern of symptoms. Moreover, many congeners, or close analogues, of LSD, such as 2-brom lysergic acid, are equally effective or more effective antagonists of serotonin without being significantly active psychologically in man. This does not disprove the hypothesis, however. In man 2-brom LSD blocks the mental effects of a subsequent dose of LSD, and in the heart of a clam it blocks the action of both LSD and serotonin. Perhaps there are "keyholes" at the sites where neurohumors act; in the case of those for serotonin it may be that LSD fits the hole and opens the lock, whereas the psychologically inactive analogues merely occupy the keyhole, blocking the action of serotonin or LSD without mimicking their effects. Certainly the re-

semblance of most of the hallucinogens to serotonin is marked, and the correlations between chemical structure and pharmacological action deserve intensive investigation. The serotonin theory of schizophrenia is far from proved, but there is strong evidence for an organic factor of some kind in the disease; it may yet turn out to involve either a specific neurohumor or an imbalance among several neurohumors.

The ingestion of LSD, mescaline or psilocybin can produce a wide range of subjective and objective effects. The subjective effects apparently depend on at least three kinds of variable: the properties and potency of the drug itself; the basic personality traits and current mood of the person ingesting it, and the social and psychological context, including the meaning to the individual of his act in taking the drug and his interpretation of the motives of those who made it available. The discussion of subjective effects that follows is compiled from many different accounts of the drug experience; it should be considered an inventory of possible effects rather than a description of a typical episode.

One subjective experience that is frequently reported is a change in visual perception. When the eyes are open, the perception of light and space is affected: colors become more vivid and seem to glow; the space between objects becomes more apparent, as though space itself had become "real," and surface details appear to be more sharply defined. Many people feel a new awareness of the physical beauty of the world, particularly of visual harmonies, colors, the play of light and the exquisiteness of detail.

The visual effects are even more striking when the eyes are closed. A constantly changing display appears, its content ranging from abstract forms to dramatic scenes involving imagined people or animals, sometimes in exotic lands or ancient times. Different individuals have recalled seeing wavy lines, cobweb or chessboard designs, gratings, mosaics, carpets, floral designs, gems, windmills, mausoleums, landscapes, "arabesques spiraling into eternity," statuesque men of the past, chariots, sequences of dramatic action, the face of Buddha, the face of Christ, the Crucifixion, "the mythical dwelling places of the gods," the immensity and blackness of space. After taking peyote Silas Weir Mitchell wrote: "To give the faintest idea of the perfectly satisfying intensity and purity of these gorgeous color fruits

WATER COLORS were done, while under the influence of a relatively large dose of a hallucinogenic drug, by a person with no art training. Originals are bright yellow, purple, green and red as well as black.

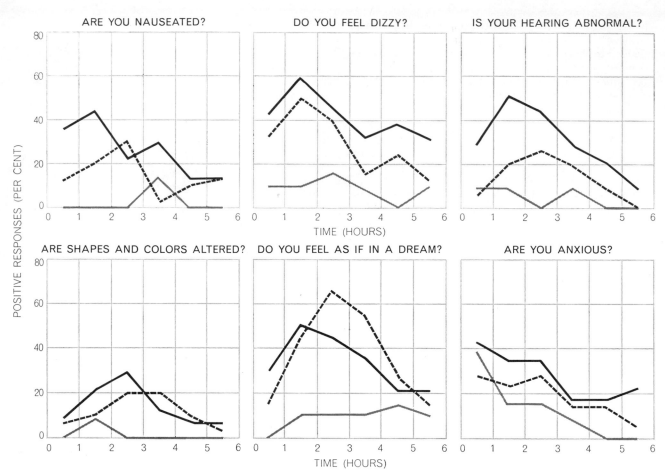

ARE YOU NAUSEATED? DO YOU FEEL DIZZY? IS YOUR HEARING ABNORMAL?

ARE SHAPES AND COLORS ALTERED? DO YOU FEEL AS IF IN A DREAM? ARE YOU ANXIOUS?

POSITIVE RESPONSES (PER CENT)

TIME (HOURS)

TIME (HOURS)

SUBJECTIVE REPORT on physiological and perceptual effects of LSD was obtained by means of a questionnaire containing 47 items, the results for six of which are presented. Volunteers were questioned at one-hour intervals beginning half an hour after they took the drug. The curves show the per cent of the group giving positive answers at each time. The gray curves are for those given an inactive substance, the broken black curves for between 25 and 75 micrograms and the solid black curves for between 100 and 225.

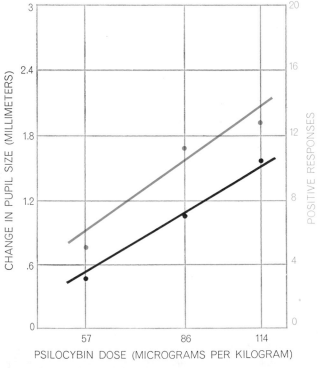

CHANGE IN PUPIL SIZE (MILLIMETERS)

POSITIVE RESPONSES

PSILOCYBIN DOSE (MICROGRAMS PER KILOGRAM)

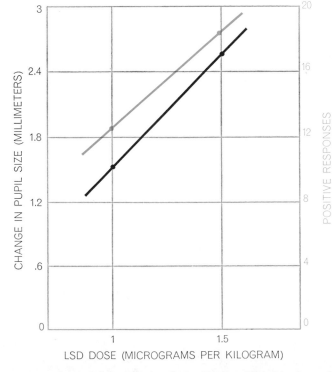

CHANGE IN PUPIL SIZE (MILLIMETERS)

POSITIVE RESPONSES

LSD DOSE (MICROGRAMS PER KILOGRAM)

OBJECTIVE AND SUBJECTIVE effects vary with dosage as shown here. The data plotted in black are for the increase in size of pupil; the number of positive responses to questions like the ones at the top of the page are shown in color. The objective and subjective measures vary in a similar manner. The data are from an experiment done by Harris Isbell of the University of Kentucky.

is quite beyond my power." A painter described the waning hours of the effects of psilocybin as follows: "As the afternoon wore on I felt very content to simply sit and stare out of the window at the snow and the trees, and at that time I recall feeling that the snow, the fire in the fireplace, the darkened and book-lined room were so perfect as to seem almost unreal."

The changes in visual perception are not always pleasant. Aldous Huxley called one of his books about mescaline *Heaven and Hell* in recognition of the contradictory sensations induced by the drug. The "hellish" experiences include an impression of blackness accompanied by feelings of gloom and isolation, a garish modification of the glowing colors observed in the "heavenly" phase, a sense of sickly greens and ugly dark reds. The subject's perception of his own body may become unpleasant: his limbs may seem to be distorted or his flesh to be decaying; in a mirror his face may appear to be a mask, his smile a meaningless grimace. Sometimes all human movements appear to be mere puppetry, or everyone seems to be dead. These experiences can be so disturbing that a residue of fear and depression persists long after the effects of the drug have worn off.

Often there are complex auditory hallucinations as well as visual ones. lengthy conversations between imaginary people, perfectly orchestrated musical compositions the subject has never heard before, voices speaking foreign languages unknown to the subject. There have also been reports of hallucinatory odors and tastes and of visceral and other bodily sensations. Frequently patterns of association normally confined to a single sense will cross over to other senses: the sound of music evokes the visual impression of jets of colored light, a "cold" human voice makes the subject shiver, pricking the skin with a pin produces the visual impression of a circle, light glinting on a Christmas tree ornament seems to shatter and to evoke the sound of sleigh bells. The time sense is altered too. The passage of time may seem to be a slow and pleasant flow or to be intolerably tedious. A "sense of timelessness" is often reported; the subject feels outside of or beyond time, or time and space seem infinite.

In some individuals one of the most basic constancies in perception is affected: the distinction between subject and object. A firm sense of personal identity depends on knowing accurately the borders of the self and on being able to distinguish what is inside from what is outside. Paranoia is the most vivid pathological instance of the breakdown of this discrimination; the paranoiac attributes to personal and impersonal forces outside himself the impulses that actually are inside him. Mystical and transcendental experiences are marked by the loss of this same basic constancy. "All is one" is the prototype of a mystical utterance. In the mystical state the distinction between subject and object disappears; the subject is seen to be one with the object. The experience is usually one of rapture or ecstasy and in religious terms is described as "holy." When the subject thus achieves complete identification with the object, the experience seems beyond words.

Some people who have taken a large dose of a hallucinogenic drug report feelings of "emptiness" or "silence," pertaining either to the interior of the self or to an "interior" of the universe—or to both as one. Such individuals have a sense of being completely undifferentiated, as though it were their personal consciousness that had been "emptied," leaving none of the usual discriminations on which the functioning of the ego depends. One man who had this experience thought later that it had been an anticipation of death, and that the regaining of the basic discriminations was like a remembrance of the very first days of life after birth.

The effect of the hallucinogens on sexual experience is not well documented. One experiment that is often quoted seemed to provide evidence that mescaline is an anaphrodisiac, an inhibitor of sexual appetite; this conclusion seemed plausible because the drugs have so often been associated with rituals emphasizing asceticism and prayer. The fact is, however, that the drugs are probably neither anaphrodisiacs nor aphrodisiacs—if indeed any drug is. There is reason to believe that if the drug-taking situation is one in which sexual relations seem appropriate, the hallucinogens simply bring to the sexual experience the same kind of change in perception that occurs in other areas of experience.

The point is that in all the hallucinogen-produced experiences it is never the drug alone that is at work. As in the case of alcohol, the effects vary widely depending on when the drug is taken, where, in the presence of whom, in what dosage and—perhaps most important of all—by whom. What happens to the individual after he takes the drug, and his changing relations to the setting and the people in it during the episode, will further influence his experience.

Since the setting is so influential in these experiments, it sometimes happens that a person who is present when someone else is taking a hallucinogenic drug, but who does not take the drug himself, behaves as though he were under the influence of a hallucinogen. In view of this effect one might expect that a person given an inactive substance he thought was a drug would respond as though he had actually received the drug. Indeed, such responses have sometimes been noted. In controlled experiments, however, subjects given an inactive substance are readily distinguishable from those who take a drug; the difference is apparent in their appearance and behavior, their answers to questionnaires and their physiological responses. Such behavioral similarities as are observed can be explained largely by a certain apprehension felt by a person who receives an inactive substance he thinks is a drug, or by anticipation on the part of someone who has taken the drug before.

In addition to the various subjective effects of the hallucinogens there are a number of observable changes in physiological function and in performance that one can measure or at least describe objectively. The basic physiological effects are those typical of a mild excitement of the sympathetic nervous system. The hallucinogens usually dilate the pupils, constrict the peripheral arterioles and raise the systolic blood pressure; they may also increase the excitability of such spinal reflexes as the knee jerk. Electroencephalograms show that the effect on electrical brain waves is usually of a fairly nonspecific "arousal" nature: the pattern is similar to that of a normally alert, attentive and problem-oriented subject, and if rhythms characteristic of drowsiness or sleep have been present, they disappear when the drug is administered. (Insomnia is common the first night after one of the drugs has been taken.) Animal experiments suggest that LSD produces these effects by stimulating the reticular formation of the midbrain, not directly but by stepping up the sensory input.

Under the influence of one of the hallucinogens there is usually some reduction in performance on standard tests of reasoning, memory, arithmetic, spelling and drawing. These findings may not indicate an inability to perform well; after taking a drug many people simply refuse to co-operate with the tester. The very fact that someone should want to

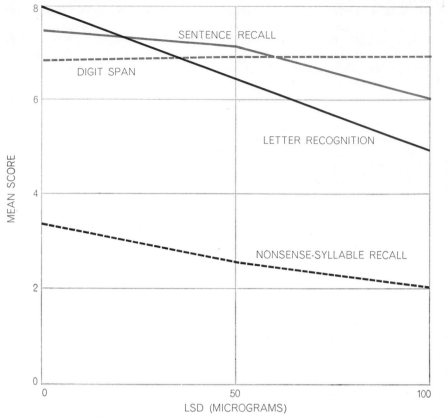

EFFECT OF LSD on memory was determined with standard tests. Curves show results of four tests for subjects given an inactive substance, 50 micrograms of the drug and 100 micrograms respectively. Effect of LSD was to decrease scores except in a test of digit-recall ability.

of psilocybin and two milligrams of LSD. No permanent effects were noted in these cases, but obviously no decisive studies of the upper limits of dosage have been undertaken.

There are also differences among the hallucinogens in the time of onset of effects and the duration of intoxication. When mescaline is given orally, the effects appear in two or three hours and last for 12 hours or more. LSD acts in less than an hour; some of its effects persist for eight or nine hours, and insomnia can last as long as 16 hours. Psilocybin usually acts within 20 or 30 minutes, and its full effect is felt for about five hours. All these estimates are for the standard dose administered orally; when any of the drugs is given intravenously, the first effects appear within minutes.

At the present time LSD and psilocybin are treated by the U.S. Food and Drug Administration like any other "experimental drug," which means that they can be legally distributed only to qualified investigators who will administer them in the course of an approved program of experimentation. In practice the drugs are legally available only to investigators working under a Government grant or for a state or Federal agency.

Nevertheless, there has probably been an increase during the past two or three years in the uncontrolled use of the drugs to satisfy personal curiosity or to experience novel sensations. This has led a number of responsible people in government, law, medicine and psychology to urge the imposition of stricter controls that would make the drugs more difficult to obtain even for basic research. These people emphasize the harmful possibilities of the drugs; citing the known cases of adverse reactions, they conclude that the prudent course is to curtail experimentation with hallucinogens.

Others—primarily those who have worked with the drugs—emphasize the constructive possibilities, insist that the hallucinogens have already opened up important leads in research and conclude that it would be shortsighted as well as contrary to the spirit of free scientific inquiry to restrict the activities of qualified investigators. Some go further, questioning whether citizens should be denied the opportunity of trying the drugs even without medical or psychological supervision and arguing that anyone who is mentally competent should have the right to explore the varieties

test them may seem absurd and may arouse either hostility or amusement. Studies by one of the authors in which tests of attention and concentration were administered to subjects who had been given different doses of LSD indicated that motivation was perhaps as important in determining scores as the subject's intellectual capacity.

The hallucinogenic drugs are not addictive—if one means by addiction that physiological dependence is established and the drug becomes necessary, usually in increasing amounts, for satisfactory physiological functioning. Some individuals become psychologically dependent on the drugs, however, and develop a "habit" in that sense; indeed, there is a tendency for those who ingest hallucinogens habitually to make the drug experience the center of all their activities. LSD, mescaline and psilocybin do produce physiological tolerance. If the same quantity of LSD is administered on three successive days, for example, it will not suffice by the third day to produce the same subjective or physiological effects; tolerance develops more slowly and less completely with mescaline and psilocybin. When an individual becomes tolerant to a given dos-

age of LSD, the ordinarily equivalent dose of psilocybin produces reduced effects. This phenomenon of cross-tolerance suggests that the two drugs have common pathways of action. Any tolerance established by daily administration of the drugs wears off rather rapidly, generally being dissipated within a few days if the drug is not taken.

The three major hallucinogens differ markedly in potency. The standard human doses—those that will cause the average adult male weighing about 150 pounds to show the full clinical effects—are 500 milligrams of mescaline, 20 milligrams of psilocybin and .1 milligram of LSD. It is assumed that in a large enough dose any of the hallucinogens would be lethal, but there are no documented cases of human deaths from the drugs alone. Death has been brought on in sensitive laboratory animals such as rabbits by LSD doses equivalent to 120 times the standard human dose. Some animals are much less susceptible; white rats have been given doses 1,000 times larger than the standard human dose without lasting harm. The maximum doses known by the authors to have been taken by human beings are 900 milligrams of mescaline, 70 milligrams

of conscious experience if he can do so without harming himself or others.

The most systematic survey of the incidence of serious adverse reactions to hallucinogens covered nearly 5,000 cases, in which LSD was administered on more than 25,000 occasions. Psychotic reactions lasting more than 48 hours were observed in fewer than two-tenths of 1 per cent of the cases. The rate of attempted suicides was slightly over a tenth of 1 per cent, and these involved psychiatric patients with histories of instability. Among those who took the drug simply as subjects in experiments there were no attempted suicides and the psychotic reactions occurred in fewer than a tenth of 1 per cent of the cases.

Recent reports do indicate that the incidence of bad reactions has been increasing, perhaps because more individuals have been taking the hallucinogens in settings that emphasize sensation-seeking or even deliberate social delinquency. Since under such circumstances there is usually no one in attendance who knows how to avert dangerous developments, a person in this situation may find himself facing an extremely frightening hallucination with no one present who can help him to recognize where the hallucination ends and reality begins. Yet the question of what is a proper setting is not a simple one. One of the criticisms of the Harvard experiments was that some were conducted in private homes rather than in a laboratory or clinical setting. The experimenters defended this as an attempt to provide a feeling of naturalness and "psychological safety." Such a setting, they hypothesized, should reduce the likelihood of negative reactions such as fear and hostility and increase the positive experiences. Controlled studies of this hypothesis have not been carried out, however.

Many psychiatrists and psychologists who have administered hallucinogens in a therapeutic setting claim specific benefits in the treatment of psychoneuroses, alcoholism and social delinquency. The published studies are difficult to evaluate because almost none have employed control groups. One summary of the available statistics on the treatment of alcoholism does indicate that about 50 per cent of the patients treated with a combination of psychotherapy and LSD abstained from alcohol for at least a year, compared with 30 per cent of the patients treated by psychotherapy alone.

In another recent study the results of psychological testing before and after

LSD therapy were comparable in most respects to the results obtained when conventional brief psychotherapy was employed. Single-treatment LSD therapy was significantly more effective, however, in relieving neurotic depression. If replicated, these results may provide an important basis for more directed study of the treatment of specific psychopathological conditions.

If the hallucinogens do have psychotherapeutic merit, it seems possible that they work by producing a shift in personal values. William James long ago noted that "the best cure for dipsomania is religiomania." There appear to be religious aspects of the drug experience that may bring about a change in behavior by causing a "change of heart." If this is so, one might be able to apply the hallucinogens in the service of moral regeneration while relying on more conventional techniques to give the patient insight into his habitual behavior patterns and motives.

In the light of the information now available about the uses and possible abuses of the hallucinogens, common sense surely decrees some form of social

control. In considering such control it should always be emphasized that the reaction to these drugs depends not only on their chemical properties and biological activity but also on the context in which they are taken, the meaning of the act and the personality and mood of the individual who takes them. If taking the drug is defined by the group or individual, or by society, as immoral or criminal, one can expect guilt and aggression and further social delinquency to result; if the aim is to help or to be helped, the experience may be therapeutic and strengthening; if the subject fears psychosis, the drug could induce psychosis. The hallucinogens, like so many other discoveries of man, are analogous to fire, which can burn down the house or spread through the house life-sustaining warmth. Purpose, planning and constructive control make the difference. The immediate research challenge presented by the hallucinogens is a practical question: Can ways be found to minimize or eliminate the hazards, and to identify and develop further the constructive potentialities, of these powerful drugs?

NATIVE AMERICAN CHURCH members take part in a peyote ceremony in Saskatchewan, Canada. Under the influence of the drug, they gaze into the fire as they pray and meditate.

12

EXPERIMENTS WITH GOGGLES

IVO KOHLER
May 1962

Of all the senses the one most intensively studied is undoubtedly vision. Much has been learned about the physical and physiological basis of visual perception, but understanding of the process remains primitive. Vision is perhaps the most complex of the senses; nonetheless it offers the investigator a tantalizing opportunity to learn how the brain processes sensory data and constructs an effective image of the outside world. Presumably this image is the result of an unconscious learning process; the image is "better" than it should be, considering the known defects in the visual system. For example, the lens of the eye is not corrected for spherical aberration; hence straight lines should look slightly curved. By the same token, lines of a certain curvature should appear straight. It is also well known that the eye is not corrected for color; as a result different wavelengths of light—originating at a common point—do not come to a common focus on the retina. One would expect this defect, called chromatic aberration, to have a noticeable effect on vision, but it does not, except under special conditions.

One way to explore the unconscious learning process that goes on in normal vision is to investigate how the visual system responds to images that are systematically distorted by specially constructed goggles. In this article I shall describe some of our studies, conducted at the University of Innsbruck in Austria, which show that the eye has a remarkable ability to discount or adapt to highly complex distortions involving both spatial geometry and color. But we have been surprised to discover that the eye does not adapt to certain other distortions that seem, superficially at least, less severe than those to which the eye does adapt. Some of these findings appear to be incompatible with traditional theories of vision in general and of color vision in particular.

In addition to contributing to the understanding of vision, experiments with goggles have immediate practical importance for ophthalmologists. If the ophthalmologist knows the extent to which the visual system can adapt to "wrongly" constructed experimental glasses, he will be less reluctant to prescribe strong glasses for his patients. The stronger a glass, meaning the higher its refractive power, the greater its capacity to distort images and produce a fringe of color around them. The ophthalmologist can tell a patient in need of strong glasses that the initially disagreeable distortions and rainbow fringes will disappear if he wears the glasses faithfully for several weeks. Or, to give another example, an operation to repair a detached retina sometimes leaves a fold in the retina that causes a bulge in the patient's visual world. On the basis of goggle experiments, the physician can assure the patient that the bulge will become less noticeable with time and will probably disappear altogether. The fold in the retina will remain, but the patient's vision will gradually adapt to discount its presence. What this implies, of course, is that an individual born with a fold or similar imperfection in his retina may never be aware of it.

We conclude, therefore, that sense organs are not rigid machines but living and variable systems, the functioning of which is itself subject to variation. If a sensory system is exposed to a new and prolonged stimulus situation that departs from the one normally experienced, the system can be expected to undergo a fundamental change in its normal mode of operation.

The use of distorting goggles seems to be the simplest way of producing novel and prolonged visual-stimulus situations. The volunteer subject can be said to be wearing the laboratory on his nose; he cannot leave the laboratory unless he closes his eyes or removes the goggles. The entire visual system, including the manifold projection regions in the brain of which we still know so little, is subjected in a certain way to a completely novel and disturbing situation. Finally it "breaks down"; established habits are abandoned and the visual system begins to respond in a new manner.

When we make the system break down and learn a new way of functioning, we do not believe we are forcing the system to function artificially or abnormally. We assume, rather, that a single mechanism is at work at all times. The mechanism that removes or minimizes an artificially created disturbance is the same one that brings about a normal

UNDISTORTED VIEW of the Union Carbide Building in New York can be compared with distorted images on opposite page.

"RUBBER WORLD" is created by prism goggles. These photographs show what the eye would see through a prism with its base held to the right. If the head is turned to the right while glancing to the left, the image expands toward the left (*top left*). If head and eye movements are reversed, the image shrinks (*top right*). If the head is moved up and down, vertical and horizontal lines tilt so as to produce a "rocking chair" effect (*two bottom pictures*). For an undistorted view of this building see the opposite page.

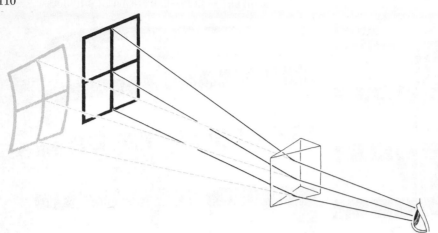

CURVATURE OF LINES is observed when looking through a prism because light rays entering the prism obliquely are bent more than those entering at right angles. A prism that has its base to the right displaces images to the left and bends the top and bottom of vertical lines still farther to the left. As a result vertical lines seem to bow to the right.

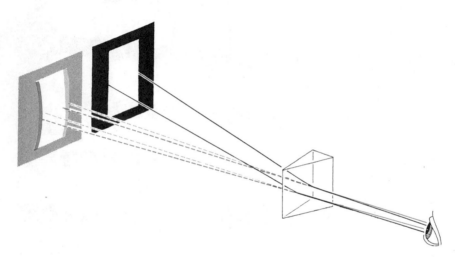

FRINGE OF COLOR borders light-colored objects because a prism bends short wavelengths of light more than long wavelengths. If the prism base is to the right, blue rays, being bent the most, are seen as a blue fringe along the left-hand border. Similarly, a yellow-red fringe of color (*shown here in gray*) appears along the right-hand border of the object.

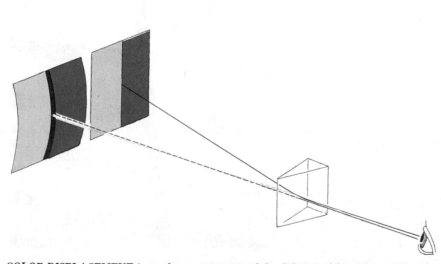

COLOR DISPLACEMENT is another consequence of the differential bending of light rays having different wavelengths. The diagram shows what happens if the green-red figure on the opposite page is viewed through a prism, base to right. The green area (*gray here*) is displaced to the left more than the red area, leaving an empty dark space between the two.

functioning of the sensory system under normal conditions. If this assumption is correct, the development of the normal visual system—in so far as its development depends on the environment—can be explored by the goggle method.

The application of distorting goggles to the study of visual adaptation dates back to the work of G. M. Stratton of the University of California, who used himself as a subject. Primarily because of the difficulty of finding subjects willing to wear goggles for days, weeks or even months, the method was little employed until about 1928. Then, independently and simultaneously, goggle experiments were undertaken by Theodor Erismann at the University of Innsbruck and by James J. Gibson at Smith College. Gibson's subjects wore goggles that placed a glass wedge, or prism, in front of each eye. Erismann experimented not only with prism goggles but also with more elaborate devices that transposed the visual field from right to left or from top to bottom. Another device allowed the subject to see only directly to the rear, as if he had eyes in the back of his head. After several weeks of wearing goggles that transposed right and left, one of Erismann's subjects became so at home in his reversed world that he was able to drive a motorcycle through Innsbruck while wearing the goggles.

Although Gibson's subjects wore goggles for only a few days at a time, they were the first to discover adaptation to the color fringes and line curvature that a prism produces. Depending on the extent to which the front and rear faces of a prism depart from the parallel, light rays passing through the glass are bent to a greater or lesser degree. This property is called the deviation of the prism. The deviation angle is approximately half the angle between the two faces. Deviations between five and 15 degrees are most useful for goggle experiments. Color fringes arise because light of short wavelength, such as blue light, is bent more than light of longer wavelength. As a result the line marking the edge of an object is spread out into a small spectrum, which becomes more noticeable the greater the contrast between the brightness of the object and that of its background [*see top illustration on opposite page*].

The curvature of lines is part of a more general prism effect that produces a variable change in the curvature, angle and distance of observed objects. The effect arises because the angle of deviation varies with the direction of the light reaching the front face of the prism.

COLOR FRINGES appear (*right*) when a simple white-on-black figure is viewed through a prism having its base to the right. The prism also bends vertical lines. The undistorted figure is shown at the left. These prismatic distortions are explained in the upper two illustrations on the opposite page. After a subject has worn prism goggles for a few days the color fringes and line curvature largely disappear. When he removes the goggles, he sees fringes of a complementary color and lines having a reverse curvature.

TEST FIGURE shows how colors are differentially shifted by a prism. When viewed through a prism with base to the right, the greater shift of the green image leaves a thin black void at the color boundary (*see bottom illustration on opposite page*). When the prism is turned around, green overlaps red, producing a thin white border. An eye with prismatic defects will see similar effects.

COLORED GOGGLES devised by the author create a blue-tinted world when the wearer looks to the left and a yellow-tinted world when he looks to the right. If the goggles are worn for several weeks, the eye adapts and the color distortions tend to disappear. Somehow the visual system learns to introduce the proper correction according to whether the eyes are turned to the left or right.

Rays entering at an oblique angle are bent more than rays entering at a right angle. Consequently straight lines appear curved, right angles seem to be acute or obtuse and distances seem to be expanded or foreshortened [*see illustrations on page 109*].

To a subject wearing prism goggles these assorted distortions produce a visual world whose appearance changes drastically as he turns his head. One of our subjects reported that it is "as if the world were made of rubber." When the head is turned to right or left, objects become broader or narrower, producing a "concertina" effect. When the head is moved up or down, objects seem to slant first one way, then the other. We have called this the rocking-chair effect.

Although the distortions arising from prism movement are severe, they might present the eye with a straightforward adaptation problem if the prism were held in rigid alignment with the central axis of the eye. In this case the rays reaching any particular area of the retina would always be deflected by the same amount and would therefore maintain a fixed angular relationship to rays striking adjacent retinal areas. Such a rigid relationship between prism and eye could be achieved if the prism could be worn as a contact lens resting directly on the cornea.

In the Erismann and Gibson experiments, however, as well as in our more recent ones, there is a small distance between the eye and the prism. As a result the eye can, and frequently does, move with respect to the glasses. Two kinds of relative motion arise. In one case the eye can be fixed on a given object while the head and goggles move. In the second case the head and goggles remain fixed while the eye moves. If one analyzes the geometry of the rays striking the retina, one finds that the adaptation problem is much more severe than if the prism and the eye could be held in rigid relationship. Let us consider a single retinal area, for example the important small region called the fovea,

near the center of the retina, where the eye has its maximum acuity. The images reaching the fovea will be distorted more when the eye is looking obliquely through the prism than they will be when it is looking straight ahead. In fact, the distortion changes with every change in the angle that the axis of the eye makes in relation to the prism.

In the accounts of his experiments Gibson neglected the free mobility of the ·eyes with respect to the glasses. Since his experiments were of short duration it is not clear how much adaptation took place among his subjects. He refers specifically only to adaptation to color fringes and to the curvature of lines. The latter is often called the Gibson effect.

In our much longer experiments, which extended the investigations begun by Erismann, a finely differentiated adaptation can be observed. Like Gibson's subjects, ours adapt rather quickly to color fringes and line curvature. We refer to these as constant distortions because they are essentially independent of head and eye movement. After wearing prism goggles for several weeks, however, our subjects also adapt to the more complex variable distortions, which are generated partly by movement of the head and goggles and partly by movement of the eyes behind the goggles.

I should like to stress the distinction between constant and variable distortions. Adaptation to the latter category apparently involves a process more complex than all previously known processes of visual adaptation. Let us suppose that the subject is provided with goggles that have prisms whose bases point to the right. When, at the start of the experiment, the subject turns his head to the left and glances to the right, he sees an image that contracts in its horizontal dimensions. Conversely, when he turns his head to the right and glances to the left, he sees an expanding image. After several weeks, however, an adaptation occurs that counteracts both of these forms of distortion. This process of double adaptation tends ultimately to eliminate the concertina effect. What seems so remarkable is that this takes place in spite of the fact that the fovea and other retinal areas have been exposed to a random mixture of these variable images. Somehow the visual system has learned a general rule: a contracted image must be expanded and an expanded image must be contracted, depending on the respective position of head and eyes.

If, after weeks or months, the subject is allowed to remove his goggles, the adaptation continues to operate when he views the normal world. The result is an apparent squeezing of images when he glances one way and an expansion when he glances the other. It is as if he were looking for the first time through prisms that have an orientation exactly opposite to those he has been wearing for so long. Moreover, all the other distortions, such as the rocking-chair effect, to which his eyes have slowly become adapted now appear in reverse when the goggles are removed. These aftereffects in their turn diminish in strength over a period of days, and the subject finally sees the stable world he used to know.

Both adaptation and aftereffects are vividly reported by our subjects. But in addition we have built devices that provide an objective measurement of the phenomena. These devices, for example, present the subject with a variety of horizontal and vertical lines that he can adjust in orientation and curvature until they look "right." Another device allows the subject to look through prisms and select the one with the strength appropriate to cancel the aftereffects induced by wearing prism goggles.

Let us now consider the adaptation to the color fringes a prism produces. If a prism with base to the right is placed before the eye and one looks at a white card on a black background, one sees a blue border along the left vertical edge of the card and a yellow-orange border along the right edge. The explanation is that the various colors of light reflected from the card and carrying its image no longer overlap precisely after passing through the prism. The result is a whole series of slightly offset colored images: yellow to left of red, green to left of yellow and blue to left of green. Across most of the area of the white card the multiplicity of colored images is not apparent because the various colors recombine to form white light. But at the left edge, where the card meets the black background, the blue image, which is shifted farthest to the left, can be seen as a blue border. Similarly, the red image appears along the right edge. (When the prism is weak, the right border looks yellow or orange rather than red because red and yellow lie so close together in the spectrum.

If one views the world through goggles with their prism bases fixed in the same direction, the rainbow fringes diminish rather quickly in intensity and within a few days virtually disappear. Here again, as a result of adaptation, a complementary aftereffect appears when the glasses are removed. The adaptation that has canceled the blue fringe on objects produces a yellowish fringe and vice versa. This complementary aftereffect, which we call the rainbow phantom, can appear after goggles have been worn for less than a day.

At first consideration the rainbow phantom may not seem surprising. Everyone is familiar with the complementary afterimage that can be induced by staring for about 20 seconds at a brightly colored pattern. Evidently the retinal elements that have been intensively exposed to a given color change in some manner, so that when they are subsequently stimulated by a neutral light, they produce a different signal from adjacent elements that are still fresh. In accordance with the work of the German psychologist Ewald Hering, we ascribe such phenomena to a process of self-regulation. The sensory response becomes shifted in such a way as to make a persisting color stimulus appear more and more neutral. As a result a second color stimulus that had previously seemed neutral now appears shifted along the spectrum; for example, toward the blue-green if the first stimulus was red.

The puzzling aspect of the rainbow phantom is that blue and yellow are themselves complementary colors. Moreover, the small foveal area, which provides most of the eye's sensitivity to color, is randomly exposed to both yellow and blue stimuli during prism-goggle experiments. Consequently the response of the fovea should become equally modified to both colors, and since each is the complement of the other their aftereffects should cancel.

Nevertheless, the rainbow adaptation and its aftereffect, the rainbow phantom, do take place. How can they be explained? As in the case of adaptation to variable distortions of geometry, we must evidently assume a similar kind of multiple (at least double) adaptation for color vision also. The two aspects are the distortion itself and the context or situation in which the distortion occurs. I have already indicated that adaptation to the concertina effect requires the visual system to learn that images contract when one looks in one direction and expand when one looks in the other. In the case of color fringing the distortion is related to a brightness gradient. The subject looking at the world through prisms that have their bases facing to the right unconsciously

learns a new rule: The boundary between a dark field on the left and a light field on the right always has a fringe of blue; when the dark field lies to the right of the light field, the fringe is always yellow. We must assume that the total adaptation process requires simultaneous adjustment to these two conditions. The rainbow phantom, which appears when the goggles are removed, can then be explained as a direct consequence of the complex adaptation process.

Once we had arrived at this explanatory concept, we undertook a further exploration of "situational color adaptation." For this purpose we designed goggles in which each lens was made up of two differently colored half-segments. For example, each lens might be half blue and half yellow [see bottom illustration on page 111]. Wearing such goggles, a subject sees a blue-tinted world when he looks to the left and a yellow-tinted world when he looks to the right. If the two colors are complementary, the situation is somewhat analogous to the rainbow effect of prism goggles. The difference is that the colors are related not to a brightness gradient but to specific positions of the head and eyes; in other words, to a "kinesthetic" gradient.

The experimental results were in accord with those obtained with prism goggles. As before, we found that the visual system adapts to complementary color stimuli so long as the colors are invariably associated with a particular situation—in this case, particular head-and-eye positions. The illustrations on pages 116 and 117 show the results of measuring color adaptation on the first day and on the 60th day of an experiment with blue-yellow glasses. The measurements are obtained through the use of an illuminated window whose color can be varied by turning a dial. The subject first looks at the window through the yellow half of his glasses and turns the dial until the window appears white or neutral in color. To achieve this condition the window must actually be made somewhat blue. The amount of blue light required is automatically recorded. The subject then readjusts the color of the window while looking through the blue half of his glasses. Finally he views the window without glasses, with his eyes turned first to the right and then to the left.

When the subject eventually removes his two-color goggles after wearing them continuously for 60 days, there is no doubt that his visual world is tinged distinctly yellow when he looks in the direction that his goggles had been blue and

blue in the direction that his goggles had been yellow. The movement of the eyes, either to right or left, seems to act as a signal for the foveal area to switch over in its color response, compensating for a yellow image in one case and a blue image in the other.

At this point in our investigations everything seemed reasonably clear, but suddenly a new and mystifying phenomenon appeared, the implications of which have not yet been fully explored. During our prism experiments we had also constructed glasses in which the prisms in front of each eye were mounted with their bases pointed in opposite directions. Similar glasses are regularly prescribed by ophthalmologists to correct strabismus, also known as squinting. People with strabismus are unable to focus both eyes on the same object because the eyes turn either inward or outward; crossed eyes are an example. Ophthalmologists are often reluctant to prescribe corrective prism glasses for strabismus because of their concern that the patient may be disturbed by the distortions and color fringes that such glasses produce.

It was partly this prejudice that prompted our experiments. Because our subjects did not have strabismus they

COLORS ACQUIRE DEPTH if viewed with the eyes partially covered by two cards (left), which exploit the chromatic aber-

found the wearing of "squint glasses" difficult until they learned to squint; that is, to turn their eyes either inward or outward, depending on the orientation of the prisms. We found, nevertheless, that adaptation is possible and that it occurs just as rapidly as it does with our usual prismatic goggles.

Our interest, however, was soon drawn to some special effects produced by squint glasses. Because the prism bases face in opposite directions, the glasses create novel stereoscopic effects in addition to those normally seen in binocular vision. The stereoscopic effects involve geometric figures and, more important, colors. If one looks at a vertical rod with prism glasses of the type described earlier, the rod will seem to bend either to the left or to the right, depending on which way the prism bases face. If the same rod is viewed with squint glasses equipped with prism bases facing outward, the rod will appear to be bent away from the observer. Similarly, plane surfaces will look concave.

But it was the stereoscopic effects involving color that took us most by surprise. On September 10, 1952, the first

day of an extended experiment with squint glasses, one of our subjects described his discovery as follows.

"In the course of a trip through town, I made the following peculiar observations: multicolored posters, traffic signs, people wearing multicolored clothes, and so on, did not appear as before to lie in one plane, but blue seemed to protrude far beyond the object plane, whereas red seemed to recede, depending on whether the background was bright or dark. A woman carrying a red bag slung over her back seemed to be transparent, and the bag to be inside her, somewhere near her stomach.... Most peculiar was a woman wearing a red blouse. She had no upper body, and the red blouse seemed to be following her about a pace behind, moving its empty sleeves in rhythm with the movement of her arms."

After explaining to ourselves this "color-stereo" effect, we were impatient to learn whether or not the subject's eyes would ultimately adapt and restore colored objects to their proper place. The explanation is not difficult. Each prism deflects colors differentially according to wavelength but in opposite

directions since the prism bases are in opposition. When the bases face outward, the blues are deflected outward more than other colors and the eyes must actually converge more to bring blue images into focus than to focus red images, which are deflected less by the two prisms. As a result, blue images seem closer to the observer than red images, and images in other colors seem to lie somewhere between the two, according to wavelength [*see illustration below*].

Again we were surprised by the outcome of the experiment. We have discovered that there is not the slightest adaptation to the color-stereo effect. This was true even in our longest test, in which a subject wore squint glasses for 52 days.

The reader can see the color-stereo effect for himself by viewing the illustration on page 112. Although the effect is more vivid with two prisms, or even one, it can be observed by making use of the chromatic aberration present in the normal eye. The procedure was described almost a century ago by the German physicist Hermann von Helmholtz. One covers the outer half of each

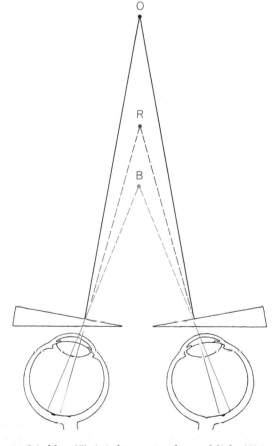

ration of the eye and simulate the effect of looking through prisms whose bases are opposed. The stereo effect works best when strong colors appear against a black background, as on page 112. If light

originating at O is blue (*B*), it is bent more than red light (*R*) in passing through the shielded eye (*center*) or a prism (*right*). The displacement makes the colors appear to be at different depths.

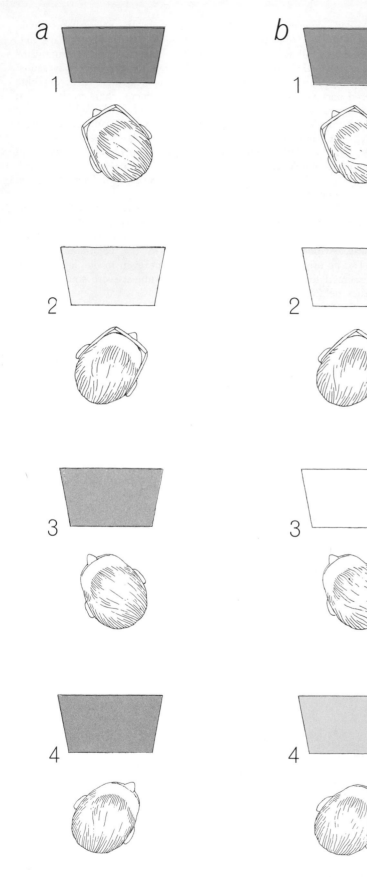

EXPERIMENTS WITH COLORED GOGGLES determine the adaptation to a split-color field, blue on the left, yellow on the right. On the first day of the experiment (*a*) the subject adjusts the color of a glass screen (*see top illustration on opposite page*) until it looks neutral through the yellow half of the goggles (*1*), the blue half (*2*) and with goggles removed (*3 and 4*). After goggles have been worn 60 days the results are different (*b*).

pupil, using two fingers or two pieces of paper. With the outer half of each lens covered, light passes only through the inner halves, which act as if they were prisms with bases facing outward. If the inner halves of the two lenses are covered, a reverse stereo effect takes place and red objects look closer than blue ones. (The reverse effect is difficult to obtain with prisms because it is hard to force the eyes to diverge enough when the bases of the prisms face inward.)

In a small percentage of people the prismatic defects of the eye are large enough so that they can obtain a color-stereo effect even without prisms or the use of Helmholtz' procedure. A sensitive check for such defects can be made with the help of the green-red figure in the middle of page 111. The figure is to be viewed with each eye separately. To a normal eye the green and red halves of the figure meet cleanly, without any noticeable peculiarity. A defective eye, however, will see either a thin black line or a thin white line where the two colors meet. A black line indicates that the green area is being displaced slightly farther to the left than the red, as it would be by a prism having its base to the right. A white line indicates that the green is being deflected to the right as by a prism with base to the left. When the green shifts to the right, it overlaps the red image, and the combination of green and red reflected light creates a white boundary. People with prismatic defects of the eye have a certain advantage over people with normal eyes, for they can differentiate colors not only by hue but also by the color-stereo effect.

Although it may not be immediately obvious, the color-stereo effect does not depend on the ability of the eye to see color. Like a prism, the lens of the eye bends light according to wavelength regardless of the hue we have come to associate with any particular wavelength. For example, if one photographed the colored pattern on page 112 in black and white using a stereoscopic camera equipped with a suitably oriented prism in front of each lens, one would obtain two pictures that would look three-dimensional when viewed through a stereoscope. The colored squares of the pattern would appear in various shades of gray, lying at various depths according to the wavelength of the original colors. It follows from this that one could enable a color-blind person to discriminate colors by providing him with prism glasses. He could be taught, for example, that the green in a traffic light will look closer to him than

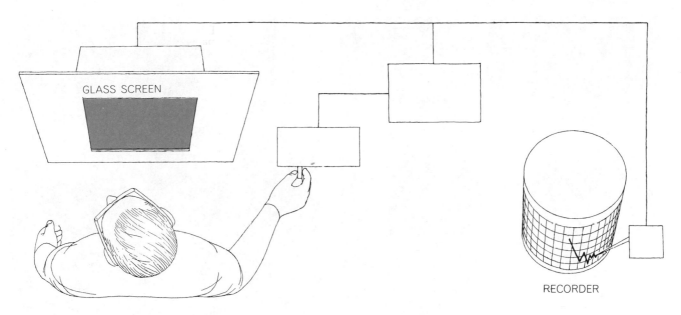

ADAPTATION-MEASURING DEVICE consists of a glass screen or panel whose color can be adjusted by the test subject. The setting of the color-selection dial is automatically transmitted to a pen recorder (*far right*). The subject is viewing the window through the yellow half of goggles that are half yellow and half blue, as shown at the bottom of page 6. His task is to make the window look neutral gray in color, which requires, in this case, that it be adjusted to look blue as seen by the normal eye.

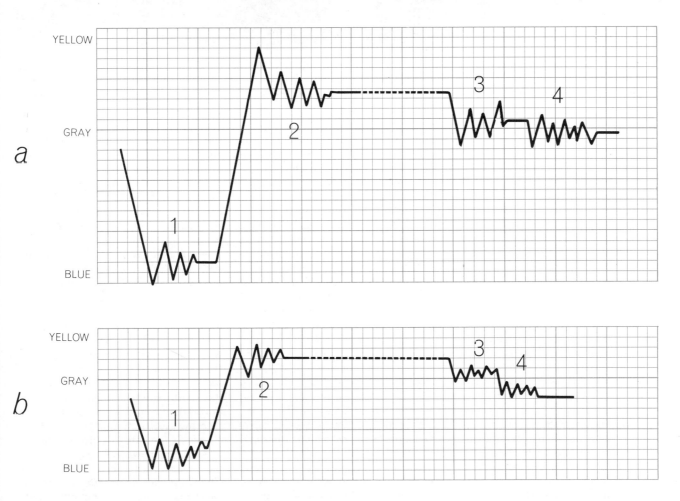

RESULTS OF COLOR-ADAPTATION TEST are shown by chart records made on the first day (*a*) and 60th day (*b*) of the experiment with blue-yellow goggles. On the first day the window of the test apparatus must be made strongly blue (*1*) to compensate for the yellow tint of the goggles and yellow (*2*) to compensate for the blue tint. When the goggles are removed after several hours, the aftereffects are negligible (*3, 4*). By the 60th day, however, the eye has adapted significantly to the color distortions produced by the goggles (*b1, b2*), and when the goggles are removed, the complementary aftereffects are significant (*b3, b4*).

REAR-LOOKING "GOGGLES," actually a mirror device, were used in early experiments by Theodor Erismann at the University of Innsbruck. Here Erismann is testing the responses of a subject.

INVERTING GOGGLES, which transposed up and down, were also devised by Erismann. This subject is balancing on a springboard to help relate the upside-down world to his bodily sensations.

yellow and that yellow will look closer than red.

The color-stereo effect may also have general implications for biology. It has always seemed strange that in the eyes of most animals, including man, the fovea lies to one side of the optical axis of the lens system. This lack of alignment may combine with the eye's chromatic aberration to produce prismatic effects that are opposite for the left and right eyes, thereby producing a weak color-stereo effect. When we consider that these defects—off-center fovea and chromatic aberration—have persisted through millions of generations of animals without being "corrected" by evolution, we cannot refrain from speculating that the defects may have functional utility. Perhaps in the development of the vertebrate eye the color-stereo effect provided the first form of color discrimination, the colors being associated not with hue but with subtle differences in the depth of images. As a matter of fact, cats, mice and other animals, which are known to be color-blind, sometimes puzzle psychologists by their apparent ability to distinguish a few strong colors in visual tests. Although this color sensitivity is likely to be demonstrated by only a few animals in any experimental group, the ability cannot be ignored, and the explanation may well be that the unusual animals possess a heightened sensitivity to the color-stereo effect.

My colleague Anton Hajos can be credited with showing, by rigorous measurement, that not the slightest adaptation to the color-stereo effect occurs among subjects wearing squint glasses. He also conceived the idea of intensifying the stereo effect to see if it heightened the sensation of color. To test this idea we were fortunate to find in Innsbruck a man who had lost his color vision as the result of an accident. When he put on a pair of our squint glasses, he reported that he was instantly able to see all the colors he had not seen for years. When he removed the glasses, the colors disappeared again. We are carrying on a further investigation of this and related cases.

What shall we make of the finding that the eye adapts rather readily to various intense distortions of geometry and color but fails totally to adapt to the type of distortion embodied in the color-stereo effect? One possible explanation is that in all cases where adaptation occurs the eye is provided with certain systematic clues as to the nature of the distortion. Straight lines always curve in the same direction; blue or yellow color fringes occur in fixed relation to light-dark boundaries; blue and yellow glasses present the eye with color fields that remain consistently either on the right or on the left; even the rubber world is rubbery in a consistent way. The color-stereo effect, however, presents the visual mechanism with a random and nearly unpredictable assortment of displaced images. As the focus of the eye shifts from one point to another, it is just as likely to encounter one color as another, and, depending on wavelength, brightness and background, the stereoscopic position of the colored image is shifted forward or back. Although the eye might conceivably learn to correlate color and displacement and thereby use the former as a basis for correcting the latter, the task is evidently beyond the power of the eye's adaptation mechanism. There is, however, an alternative possibility: the color-stereo effect may represent a primitive way of identifying colors. The failure of the visual system to adapt to this effect, when presented in exaggerated form by squint glasses, may be evidence that spatial displacement of colors indeed played such an evolutionary role.

13

THE SPLIT BRAIN IN MAN

MICHAEL S. GAZZANIGA
August 1967

The brain of the higher animals, including man, is a double organ, consisting of right and left hemispheres connected by an isthmus of nerve tissue called the corpus callosum. Some 15 years ago Ronald E. Myers and R. W. Sperry, then at the University of Chicago, made a surprising discovery: When this connection between the two halves of the cerebrum was cut, each hemisphere functioned independently as if it were a complete brain. The phenomenon was first investigated in a cat in which not only the brain but also the optic chiasm, the crossover of the optic nerves, was divided, so that visual information from the left eye was dispatched only to the left brain and information from the right eye only to the right brain. Working on a problem with one eye, the animal could respond normally and learn to perform a task; when that eye was covered and the same problem was presented to the other eye, the animal evinced no recognition of the problem and had to learn it again from the beginning with the other half of the brain.

The finding introduced entirely new questions in the study of brain mechanisms. Was the corpus callosum responsible for integration of the operations of the two cerebral hemispheres in the intact brain? Did it serve to keep each hemisphere informed about what was going on in the other? To put the question another way, would cutting the corpus callosum literally result in the right hand not knowing what the left was doing? To what extent were the two half-brains actually independent when they were separated? Could they have separate thoughts, even separate emotions?

Such questions have been pursued by Sperry and his co-workers in a wide-ranging series of animal studies at the California Institute of Technology over the past decade [see "The Great Cerebral Commissure," by R. W. Sperry; SCIENTIFIC AMERICAN Offprint 74]. Recently these questions have been investigated in human patients who underwent the brain-splitting operation for medical reasons. The demonstration in experimental animals that sectioning of the corpus callosum did not seriously impair mental faculties had encouraged surgeons to resort to this operation for people afflicted with uncontrollable epilepsy. The hope was to confine a seizure to one hemisphere. The operation proved to be remarkably successful; curiously there is an almost total elimination of all attacks, including unilateral ones. It is as if the intact callosum had served in these patients to facilitate seizure activity.

This article is a brief survey of investigations Sperry and I have carried out at Cal Tech over the past five years with some of these patients. The operations were performed by P. J. Vogel and J. E. Bogen of the California College of Medicine. Our studies date back to 1961, when the first patient, a 48-year-old war veteran, underwent the operation: cutting of the corpus callosum and other commissure structures connecting the two halves of the cerebral cortex [see illustration on page 121]. As of today 10 patients have had the operation, and we have examined four thoroughly over a long period with many tests.

From the beginning one of the most striking observations was that the operation produced no noticeable change in the patients' temperament, personality or general intelligence. In the first case the patient could not speak for 30 days after the operation, but he then recovered his speech. More typical was the third case: on awaking from the surgery the patient quipped that he had a "splitting headache," and in his still drowsy state he was able to repeat the tongue twister "Peter Piper picked a peck of pickled peppers."

Close observation, however, soon revealed some changes in the patients' everyday behavior. For example, it could be seen that in moving about and responding to sensory stimuli the patients favored the right side of the body, which is controlled by the dominant left half of the brain. For a considerable period after the operation the left side of the body rarely showed spontaneous activity, and the patient generally did not respond to stimulation of that side: when he brushed against something with his left side he did not notice that he had done so, and when an object was placed in his left hand he generally denied its presence.

More specific tests identified the main features of the bisected-brain syndrome. One of these tests examined responses to visual stimulation. While the patient fixed his gaze on a central point on a board, spots of light were flashed (for a tenth of a second) in a row across the board that spanned both the left and the right half of his visual field. The patient was asked to tell what he had seen. Each patient reported that lights had been flashed in the right half of the visual field. When lights were flashed only in the left half of the field, however, the patients generally denied having seen any lights. Since the right side of the visual field is normally projected to the left hemisphere of the brain and the left field to the right hemisphere, one might have concluded that in these patients with divided brains the right hemisphere was in effect blind. We found, however, that this was not the case when the patients were directed to point to the lights that had flashed instead of giving a verbal report. With this manual response they were able to indicate when lights had

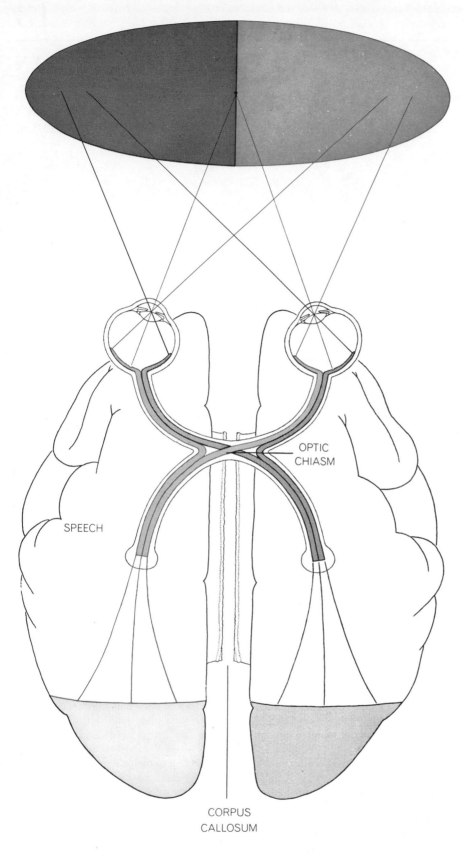

OPTIC CHIASM

SPEECH

CORPUS CALLOSUM

VISUAL INPUT to bisected brain was limited to one hemisphere by presenting information only in one visual field. The right and left fields of view are projected, via the optic chiasm, to the left and right hemispheres of the brain respectively. If a person fixes his gaze on a point, therefore, information to the left of the point goes only to the right hemisphere and information to the right of the point goes to the left hemisphere. Stimuli in the left visual field cannot be described by a split-brain patient because of the disconnection between the right hemisphere and the speech center, which is in the left hemisphere.

been flashed in the left visual field, and perception with the brain's right hemisphere proved to be almost equal to perception with the left. Clearly, then, the patients' failure to report the right hemisphere's perception verbally was due to the fact that the speech centers of the brain are located in the left hemisphere.

Our tests of the patients' ability to recognize objects by touch at first resulted in the same general finding. When the object was held in the right hand, from which sensory information is sent to the left hemisphere, the patient was able to name and describe the object. When it was held in the left hand (from which information goes primarily to the right hemisphere), the patient could not describe the object verbally but was able to identify it in a nonverbal test—matching it, for example, to the same object in a varied collection of things. We soon realized, however, that each hemisphere receives, in addition to the main input from the opposite side of the body, some input from the same side. This "ipsilateral" input is crude; it is apparently good mainly for "cuing in" the hemisphere as to the presence or absence of stimulation and relaying fairly gross information about the location of a stimulus on the surface of the body. It is unable, as a rule, to relay information concerning the qualitative nature of an object.

Tests of motor control in these split-brain patients revealed that the left hemisphere of the brain exercised normal control over the right hand but had less than full control of the left hand (for instance, it was poor at directing individual movements of the fingers). Similarly, the right hemisphere had full control of the left hand but not of the right hand. When the two hemispheres were in conflict, dictating different movements for the same hand, the hemisphere on the side opposite the hand generally took charge and overruled the orders of the side of the brain with the weaker control. In general the motor findings in the human patients were much the same as those in split-brain monkeys.

We come now to the main question on which we centered our studies, namely how the separation of the hemispheres affects the mental capacities of the human brain. For these psychological tests we used two different devices. One was visual: a picture or written information was flashed (for a tenth of a second) in either the right or the left visual field, so that the information was transmitted only to the left or to the right brain hemisphere [see illustration on page 122]. The other type of test was tactile: an object was placed out of view in the patient's right or left hand, again for the purpose of conveying the information to just one hemisphere—the hemisphere on the side opposite the hand.

When the information (visual or tactile) was presented to the dominant left hemisphere, the patients were able to deal with and describe it quite normally, both orally and in writing. For example, when a picture of a spoon was shown in the right visual field or a spoon was placed in the right hand, all the patients readily identified and described it. They were able to read out written messages and to perform problems in calculation that were presented to the left hemisphere.

In contrast, when the same information was presented to the right hemisphere, it failed to elicit such spoken or written responses. A picture transmitted to the right hemisphere evoked either a haphazard guess or no verbal response at all. Similarly, a pencil placed in the left hand (behind a screen that cut off vision) might be called a can opener or a cigarette lighter, or the patient might not even attempt to describe it. The verbal guesses presumably came not from the right hemisphere but from the left, which had no perception of the object but might attempt to identify it from indirect clues.

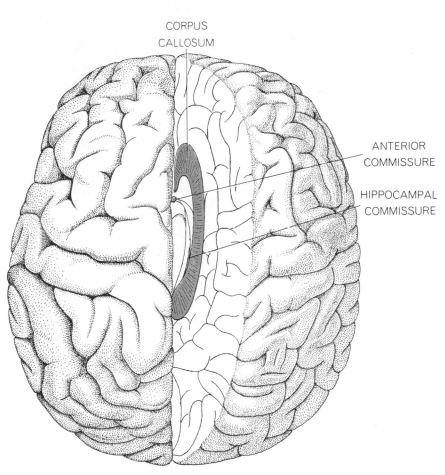

TWO HEMISPHERES of the human brain are divided by neurosurgeons to control epileptic seizures. In this top view of the brain the right hemisphere is retracted and the corpus callosum and other commissures, or connectors, that are generally cut are shown in color.

Did this impotence of the right hemisphere mean that its surgical separation from the left had reduced its mental powers to an imbecilic level? The earlier tests of its nonverbal capacities suggested that this was almost certainly not so. Indeed, when we switched to asking for nonverbal answers to the visual and tactile information presented in our new psychological tests, the right hemisphere in several patients showed considerable capacity for accurate performance. For example, when a picture of a spoon was presented to the right hemisphere, the patients were able to feel around with the left hand among a varied group of objects (screened from sight) and select a spoon as a match for the picture. Furthermore, when they were shown a picture of a cigarette they succeeded in selecting an ashtray, from a group of 10 objects that did not include a cigarette, as the article most closely related to the picture. Oddly enough, however, even after their correct response, and while they were holding the spoon or the ashtray in their left hand, they were unable to name or describe the object or the picture. Evidently the left hemisphere was completely divorced, in perception and knowledge, from the right.

Other tests showed that the right hemisphere did possess a certain amount of language comprehension. For example, when the word "pencil" was flashed to the right hemisphere, the patients were able to pick out a pencil from a group of unseen objects with the left hand. And when a patient held an object in the left hand (out of view), although he could not say its name or describe it, he was later able to point to a card on which the name of the object was written.

In one particularly interesting test the word "heart" was flashed across the center of the visual field, with the "he" portion to the left of the center and "art" to the right. Asked to tell what the word was, the patients would say they had seen "art"—the portion projected to the left brain hemisphere (which is responsible for speech). Curiously when, after "heart" had been flashed in the same way, the patients were asked to point with the left hand to one of two cards— "art" or "he"—to identify the word they had seen, they invariably pointed to "he." The experiment showed clearly that both hemispheres had simultaneously observed the portions of the word available to them and that in this particular case the right hemisphere, when it had had the opportunity to express itself, had prevailed over the left.

Because an auditory input to one ear goes to both sides of the brain, we conducted tests for the comprehension of words presented audibly to the right hemisphere not by trying to limit the original input but by limiting the ability to answer to the right hemisphere. This was done most easily by having a patient use his left hand to retrieve, from a grab bag held out of view, an object named by the examiner. We found that the patients could easily retrieve such objects as a watch, comb, marble or coin. The object to be retrieved did not even have to be named; it might simply be described or alluded to. For example, the command "Retrieve the fruit monkeys like best" results in the patients' pulling out a banana from a grab bag full of plastic fruit; at the command "Sunkist sells a lot of them" the patients retrieve an orange. We knew that touch information from the left hand was going exclusively to the right hemisphere because moments later, when the patients were asked to name various pieces of fruit placed in the left hand, they were unable to score above a chance level.

The upper limit of linguistic abilities in each hemisphere varies from subject to subject. In one case there was little or no evidence for language abilities in the right hemisphere, whereas in the other three the amount and extent of the capacities varied. The most adept patient showed some evidence of even being able to spell simple words by placing plastic letters on a table with his left hand. The subject was told to spell a word such as "pie," and the examiner then placed the three appropriate letters, one at a time in a random order, in his left hand to be arranged on the table. The patient was able to spell even more abstract words such as "how," "what" and "the." In another test three or four letters were placed in a pile, again out of view, to be felt with the left hand. The letters available in each trial would spell only one word, and the instructions to the subject were "Spell a word." The patient was able to spell such words as "cup" and "love." Yet after he had completed this task, the patient was unable to name the word he had just spelled!

The possibility that the right hemisphere has not only some language but even some speech capabilities cannot be ruled out, although at present there is no firm evidence for this. It would not be surprising to discover that the patients are capable of a few simple exclamatory remarks, particularly when under emotional stress. The possibility also remains, of course, that speech of some type could be trained into the right hemisphere. Tests aimed at this question, however, would have to be closely scrutinized and controlled.

The reason is that here, as in many of the tests, "cross-cuing" from one hemisphere to the other could be held responsible for any positive findings. We had a case of such cross-cuing during a series of tests of whether the right hemisphere could respond verbally to simple red or green stimuli. At first, after either a red or a green light was flashed to the right hemisphere, the patient would guess the color at a chance level, as might be expected if the speech mechanism is solely represented in the left hemisphere. After a few trials, however, the score improved whenever the examiner allowed a second guess.

We soon caught on to the strategy the patient used. If a red light was flashed and the patient by chance guessed red, he would stick with that answer. If the flashed light was red and the patient by chance guessed green, he would frown,

shake his head and then say, "Oh no, I meant red." What was happening was that the right hemisphere saw the red light and heard the left hemisphere make the guess "green." Knowing that the answer was wrong, the right hemisphere precipitated a frown and a shake of the head, which in turn cued in the left hemisphere to the fact that the answer was wrong and that it had better correct itself! We have learned that this cross-cuing mechanism can become extremely refined. The realization that the neurological patient has various strategies at his command emphasizes how difficult it is to obtain a clear neurological description of a human being with brain damage.

Is the language comprehension by the right hemisphere that the patients exhibited in these tests a normal capability of that hemisphere or was it acquired by learning after their operation, perhaps during the course of the experiments themselves? The issue is difficult to decide. We must remember that we are examining a half of the human brain, a system easily capable of learning from a single trial in a test. We do know that the right hemisphere is decidedly inferior to the left in its overall command of language. We have established, for instance, that although the right hemisphere can respond to a concrete noun such as "pencil," it cannot do as well with verbs; patients are unable to re-

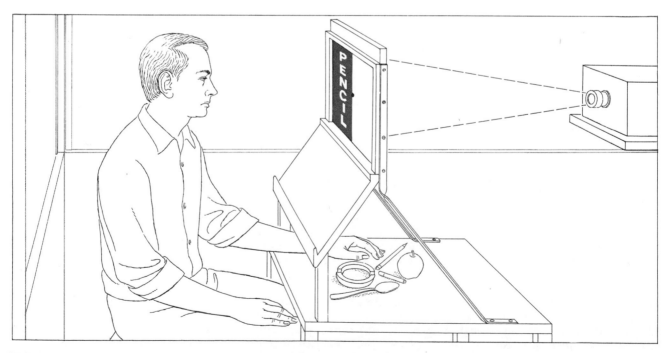

RESPONSE TO VISUAL STIMULUS is tested by flashing a word or a picture of an object on a translucent screen. The examiner first checks the subject's gaze to be sure it is fixed on a dot that marks the center of the visual field. The examiner may call for a verbal response—reading the flashed word, for example—or for a non-verbal one, such as picking up the object that is named from among a number of things spread on the table. The objects are hidden from the subject's view so that they can be identified only by touch.

spond appropriately to simple printed instructions, such as "smile" or "frown," when these words are flashed to the right hemisphere, nor can they point to a picture that corresponds to a flashed verb. Some of our recent studies at the University of California at Santa Barbara also indicate that the right hemisphere has a very poorly developed grammar; it seems to be incapable of forming the plural of a given word, for example.

In general, then, the extent of language present in the adult right hemisphere in no way compares with that present in the left hemisphere or, for that matter, with the extent of language present in the child's right hemisphere. Up to the age of four or so, it would appear from a variety of neurological observations, the right hemisphere is about as proficient in handling language as the left. Moreover, studies of the child's development of language, particularly with respect to grammar, strongly suggest that the foundations of grammar—a ground plan for language, so to speak—are somehow inherent in the human organism and are fully realized between the ages of two and three. In other words, in the young child each hemisphere is about equally developed with respect to language and speech function. We are thus faced with the interesting question of why the right hemisphere at an early age and stage of development possesses substantial language capacity whereas at a more adult stage it possesses a rather poor capacity. It is difficult indeed to conceive of the underlying neurological mechanism that would allow for the establishment of a capacity of a high order in a particular hemisphere on a temporary basis. The implication is that during maturation the processes and systems active in making this capacity manifest are somehow inhibited and dismantled in the right hemisphere and allowed to reside only in the dominant left hemisphere.

Yet the right hemisphere is not in all respects inferior or subordinate to the left. Tests have demonstrated that it excels the left in some specialized functions. As an example, tests by us and by Bogen have shown that in these patients the left hand is capable of arranging blocks to match a pictured design and of drawing a cube in three dimensions, whereas the right hand, deprived of instructions from the right hemisphere, could not perform either of these tasks.

It is of interest to note, however, that although the patients (our first subject in particular) could not execute such tasks

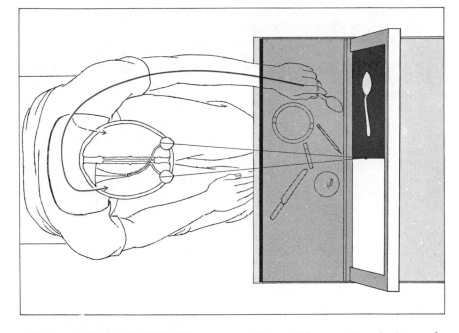

VISUAL-TACTILE ASSOCIATION is performed by a split-brain patient. A picture of a spoon is flashed to the right hemisphere; with the left hand he retrieves a spoon from behind the screen. The touch information from the left hand projects (*color*) mainly to the right hemisphere, but a weak "ipsilateral" component goes to the left hemisphere. This is usually not enough to enable him to say (using the left hemisphere) what he has picked up.

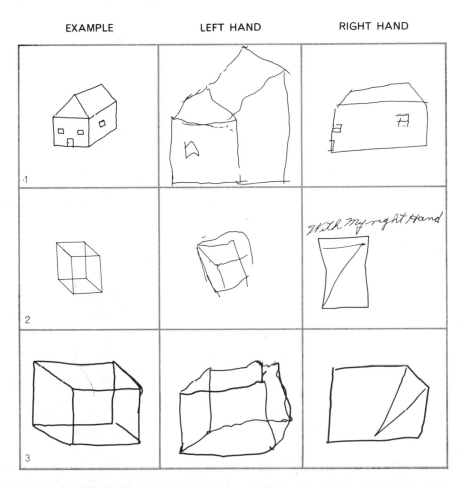

EXAMPLE	LEFT HAND	RIGHT HAND

"VISUAL-CONSTRUCTIONAL" tasks are handled better by the right hemisphere. This was seen most clearly in the first patient, who had poor ipsilateral control of his right hand. Although right-handed, he could copy the examples only with his left hand.

with the right hand, they were capable of matching a test stimulus to the correct design when it appeared among five related patterns presented in their right visual field. This showed that the dominant left hemisphere is capable of discriminating between correct and incorrect stimuli. Since it is also true that the patients have no motor problems with their right hand, the patients' inability to perform these tasks must reflect a breakdown of an integrative process somewhere between the sensory system and the motor system.

We found that in certain other mental processes the right hemisphere is on a par with the left. In particular, it can independently generate an emotional reaction. In one of our experiments exploring the matter we would present a series of ordinary objects and then suddenly flash a picture of a nude woman. This evoked an amused reaction regardless of whether the picture was presented to the left hemisphere or to the right. When the picture was flashed to the left hemisphere of a female patient, she laughed and verbally identified the picture as a nude. When it was later presented to the right hemisphere, she said in reply to a question that she saw nothing, but almost immediately a sly smile spread over her face and she began to chuckle. Asked what she was laughing at, she said: "I don't know...nothing...oh—that funny machine." Although the right hemisphere could not describe what it had seen, the sight nevertheless elicited an emotional response like the one evoked from the left hemisphere.

Taken together, our studies seem to demonstrate conclusively that in a split-brain situation we are really dealing with two brains, each separately capable of mental functions of a high order. This implies that the two brains should have twice as large a span of attention—that is, should be able to handle twice as much information—as a normal whole brain. We have not yet tested this precisely in human patients, but E. D. Young and I have found that a split-brain monkey can indeed deal with nearly twice as much information as a normal animal [see illustration below]. We have so far determined also that brain-bisected patients can carry out two tasks as fast as a normal person can do one.

Just how does the corpus callosum of the intact brain combine and integrate the perceptions and knowledge of the two cerebral hemispheres? This has been investigated recently by Giovanni Berlucchi, Giacomo Rizzolati and me at the Istituto di Fisiologia Umana in Pisa. We made recordings of neural activity in the posterior part of the callosum of the cat with the hope of relating the responses of that structure to stimulation of the animal's visual fields. The kinds of responses recorded turned out to be similar to those observed in the visual cortex of the cat. In other words, the results suggest that visual pattern information can be transmitted through the callosum. This finding militates against the notion that learning and memory are transferred across the callosum, as has usually been suggested. Instead, it looks as though in animals with an intact callosum a copy of the visual world as seen in one hemisphere is sent over to the other, with the result that both hemispheres can learn together a discrimination presented to just one hemisphere. In the split-brain animal this extension of the visual pathway is cut off; this would explain rather simply why no learning proceeds in the visually isolated hemisphere and why it has to learn the discrimination from scratch.

Curiously, however, the neural activity in the callosum came only in response to stimuli at the midline of the visual field. This finding raises difficult questions. How can it be reconciled with the well-established observation that the left hemisphere of a normal person can give a running description of all the visual information presented throughout the entire half-field projected to the right hemisphere? For this reason alone one is wearily driven back to the conclusion that somewhere and somehow all or part of the callosum transmits not only a visual scene but also a complicated neural code of a higher order.

All the evidence indicates that separation of the hemispheres creates two independent spheres of consciousness within a single cranium, that is to say, within a single organism. This conclusion is disturbing to some people who view consciousness as an indivisible property of the human brain. It seems premature to others, who insist that the capacities revealed thus far for the right hemisphere are at the level of an automaton. There is, to be sure, hemispheric inequality in the present cases, but it may well be a characteristic of the individuals we have studied. It is entirely possible that if a human brain were divided in a very young person, both hemispheres could as a result separately and independently develop mental functions of a high order at the level attained only in the left hemisphere of normal individuals.

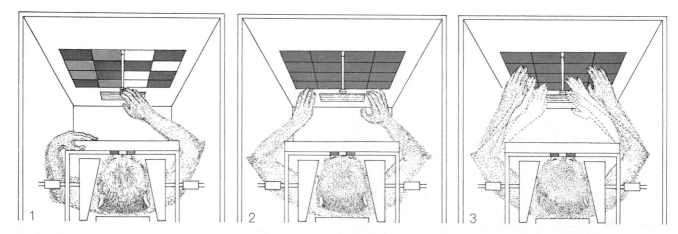

SPLIT-BRAIN MONKEYS can handle more visual information than normal animals. When the monkey pulls a knob (1), eight of the 16 panels light momentarily. The monkey must then start at the bottom and punch the lights that were lit and no others (2). With the panels lit for 600 milliseconds normal monkeys get up to the third row from the bottom before forgetting which panels were lit (3). Split-brain monkeys complete the entire task with the panels lit only 200 milliseconds. The monkeys look at the panels through filters; since the optic chiasm is cut in these animals, the filters allow each hemisphere to see the colored panels on one side only.

14

THE PHYSIOLOGY OF MEDITATION

ROBERT KEITH WALLACE AND HERBERT BENSON
February 1972

How capable is the human organism of adjusting to psychologically disturbing changes in the environment? Our technological age is probably testing this capacity more severely than it was ever tested in the past. The impact of the rapid changes—unprecedented in scale, complexity and novelty—that technology is bringing about in our world seems to be having a deleterious effect on the mental and physical health of modern man. Some of the common disorders of our age, notably "nervous stomach" and high blood pressure, may well be attributable in part to the uncertainties that are burgeoning in our environment and daily lives. Since the environment is not likely to grow less complex or more predictable, it seems only prudent to devote some investigative attention to the human body's resources for coping with the vicissitudes of the environment.

There are in fact several ways in which an individual can control his physiological reactions to psychological events. Among the claims for such control the most notable have come from practitioners of meditation systems of the East: yoga and Zen Buddhism. This article will review and discuss recent studies of the effects of meditation that have been made by ourselves and by other investigators.

Yogis in India have long been reputed to perform phenomenal feats such as voluntarily stopping the heartbeat or surviving for extended periods in an "airtight" pit or in extreme cold without food or in a distorted physical posture. One of the first investigators to look into these claims in an objective way was a French cardiologist, Thérèse Brosse, who went to India in 1935 equipped with a portable electrocardiograph so that she could monitor the activity of the heart. Brosse concluded from her tests that one of her subjects actually was able to stop his heart. In 1957 two American physiologists, M. A. Wenger of the University of California at Los Angeles and B. K. Bagchi of the University of Michigan Medical School, conducted a more extensive investigation in collaboration with B. K. Anand of the All-India Institute of Medical Sciences in New Delhi. None of the yogis they studied, with more elaborate equipment than Brosse had used, showed a capability for stopping the heart. Wenger and Bagchi concluded that the disappearance of the signal of heart activity in Brosse's electrocardiogram was probably an artifact, since the heart impulse is sometimes obscured by electrical signals from contracting muscles of the thorax. (In attempting to stop the heart the yogis usually performed what is called the Valsalva maneuver, which increases the pressure within the chest; it can be done by holding one's breath and straining downward.) Wenger, Bagchi and Anand did find, however, that some of the yogis could slow both heartbeat and respiration rate.

Reports of a number of other investigations by researchers in the 1950's and 1960's indicated that meditation as practiced by yoga or Zen meditators could produce a variety of physiological effects. One of the demonstrated effects was reduction of the rate of metabolism. Examining Zen monks in Japan who had had many years of experience in the practice of deep meditation, Y. Sugi and K. Akutsu found that during meditation the subjects decreased their consumption of oxygen by about 20 percent and reduced their output of carbon dioxide. These signs of course constitute evidence of a slowing of metabolism. In New Delhi, Anand and two collaborators, G. S. Chhina and Baldeu Singh, made a similar finding in examination of a yoga practitioner; confined in a sealed metal box, the meditating yogi markedly reduced his oxygen consumption and carbon dioxide elimination.

These tests strongly indicated that meditation produced the effects through control of an "involuntary" mechanism in the body, presumably the autonomic nervous system. The reduction of carbon dioxide elimination might have been accounted for by a recognizably voluntary action of the subject—slowing the breathing—but such action should not markedly affect the uptake of oxygen by the body tissues. Consequently it was a reasonable supposition that the drop in oxygen consumption, reflecting a decrease in the need for inhaled oxygen, must be due to modification of a process not subject to manipulation in the usual sense.

Explorations with the electroencephalograph showed further that meditation produced changes in the electrical activity of the brain. In studies of Zen monks A. Kasamatsu and T. Hirai of the University of Tokyo found that during meditation with their eyes half-open the monks developed a predominance of alpha waves—the waves that ordinarily become prominent when a person is thoroughly relaxed with his eyes closed. In the meditating monks the alpha waves increased in amplitude and regularity, particularly in the frontal and central regions of the brain. Subjects with a great deal of experience in meditation showed other changes: the alpha waves slowed from the usual frequency of nine to 12 cycles per second to seven or eight cycles per second, and rhythmical theta waves at six to seven cycles per second appeared. Anand and other investigators in India found that yogis, like the Zen monks, also showed a heightening of alpha activity during meditation. N. N. Das and H. Gastaut, in an electroencephalographic examination of seven yogis,

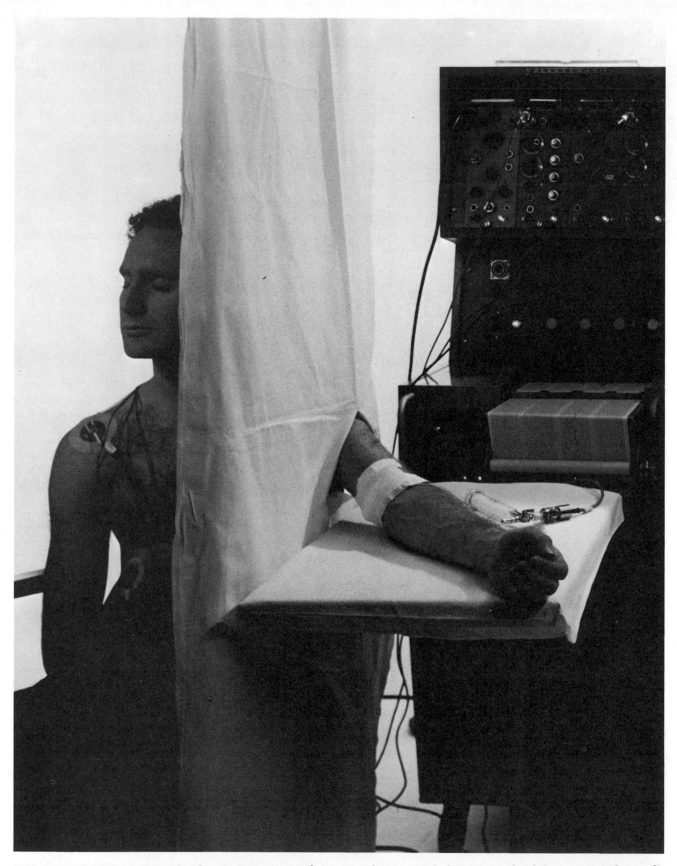

ISOLATED SUBJECT is connected with an instrument array that continuously records such physiological variables as heart rate and blood pressure. A catheter in the subject's left arm draws samples of arterial blood at 10-minute intervals; these samples are analyzed for oxygen and carbon dioxide content and for blood acidity and blood-lactate level. The subject's arm is screened from his view to minimize the psychological effects of blood withdrawal. Each sub-

ject first sat quietly for an interval and then was invited to meditate for a 30-minute period. At the end of the period the subject was asked to stop meditating but to continue sitting quietly during a further recording interval. Thirty-six qualified "transcendental" meditators from 17 to 41 years old volunteered as subjects for the study, which was conducted both at the Harvard Medical Unit of the Boston City Hospital and at the University of California at Irvine.

observed that as the meditation progressed the alpha waves gave way to fast-wave activity at the rate of 40 to 45 cycles per second and these waves in turn subsided with a return of the slow alpha and theta waves.

Another physiological response tested by the early investigators was the resistance of the skin to an electric current. This measure is thought by some to reflect the level of "anxiety": a decrease in skin resistance representing greater anxiety; a rise in resistance, greater relaxation. It turns out that meditation increases the skin resistance in yogis and somewhat stabilizes the resistance in Zen meditators.

We decided to undertake a systematic study of the physiological "effects," or, as we prefer to say, the physiological correlates, of meditation. In our review of the literature we had found a bewildering range of variation in the cases and the results of the different studies. The subjects varied greatly in their meditation techniques, their expertise and their performance. This was not so true of the Zen practitioners, all of whom employ the same technique, but it was quite characteristic of the practice of yoga, which has many more adherents. The state called yoga (meaning "union") has a generally agreed definition: a "higher" consciousness achieved through a fully rested and relaxed body and a fully awake and relaxed mind. In the endeavor to arrive at this state, however, the practitioners in India use a variety of approaches. Some seek the goal through strenuous physical exercise; others concentrate on controlling a particular overt function, such as the respiratory rate; others focus on purely mental processes, based on some device for concentration or contemplation. The difference in technique may produce a dichotomy of physiological effects; for instance, whereas those who use contemplation show a decrease in oxygen consumption, those who use physical exercise to achieve yoga show an oxygen-consumption increase. Moreover, since most of the techniques require rigorous discipline and long training, the range in abilities is wide, and it is difficult to know who is an "expert" or how expert he may be. Obviously all these complications made the problem of selecting suitable subjects for our systematic study a formidable one.

Fortunately one widely practiced yoga technique is so well standardized that it enabled us to carry out large-scale studies under reasonably uniform conditions. This technique, called "transcendental meditation," was developed by

Maharishi Mahesh Yogi and is taught by an organization of instructors whom he personally qualifies. The technique does not require intense concentration or any form of rigorous mental or physical control, and it is easily learned, so that all subjects who have been through a relatively short period of training are "experts." The training does not involve devotion to any specific beliefs or life-style. It consists simply in two daily sessions of practice, each for 15 to 20 minutes.

The practitioner sits in a comfortable position with eyes closed. By a systematic method that he has been taught, he perceives a "suitable" sound or thought. Without attempting to concentrate specifically on this cue, he allows his mind to experience it freely, and his thinking, as the practitioners themselves report, rises to a "finer and more creative level in an easy and natural manner." More than 90,000 men and women in the U.S. are said to have received instruction in transcendental meditation by the organization teaching it. Hence large numbers of uniformly trained subjects were available for our studies.

What follows is a report of the detailed measurements made on a group of 36 subjects. Some were observed at the Thorndike Memorial Laboratory, a part

of the Harvard Medical Unit at the Boston City Hospital. The others were observed at the University of California at Irvine. Twenty-eight were males and eight were females; they ranged in age from 17 to 41. Their experience in meditation ranged from less than a month to nine years, with the majority having had two to three years of experience.

During each test the subject served as his own control, spending part of the session in meditation and part in a normal, nonmeditative state. Devices for continuous measurement of blood pressure, heart rate, rectal temperature, skin resistance and electroencephalographic events were attached to the subject, and during the period of measurement samples were taken at 10-minute intervals for analysis of oxygen consumption, carbon dioxide elimination and other parameters. The subject sat in a chair. After a 30-minute period of habituation, measurements were started and continued for three periods: 20 to 30 minutes of a quiet, premeditative state, then 20 to 30 minutes of meditation, and finally 20 to 30 minutes after the subject was asked to stop meditating.

The measurements of oxygen consumption and carbon dioxide elimination confirmed in precise detail what had

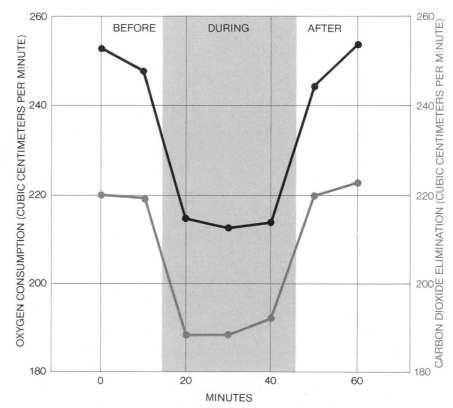

EFFECT OF MEDITATION on the subjects' oxygen consumption (*black*) and carbon dioxide elimination (*color*) was recorded in 20 and 15 cases respectively. After the subjects were invited to meditate both rates decreased markedly (*colored area*). Consumption and elimination returned to the premeditation level soon after the subjects stopped meditating.

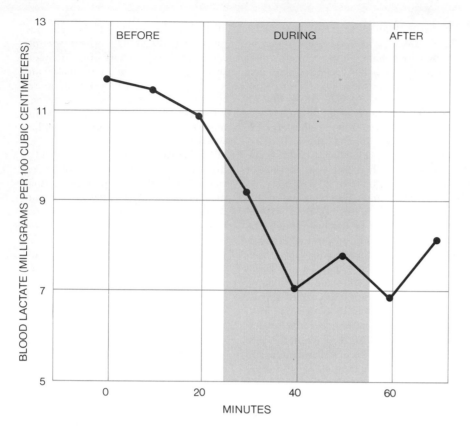

RAPID DECLINE in the concentration of blood lactate is apparent following the invitation to start meditating (*colored area*). Lactate is produced by anaerobic metabolism, mainly in muscle tissue. Its concentration normally falls in a subject at rest, but the rate of decline during meditation proved to be more than three times faster than the normal rate.

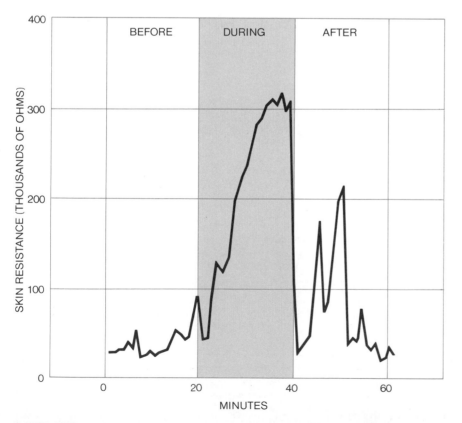

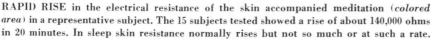

RAPID RISE in the electrical resistance of the skin accompanied meditation (*colored area*) in a representative subject. The 15 subjects tested showed a rise of about 140,000 ohms in 20 minutes. In sleep skin resistance normally rises but not so much or at such a rate.

been reported earlier. Oxygen consumption fell sharply from 251 cubic centimeters per minute in the premeditation period to 211 cubic centimeters during meditation, and in the postmeditation period it rose gradually to 242 cubic centimeters. Similarly, carbon dioxide elimination decreased, from 219 centimeters per minute beforehand to 187 cubic centimeters during meditation, and then returned to about the premeditation level afterward. The ratio of carbon dioxide elimination to oxygen consumption (in volume) remained essentially unchanged throughout the three periods, which indicates that the controlling factor for both was the rate of metabolism. The reduction in metabolic rate (and hence in the need for oxygen) during meditation was reflected in a decrease, essentially involuntary, in the rate of respiration (off two breaths per minute) and in the volume of air breathed (one liter less per minute).

For the measurement of arterial blood pressure and the taking of blood samples we used a catheter, which was inserted in the brachial artery and hidden with a curtain so that the subject would not be exposed to possible psychological trauma from witnessing the drawing of blood. Since local anesthesia was used at the site of the catheter insertion in the forearm, the subject felt no sensation when blood samples were taken. The blood pressure was measured continuously by means of a measuring device connected to the catheter.

We found that the subjects' arterial blood pressure remained at a rather low level throughout the examination; it fell to this level during the quiet premeditation period and did not change significantly during meditation or afterward. On the average the systolic pressure was equal to 106 millimeters of mercury, the diastolic pressure to 57 and the mean pressure to 75. The partial pressures of carbon dioxide and oxygen in the arterial blood also remained essentially unchanged during meditation. There was a slight increase in the acidity of the blood, indicating a slight metabolic acidosis, during meditation, but the acidity was within the normal range of variation.

Measurements of the lactate concentration in the blood (an indication of anaerobic metabolism, or metabolism in the absence of free oxygen) showed that during meditation the subjects' lactate level declined precipitously. During the first 10 minutes of meditation the lactate level in the subjects' arterial blood decreased at the rate of 10.26 milligrams per 100 cubic centimeters per hour, nearly four times faster than the rate of decrease in people normally resting in a supine position or in the subjects themselves during their premeditation period. After the subjects ceased meditating the lactate level continued to fall for a few minutes and then began to rise, but at the end of the postmeditation period it was still considerably below the premeditation level. The mean level during the premeditation period was 11.4 milligrams per 100 cubic centimeters, during meditation 8.0 milligrams and during postmeditation 7.3 milligrams.

How could one account for the fact that lactate production, which reflects anaerobic metabolism, was reduced so much during meditation? New experiments furnished a possible answer. These had to do with the rate of blood flow in meditating subjects; the explanation they suggest appears significant with respect to the psychological benefits that can be obtained from meditation.

In studies H. Rieckert conducted at the University of Tübingen, he reported that during transcendental meditation his subjects showed a 300 percent increase in the flow of blood in the forearm. In similar measurements on our subjects we found the increase in forearm blood flow to be much less: 32 percent. Still, this increase was interesting, and it offered an explanation of the relatively large decrease in blood-lactate concentration. The main site of lactate production in the body is the skeletal muscle tissue. Presumably the observed acceleration of blood flow to the forearm muscles during meditation speeds up the delivery of oxygen to the muscles. The resulting gain in oxidative metabolism may substitute for anaerobic metabolism, and this would explain the sharp drop in the production of lactate that accompanies meditation.

The intriguing consequence of this view is that it brings the autonomic nervous system further into the picture. In a situation of constant blood pressure (which is the case during meditation) the rate of blood flow is controlled basically by dilation or constriction of the blood vessels. The autonomic nervous system, in turn, controls this blood-vessel behavior. One element in this system, a part of the sympathetic nerve network, sometimes gives rise to the secretion of acetylcholine through special fibers and thereby stimulates the blood vessels to dilate. Conversely, the major part of the sympathetic nerve network stimulates the secretion of norepinephrine and thus causes constriction of the blood vessels. Rieckert's finding of a large increase in blood flow during meditation suggested that meditation increased the activity of the sympathetic nerve network that secretes the dilating substance. Our own finding of a much more modest enhancement of blood flow indicated a different view: that meditation reduces the activity of the major part of the sympathetic nerve network, so that its constriction of the blood vessels is absent. This interpretation also helps to account for the great decrease in the production of lactate during meditation; norepinephrine is known to stimulate lactate production, and a reduction in the secretion of norepinephrine, through inhibition of the major sympathetic network, should be expected to diminish the output of lactate.

Whatever the explanation of the fall in the blood-lactate level, it is clear that this could have a beneficial psychological effect. Patients with anxiety neurosis show a large rise in blood lactate when they are placed under stress [see "The Biochemistry of Anxiety," by Ferris N. Pitts, Jr.; SCIENTIFIC AMERICAN Offprint 521]. Indeed, Pitts and J. N. McClure, Jr., a co-worker of Pitts's at the Washington University School of Medicine, showed experimentally that an infusion of lactate could bring on attacks of anxiety in such patients and could even produce anxiety symptoms in normal subjects. Furthermore, it is significant that patients with hypertension (essential and renal) show higher blood-lactate levels in a resting state than patients without hypertension, whereas in contrast the low lactate level in transcendental meditators is associated with low blood pressure. All in all, it is reasonable to hypothesize that the low level of lactate found in subjects during and after transcendental meditation may be responsible in part for the meditators' thoroughly relaxed state.

Other measurements on the meditators confirmed the picture of a highly relaxed, although wakeful, condition. During meditation their skin resistance to an electric current increased markedly, in some cases more than fourfold. Their heart rate slowed by about three beats per minute on the average. Electroencephalographic recordings disclosed a marked intensification of alpha waves in all the subjects. We recorded the waves from seven main areas of the brain on magnetic tape and then analyzed the patterns with a computer. Typically there was an increase in intensity of slow alpha waves at eight or nine cycles per second in the frontal and central regions of the brain during meditation. In several subjects this change was also accompanied by prominent theta waves in the frontal area.

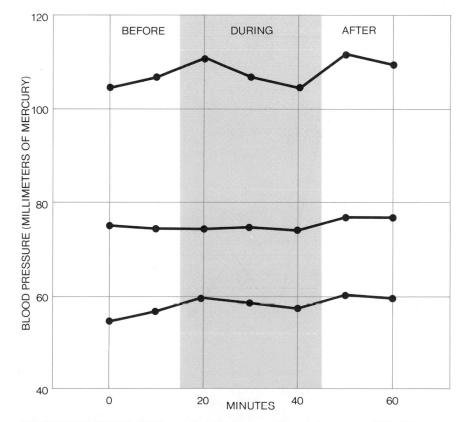

NO SIGNIFICANT CHANGE was observed in nine subjects whose arterial blood pressure was recorded before, during and after meditation. Systolic pressure (*top*), mean pressure (*middle*) and diastolic pressure (*bottom*), however, stayed relatively low throughout.

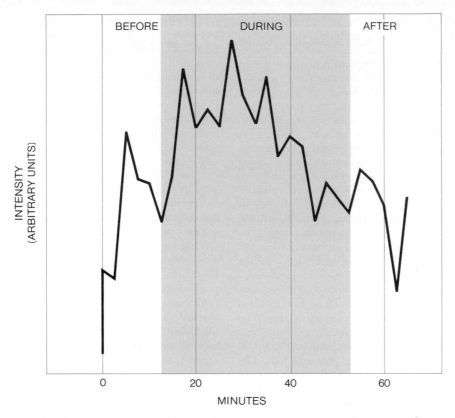

INCREASE IN INTENSITY of "slow" alpha waves, at eight to nine cycles per second, was evident during meditation (*colored area*) in electroencephalograph readings of the subjects' frontal and central brain regions. This is a representative subject's frontal reading. Before meditation most subjects' frontal readings showed alpha waves of lower intensity.

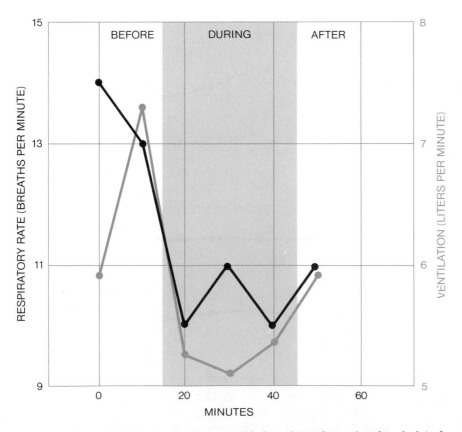

DECREASES OCCURRED in respiratory rate (*black*) and in volume of air breathed (*color*) during meditation. The ratio between carbon dioxide expired and oxygen consumed, however, continued unchanged and in the normal range during the entire test period.

To sum up, our subjects during the practice of transcendental meditation manifested the physiological signs of what we describe as a "wakeful, hypometabolic" state: reductions in oxygen consumption, carbon dioxide elimination and the rate and volume of respiration; a slight increase in the acidity of the arterial blood; a marked decrease in the blood-lactate level; a slowing of the heartbeat; a considerable increase in skin resistance, and an electroencephalogram pattern of intensification of slow alpha waves with occasional theta-wave activity. These physiological modifications, in people who were practicing the easily learned technique of transcendental meditation, were very similar to those that have been observed in highly trained experts in yoga and in Zen monks who have had 15 to 20 years of experience in meditation.

How do the physiological changes during meditation compare with those in other relaxed states, such as sleep and hypnosis? There is little resemblance. Whereas oxygen consumption drops rapidly within the first five or 10 minutes of transcendental meditation, hypnosis produces no noticeable change in this metabolic index, and during sleep the consumption of oxygen decreases appreciably only after several hours. During sleep the concentration of carbon dioxide in the blood increases significantly, indicating a reduction in respiration. There is a slight increase in the acidity of the blood; this is clearly due to the decrease in ventilation and not to a change in metabolism such as occurs during meditation. Skin resistance commonly increases during sleep, but the rate and amount of this increase are on a much smaller scale than they are in transcendental meditation. The electroencephalogram patterns characteristic of sleep are different; they consist predominantly of high-voltage (strong) activity of slow waves at 12 to 14 cycles per second and a mixture of weaker waves at various frequencies—a pattern that does not occur during transcendental meditation. The patterns during hypnosis have no relation to those of the meditative state; in a hypnotized subject the brain-wave activity takes the form characteristic of the mental state that has been suggested to the subject. The same is true of changes in heart rate, blood pressure, skin resistance and respiration; all these visceral adjustments in a hypnotized person merely reflect the suggested state.

It is interesting to compare the effects obtained through meditation with those that can be established by means of operant conditioning. By such conditioning animals and people have been trained to increase or decrease their heart rate, blood pressure, urine formation and certain other autonomic functions [see the article beginning on page 74, "Learning in the Autonomic Nervous System," by Leo V. DiCara]. Through the use of rewards that act as reinforcers a subject is taught to make a specific visceral response to a given stimulus. This procedure and the result are quite different, however, from what occurs in transcendental meditation. Whereas operant conditioning is limited to producing specific responses and depends on a stimulus and feedback of a reinforcer, meditation is independent of such assistance and produces not a single specific response but a complex of responses that marks a highly relaxed state.

The pattern of changes suggests that meditation generates an integrated response, or reflex, that is mediated by the central nervous system. A well-known reflex of such a nature was described many years ago by the noted Harvard physiologist Walter B. Cannon; it is called the "fight or flight" or "defense alarm" reaction. The aroused sympathetic nervous system mobilizes a set of physiological responses marked by increases in the blood pressure, heart rate, blood flow to the muscles and oxygen consumption.

The hypometabolic state produced by meditation is of course opposite to this in almost all respects. It looks very much like a counterpart of the fight-or-flight reaction.

During man's early history the defense-alarm reaction may well have had high survival value and thus have become strongly established in his genetic makeup. It continues to be aroused in all its visceral aspects when the individual feels threatened. Yet in the environment of our time the reaction is often an anachronism. Although the defense-alarm reaction is generally no longer appropriate, the visceral response is evoked with considerable frequency by the rapid and unsettling changes that are buffeting modern society. There is good reason to believe the changing environment's incessant stimulations of the sympathetic nervous system are largely responsible for the high incidence of hypertension and similar serious diseases that are prevalent in our society.

In these circumstances the hypometabolic state, representing quiescence rather than hyperactivation of the sympathetic nervous system, may indicate a guidepost to better health. It should be well worthwhile to investigate the possibilities for clinical application of this state of wakeful rest and relaxation.

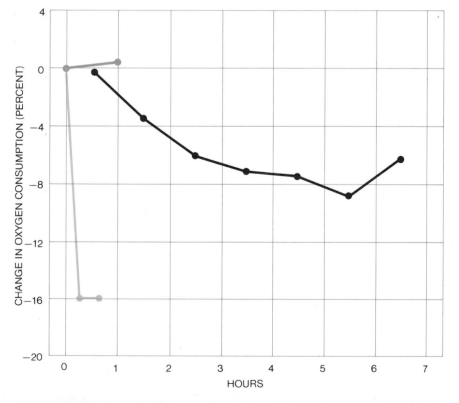

CONSUMPTION OF OXYGEN is compared in three different circumstances: during hypnosis (color), sleep (black) and meditation (light color). No significant change occurs under hypnosis. One study shows that oxygen consumption is reduced by about 8 percent after five hours' sleep. Meditation brings twice the reduction in a fraction of the time.

BIBLIOGRAPHY

I BRAIN AND AWARENESS

1. The Electrical Activity of the Brain

ELECTROENCEPHALOGRAPHY. W. Grey Walter in *Endeavour*, Vol. 8, No. 32, pages 194–199; October, 1949.

THE LIVING BRAIN. W. Grey Walter. W. W. Norton & Company, Inc., 1953.

2. The Analysis of Brain Waves

COMPUTER TECHNIQUES IN EEG ANALYSIS. Edited by Mary A. B. Brazier. *Electroencephalography and Clinical Neurophysiology*, Suppl. 20; 1961.

THE ELECTRICAL ACTIVITY OF THE NERVOUS SYSTEM. Mary A. B. Brazier. The Macmillan Co., 1960.

PROCESSING NEUROELECTRIC DATA. Communications Biophysics Group of Research Laboratory of Electronics and William M. Siebert. The Technology Press of the Massachusetts Institute of Technology, 1959.

SOME USES OF COMPUTERS IN EXPERIMENTAL NEUROLOGY. Mary A. B. Brazier in *Experimental Neurology*, Vol. 2, No. 2, pages 123–143; April, 1960.

THE WAKING BRAIN. H. W. Magoun. Charles C Thomas, Publisher, 1958.

3. The Reticular Formation

BRAIN MECHANISMS AND CONSCIOUSNESS. J. F. Delafresnaye. Blackwell Scientific Publications, 1954.

BRAIN STEM RETICULAR FORMATION AND ACTIVATION OF THE EEG. G. Moruzzi and H. W. Magoun in *Electroencephalography and Clinical Neurophysiology*, Vol. 1, No. 4, pages 455–473; November, 1949.

PATTERNS OF ORGANIZATION IN THE CENTRAL NERVOUS SYSTEM. Edited by Philip Bard. The Williams & Wilkins Company, 1952.

SPASTICITY: THE STRETCH-REFLEX AND EXTRAPYRAMIDAL SYSTEMS. H. W. Magoun and Ruth Rhines. Charles C. Thomas, 1947.

4. The Physiology of Imagination

COMPLEXITY-SIMPLICITY AS A PERSONALITY DIMENSION. Frank Barron in *The Journal of Abnormal and Social Psychology*, Vol. 48, No. 2, pages 163–172; April, 1953.

THE CREATIVE PROCESS: A SYMPOSIUM. Brewster Ghiselin. University of California Press, 1952.

THE DISPOSITION TOWARD ORIGINALITY. Frank Barron in *The Journal of Abnormal and Social Psychology*, Vol. 51, No. 3, pages 478–485; November, 1955.

SOME PERSONALITY CORRELATES OF INDEPENDENCE OF JUDGMENT. Frank Barron in *Character and Personality (Journal of Personality)*, Vol. 21, No. 3, pages 287–297; March, 1953.

II ALTERED STATES OF AWARENESS: INTERNAL CONTROL

5. Patterns of Dreaming

A COMPARISON OF "DREAMERS" AND "NONDREAMERS": EYE MOVEMENTS, ELECTROENCEPHALOGRAMS AND THE RECALL OF DREAMS. Donald R. Goodenough, Arthur Shapiro, Melvin Holden and Leonard Steinschriber in *The Journal of Abnormal and Social Psychology*, Vol. 59, No. 3, pages 295–302; November, 1959.

CYCLIC VARIATIONS IN EEG DURING SLEEP AND THEIR RELATION TO EYE MOVEMENTS, BODY MOTILITY, AND DREAMING. William Dement and Nathaniel Kleitman in *Electroencephalography and Clinical Neurophysiology*, Vol. 9, No. 4, pages 673–690; November, 1957.

THE RELATION OF EYE MOVEMENTS DURING SLEEP TO DREAM ACTIVITY: AN OBJECTIVE METHOD FOR THE STUDY OF DREAMING. W. Dement and N. Kleitman in *Journal of Experimental Psychology*, Vol. 53, No. 5, pages 339–346; May, 1957.

STUDIES IN PSYCHOPHYSIOLOGY OF DREAMS. I: EX-
PERIMENTAL EVOCATION OF SEQUENTIAL DREAM
EPISODES. Edward A. Wolpert and Harry Trosman
in *A.M.A. Archives of Neurology and Psychiatry*,
Vol. 79, No. 4, pages 603–606; April, 1958.
TWO TYPES OF OCULAR MOTILITY OCCURRING IN
SLEEP. E. Aserinsky and N. Kleitman in *Journal
of Applied Physiology*, Vol. 8, No. 1, pages 1–10;
July, 1955.

6. The States of Sleep

ASPECTS ANATOMO-FONCTIONNELS DE LA PHYSIOL-
OGIE DU SOMMEIL. Edited by M. Jouvet. Centre
National de la Recherche Scientifique, 1965.
AN ESSAY ON DREAMS: THE ROLE OF PHYSIOLOGY IN
UNDERSTANDING THEIR NATURE. W. C. Dement in
New Directions in Psychology: Vol. II. Holt, Rine-
hart & Winston, Inc., 1965.
SLEEP AND WAKEFULNESS. Nathaniel Kleitman. The
University of Chicago Press, 1963.
SLEEPING AND WAKING. Ian Oswald. American Elsevier
Publishing Company, Inc., 1962.
SLEEP MECHANISMS. Edited by K. Akert, C. Bally and
J. P. Schadé. American Elsevier Publishing Com-
pany, Inc., 1965.

7. The Pathology of Boredom

EFFECTS OF DECREASED VARIATION IN THE SENSORY
ENVIRONMENT. W. H. Bexton, W. Heron and T. H.
Scott in *Canadian Journal of Psychology*, Vol. 8,
No. 2, pages 70–76; June, 1954.
THE MAMMAL AND HIS ENVIRONMENT. D. O. Hebb in
The American Journal of Psychiatry, Vol. 111, No.
11, pages 826–831; May, 1955.
VISUAL DISTURBANCES AFTER PROLONGED PERCEP-
TUAL ISOLATION. Woodburn Heron, B. K. Doane

and T. H. Scott in *Canadian Journal of Psychology*,
Vol. 10, No. 1, pages 13–18; March, 1956.

8. On Telling Left from Right

THE ANALYSIS OF SENSATIONS AND THE RELATION OF
THE PHYSICAL TO THE PSYCHICAL. Ernst Mach.
Dover Publications, Inc., 1959.
THE AMBIDEXTROUS UNIVERSE. Martin Gardner. Basic
Books, Inc., 1964.
LEFT AND RIGHT IN SCIENCE AND LIFE. Vilma Fritsch.
Barrie & Rockliff, 1968.
BILATERAL SYMMETRY AND BEHAVIOR. M. C. Corballis
and I. L. Beale in *Psychological Review*, Vol. 77,
No. 5, pages 451–464; September, 1970.

9. Learning in the Autonomic Nervous System

INSTRUMENTAL LEARNING OF HEART RATE CHANGES
IN CURARIZED RATS: SHAPING, AND SPECIFICITY
TO DISCRIMINATIVE STIMULUS. Neal E. Miller
and Leo DiCara in *Journal of Comparative & Phys-
iological Psychology*, Vol. 63, No. 1, pages 12–19;
February, 1967.
INSTRUMENTAL LEARNING OF VASOMOTOR RESPONSES
BY RATS: LEARNING TO RESPOND DIFFEREN-
TIALLY IN THE TWO EARS. Leo V. DiCara and
Neal E. Miller in *Science*, Vol. 159, No. 3822, pages
1485–1486; March 29, 1968.
HOMEOSTASIS AND REWARD: T-MAZE LEARNING IN-
DUCED BY MANIPULATING ANTIDIURETIC HOR-
MONE. Neal E. Miller, Leo V. DiCara and George
Wolf in *American Journal of Physiology*, Vol. 215,
No. 3, pages 684–686; September, 1968.
LEARNING OF VISCERAL AND GLANDULAR RESPONSES.
Neal E. Miller in *Science*, Vol. 163, No. 3866, pages
434–445; January 31, 1969.

III   ALTERED STATES OF AWARENESS: EXTERNAL CONTROL

10. Marihuana

THE MARIHUANA PAPERS. Edited by David Solomon.
The Bobbs-Merrill Company, Inc., 1966.
SOCIAL AND PARA-MEDICAL ASPECTS OF HALLUCINO-
GENIC DRUGS. William H. McGlothlin in *The Use
of LSD in Psychotherapy and Alcoholism*, edited
by Harold A. Abramson. The Bobbs-Merrill Com-
pany, Inc., 1967.
CLINICAL AND PSYCHOLOGICAL EFFECTS OF MARI-
HUANA IN MAN. Andrew T. Weil, Norman E. Zin-
berg and Judith M. Nelsen in *Science*, Vol. 162,
No. 3859, pages 1234–1242; December 13, 1968.

11. The Hallucinogenic Drugs

THE CLINICAL PHARMACOLOGY OF THE HALLUCINO-
GENS. Erik Jacobsen in *Clinical Pharmacology
and Therapeutics*, Vol. 4, pages 480–504; July–
August, 1963.
LYSERGIC ACID DIETHYLAMIDE (LSD-25) AND EGO
FUNCTIONS. G. D. Klee in *Archives of General
Psychiatry*, Vol. 8, No. 5, pages 461–474; May, 1963.
PROLONGED ADVERSE REACTIONS TO LYSERGIC ACID
DIETHYLAMIDE. S. Cohen and K. S. Ditman in
Archives of General Psychiatry, Vol. 8, No. 5, pages
475–480; May, 1963.

THE PSYCHOTOMIMETIC DRUGS: AN OVERVIEW. Jonathan O. Cole and Martin M. Katz in *The Journal of the American Medical Association*, Vol. 187, No. 10, pages 758–761; March, 1964.

12. Experiments with Goggles

ADAPTATION, AFTER-EFFECT AND CONTRAST IN THE PERCEPTION OF CURVED LINES. James J. Gibson in *Journal of Experimental Psychology*, Vol. 16, No. 1, pages 1–31; February, 1933.

SOME PRELIMINARY EXPERIMENTS ON VISION WITHOUT INVERSION OF THE RETINAL IMAGE. George M. Stratton in *The Psychological Review*, Vol. 3, No. 6, pages 611–617; November, 1896.

VISION WITHOUT INVERSION OF THE RETINAL IMAGE. George M. Stratton in *The Psychological Review*, Vol. 4, No. 4, pages 341–360; July, 1897.

VISION WITHOUT INVERSION OF THE RETINAL IMAGE (CONCLUDED). George M. Stratton in *The Psychological Review*, Vol. 4, No. 5, pages 463–481; September, 1897.

13. The Split Brain in Man

CEREBRAL COMMISSUROTOMY. J. E. Bogen, E. D. Fisher and P. J. Vogel in *Journal of the American Medical Association*, Vol. 194, No. 12, pages 1328–1329; December 20, 1965.

CEREBRAL ORGANIZATION AND BEHAVIOR. R. W. Sperry in *Science*, Vol 133, No. 3466, pages 1749–1757; June 2, 1961.

LANGUAGE AFTER SECTION OF THE CEREBRAL COMMISSURES. M. S. Gazzaniga and R. W. Sperry in *Brain*, Vol. 90, Part 1, pages 131–148; 1967.

MICROELECTRODE ANALYSIS OF TRANSFER OF VISUAL INFORMATION BY THE CORPUS CALLOSUM. G. Berlucchi, M. S. Gazzaniga and G. Rizzolati in *Archives Italiennes de Biologie*, Vol. 105, pages 583–596; 1967.

OBSERVATIONS ON VISUAL PERCEPTION AFTER DISCONNEXION OF THE CEREBRAL HEMISPHERES IN MAN. M. S. Gazzaniga, J. E. Bogen and R. W. Sperry in *Brain*, Vol. 88, Part 2, pages 221–236; 1965.

14. The Physiology of Meditation

STUDIES ON SHRI RAMANAND YOGI DURING HIS STAY IN AN AIR-TIGHT BOX. B. K. Anand, G. S. Chhina and Baldev Singh in *The Indian Journal of Medical Research*, Vol 49, No. 1, pages 82–89; January, 1961.

PHYSIOLOGICAL EFFECTS OF TRANSCENDENTAL MEDITATION. Robert Keith Wallace in *Science*, Vol. 167, No. 3926, pages 1751–1754; March 27, 1970.

A WAKEFUL HYPOMETABOLIC PHYSIOLOGIC STATE. Robert Keith Wallace, Herbert Benson and Archie F. Wilson in *American Journal of Physiology*, Vol. 221, No. 3, pages 795–799; September, 1971.